Global Governance in Question

Critical Introductions to World Politics
Series Editors: Alejandro Colás (Birkbeck College, University of London)
Richard Saull (Department of Politics and International Relations,
University of Leicester)

Also available:

Ray Kiely
Empire in the Age of Globalisation:
US Hegemony and Neoliberal Disorder

Global Governance in Question

Empire, Class, and the New Common Sense in Managing North–South Relations

Susanne Soederberg

Pluto Press

LONDON • ANN ARBOR, MI

First published 2006 by Pluto Press
345 Archway Road, London N6 5AA
and 839 Greene Street, Ann Arbor, MI 48106

www.plutobooks.com

British Library Cataloguing in Publication Data
A catalogue record for this book is available from the British Library

ISBN   0 7453 2070 8 hardback
ISBN   0 7453 2069 4 paperback

Library of Congress Cataloging in Publication Data applied for

10   9   8   7   6   5   4   3   2   1

Designed and produced for Pluto Press by
Chase Publishing Services Ltd, Fortescue, Sidmouth, EX10 9QG, England
Typeset from disk by Stanford DTP Services, Northampton
Printed and bound by CPI Group (UK) Ltd, Croydon, CR0 4YY

Contents

TABLES

BOXES

Series Introduction

Critical Introductions to World Politics
Series Editors: Alejandro Colás (Birkbeck College, University of London)
Richard Saull (Department of Politics and International Relations, University of Leicester)

World politics in all its socio-economic, cultural, institutional and military dimensions affects the lives of billions across the globe. Yet international relations is still an area of study associated with the 'high politics' of statecraft, strategy and diplomacy, or with distant and seemingly uncontrollable global flows of money, people and commodities. Critical Introductions to World Politics aims to reverse this prevailing elitism by illuminating and explaining the causes and consequences of these diverse aspects of international relations in an accessible way, thereby highlighting the impact of international processes and developments on the lives of ordinary people. The series will bring together a range of theoretical and empirical studies into the workings of world politics, while also identifying areas for political intervention by those seeking not just to interpret the world, but also to participate in political struggles to change it.

The series engages with key areas, providing succinct, informative and accessible overviews to central debates in global affairs. It draws mainly, although not exclusively, on Marxist approaches to international relations concerned with the analysis of, among other issues, transnational class formation, the role of international organisations in sustaining global capitalist hegemony, the sources of violent conflict and war, and the nature and evolution of state sovereignty. Empirically, it focuses on such issues as the origins of the modern international system, the Cold War and the consequences of its end, globalisation, and the character of American global power.

Critical Introductions to World Politics builds on a new, distinctly historical-materialist approach to global affairs, serving as a key reference point and resource for those studying and teaching international relations from a critical perspective, as well as those involved in the various movements for a more just, equal and sustainable world.

Acknowledgements

I first taught upper-level and graduate seminars on the topic of the Political Economy of Global Governance in the Department of Political Science at the University of Alberta, Canada in 2001. From this time onwards, I have been struck by not only the lack of Marxist analyses of global governance, but also the mainstream literature's neglect of the Third World in the conceptualizations of power and policy-making in the international arena. This book is motivated by these gaps in our knowledge and the enthusiasm of my students in the Department of Political Science at the University of Alberta, and, presently, in the Development Studies Programme at Queen's University, Kingston, Ontario. The first round of thanks and acknowledgements therefore are for my students, from whom I continue to learn and draw my passion to understand the world.

I would also like to thank Alejandro Colás and Richard Saull, the Editors for Pluto Press, for inviting me to contribute to the exciting new series: Critical Studies in World Politics, as well as providing excellent guidance on how to improve the overall argument of the book. Roger van Zwanenberg, the Managing Director at Pluto Press, provided much needed patience and support throughout the entire process. I received a stream of helpful suggestions and support from colleagues and friends: Elmar Altvater, Karyn Ball, Patrick Bond, Janine Brodie, Phil Cerny, Lois Harder, Gail Faurschou, Stella Gaon, Satoshi Ikeda, Yoshie Hayashi, Otto Holman, Fred Judson, Catherine Kellogg, Paul Langley, Ronnie Lipschutz, Sourayan Mookerjea, Leo Panitch, Philip McMichael, and Kees van der Pijl. I would also like to thank the Faculty of Arts at the University of Alberta, the Social Sciences Humanities Research Council of Canada, and the Faculty of Arts and Science at Queen's University at Kingston for their generous financial support. Ryan Foster's assistance has been invaluable in terms of the background research for this project, and for providing input as to how the manuscript could be improved in terms of accessibility from a student's perspective. I would also like to thank *Third World Quarterly* for permission to reprint Chapters 4 and 5. Finally, I would like to thank Marcus Taylor for his support throughout this project.

Acronyms

AFL-CIO	American Federation of Labor and Congress of Industrial Organizations
BWS	Bretton Woods system
CACs	collection action clauses
CERES	Coalition for Environmentally Responsible Economics
CGG	Commission on Global Governance
CSR	corporate social responsibility
ECLA	Economic Commission for Latin America
ECLAC	Economic Commission on Latin America and the Caribbean
ECOSOC	Economic and Social Council
EPZs	export processing zones
ESAF	Enhanced Structural Adjustment Facility
ETOSS	Ente Tripartito de Obras y Servicios Sanitarios
FDI	foreign direct investment
FLA	Fair Labour Association
FPI	foreign portfolio investment
FOCAL	Canadian Federation of the Americas
FY	fiscal year
FLA	Fair Labour Association
G-7	Group of 7
G-8	Group of 8
G-20	Group of 20
G-77	Group of 77
GATS	General Agreement on Trade in Services
GATT	General Agreement on Tariffs and Trade
GC	Global Compact
GCAB	Global Committee on Argentine Bondholders
GDP	gross domestic product
GNI	gross national income
GRI	Global Reporting Initiative
HIPCs	Highly Indebted Poor Countries
ICC	International Chamber of Commerce
ICCR	Interfaith Center on Corporate Responsibility
ICFTU	International Confederation of Free Trade Unions
IDA	International Development Association
IDC	International Debt Commission
IEO	Independent Evaluation Office
IFIs	international financial institutions (e.g., the IMF and the World Bank)

ILO	International Labour Organization
IMF	International Monetary Fund
IMFC	International Monetary and Financial Committee
IRRC	Investor Responsibility Research Center
M&As	mergers and acquisitions
MCA	Millennium Challenge Account
MCC	Millennium Challenge Corporation
MDGs	Millennium Development Goals
MFN	most favoured nation
MNCs	multinational corporations
NAFTA	North American Free Trade Agreement
NAM	Non-Aligned Movement
NGOs	non-governmental organizations
NICs	newly industrializing countries
NIDL	New International Division of Labour
NIEO	New International Economic Order
NIFA	New International Financial Architecture
NSS	National Security Strategy
OECD	Organization for Economic Co-operation and Development
OPEC	Organization of Petroleum Exporting Countries
PINs	Public Information Notices
PRGF	Poverty Reduction Growth Facility
PRSP	Poverty Reduction Strategy Papers
R&D	research and development
ROSC	Reports on Observances of Standards and Codes
SAPs	structural adjustment programmes
SDRM	Sovereign Debt Restructuring Mechanism
TNCs	transnational corporations
TRIMS	trade-related investment measures
TRIPS	trade-related intellectual property rights
TUAC	Trade Union Advisory Council
UDHR	Universal Declaration of Human Rights
UN	United Nations
UNCTAD	United Nations Conference on Trade and Development
UNCTC	United Nations Centre on Transnational Corporations
UNEP	United Nations Environment Programme
UNESCO	United Nations Educational, Scientific and Cultural Organization
UNIFEM	United Nations Development Fund for Women
USAID	United States Agency for International Development
WIR	World Investment Report
WTO	World Trade Organization

1
Global Governance in Question

The international system that the UN Charter put in place needs to be renewed. The flaws and inadequacies of existing institutions have to be overcome. There is a need to weave a tighter fabric of international norms, expanding the rule of law world-wide and enabling citizens to exert their democratic influence on global processes. We also believe the world's arrangements for the conduct of its affairs must be underpinned by certain common values. Ultimately, no organisation will work and no law be upheld unless they rest on a foundation made strong by shared values. These values must be informed by a sense of common responsibility for both present and future generations.

Commission on Global Governance, *Our Global Neighbourhood*, 1995: xiv.

Global governance is often used by international policy-makers and scholars to describe and explain the socio-political infrastructure of globalization. Despite its growing popularity, however, this term remains, with a few notable exceptions, notoriously ill defined and devoid of any critical theorization (Hewson and Sinclair, 1999; Murphy, 1994; 2000; Wilkinson and Hughes, 2002; Overbeek, 2004). Global governance has therefore come to serve as a catchall phrase, rather than a concise descriptor. To conduct a critical evaluation of this term, it is imperative that we establish a clear definition of global governance at the outset of our discussion. While there is no consensus over this term, we can identify a generally accepted usage found in the highly influential Report of the Commission on Global Governance (CGG). According to the CGG,

> [g]overnance is the sum of the many ways individuals and institutions, public and private, manage their common affairs. It is a continuing process through which conflicting or diverse interests may be accommodated and co-operative action may be taken. It includes formal institutions and regimes empowered to enforce compliance, as well as informal arrangements that people and institutions either have agreed to or perceive to be in their interests (CGG, 1995: 2).

The CGG goes on to suggest that governance occurs not only at the national and global, but also at the local level. At each of these levels of analysis, there exists a multiplicity of actors, ranging from local producers to transnational corporations, from local and international non-governmental organisations (NGOs) to the World Bank. According to the CGG, this understanding of global governance allows for more diversity and lateral forms of decision-making than the traditional state-centric, top-down perspective that dominated much of the post-war period: 'There is no single model or form of global governance, nor is there a single structure or set of structures. It is a broad, dynamic, complex process of interactive decision-making that is constantly evolving and responding to changing circumstances' (CGG, 1995: 4). We should underscore that this particular meaning of global governance precludes global or world government.

There is much to commend the CGG's account of global governance – above all its humanitarian concerns for world peace, human security, and democratic forms of international co-operation. At the same time, however, the Commission's portrayal of global governance must be criticised for its lack of historical insight into the unequal human relations that comprise its multi-level governance structure. The CGG has been so intent on describing the harmony of difference brought about by globalization that it has failed to acknowledge not only the inequality and exclusion inherent in the 'global neighbourhood', but also the increasingly unilateral policies of the United States government, particularly vis-à-vis the South. Examples of these charges are not difficult to find. The unwillingness of the majority of the world's population to continue to adhere to global rules governing trade, which have been written largely by a select number of wealthy states, was evident in the breakdown of the World Trade Organization's (WTO) Ministerial Meeting held in Cancún, Mexico in September 2003. In very broad terms, poorer member states (for example, the Group of 20+ and Group of 77), representing 65 per cent of the world population, 72 per cent of its farmers and 22 per cent of its agricultural output, refused to ratify the global trade pact, as they felt that key trade issues, such as agriculture, market access and drug patent rules – not to mention the four new issues introduced at Cancún (investment, competition policy, transparency in government procurement, and trade facilitation – i.e. customs procedures) were not in the interests of the developing world, but rather of large corporate profits.[1] It should be emphasized here that, while coalitions of the Third World work together to strengthen their position in relation to the G-7 countries, this should not be construed as the developing world speaking with one voice.

Indeed, there were, and remain, many fundamental differences and tensions between countries of the global South, such as trade and development issues.

With regard to the (ongoing) exclusionary practices in the global neighbourhood, large segments of civil society – particularly the more 'radical' elements that disagree with neoliberal-led globalization – have been consistently barred at significant international conferences such as the joint annual meetings of the IMF and the World Bank, and that of the WTO, or G-7/8 meetings (see Drainville, 2004). Other examples of exclusion at the global level are readily available. The majority of civil society members from both the developed and developing world were excluded from the Financing for Development Conference in Monterrey, Mexico in March 2002, which was initiated and conducted by the United Nations, while only a select handful of what the G-7 has termed 'systematically important' emerging markets were included in one of the key institutional features of the New International Financial Architecture, namely the G-20 (Soederberg, 2004).

The most spectacular example of the unilateral behaviour of the American government was its reaction, along with the 'coalition of the willing', to the bombings of the World Trade Center on September 11, 2001: a non-UN-sanctioned military invasion ('pre-emptive strike' to prevent the use of weapons of mass destruction) and subsequent illegal occupation of Iraq in 2002. Against this backdrop of 'go it alone' policies, conceptualizations of 'empire' have become, once again, popular on both the right and the left (Hardt and Negri, 2000; Panitch and Gindin, 2003; Harvey, 2003a, 2003b; Kagan, 2003; Eland, 2002; Newhouse, 2003; Slaughter, 2004). Influential Washington neoconservatives, for example, have been using the 'E-word' freely, insisting that the United States is the world's most benevolent nation and that it should use its imperial power forcefully to expand 'freedom' and 'democracy' across the globe (Kagan, 2003; see also the Project for a New American Century: www.newamericancentury.org).

The fact that these relations of inequality, exclusion and dominance have been ignored by the CGG and other global governance sympathizers prompts us to ask some tough questions. Who benefits from global governance and why? Who is excluded, and why? Why has neoliberalism been largely neglected in the debates about global governance? Why does the United Nations – and particularly its 'special institutions', such as the World Bank and the IMF – stand above reproach in the CGG's understanding of global governance? What roles have states, particularly the US state, played in global governance? And finally, what is the connection between global governance and global capitalism? The objective of this book is to provide answers to these questions.

In very broad terms, the central argument running through this book is that mainstream understandings of global economic governance, particularly as represented by the CGG, fail to engage with the wider social relations and contradictions that characterize global capitalism. The immediate consequences of this neglect are, first, that there is no explanation of the changing nature of American empire and capitalist power in the world; and second, that the CGG's notion of global governance acts to normalize, neutralize, and legitimate increasingly austere forms of capitalist restructuring and expansion, which may be regarded as a deepening, heightening, and broadening of neoliberal domination.

Before I continue with an outline of the chapter and an historical contextualization of global governance, three caveats are in order. First, I do not claim to provide an exhaustive survey of global governance, which, of course, would be impossible, given that by its very definition it includes a system of rule anywhere from the individual to international organizations. In other words, while global governance covers a multiplicity of significant issues, such as gender, health, migration, race and identity politics, culture, environment, new security concerns, and so forth, my focus will be limited to global economic governance.[2] This should not be construed as an attempt at economic reductionism, but instead as an historically sensitive exploration of the social, political, and ideological dimensions of issues largely ignored in the global economic governance debates – namely, the increasingly coercive power of corporations, debt, and official development assistance. Thus, within the parameters of this book, the terms 'global governance' and 'global economic governance' should be taken as interchangeable. Second, our discussion focuses specifically on the Report of the CGG (*Our Global Neighbourhood*), not only because this helps us narrow the scope of our inquiry into global economic governance, but also because the Report represents the ideas and values of an elite group of scholars and policy-makers from both the advanced industrialized countries and the global South. Moreover, instead of merely focusing on yet another scholarly discussion of global governance, I thought it more interesting and relevant to explore the underlying premises of a document that has greatly influenced the understanding of the way those in power (the United Nations, national governments, multilateral lending organisations, and so on) think about global governance. Moreover, given the fact that *Our Global Neighbourhood* was written over a decade ago, we are able to evaluate the recent history surrounding the CGG's claims and observations. Finally, the third caveat relates to my attempts at balancing clarity with complexity. In this regard, the reader should be aware that, whenever possible, I have attempted to provide definitions of technical terms in the endnotes.

I have organized this introductory chapter into three sections. The first section provides a general account of the wider historical context from which global governance, and more specifically the CGG, emerged in the post-war era. Building on this discussion, the second section highlights some of the key premises underpinning global governance by drawing on James Rosenau's seminal work. A few words regarding the rationale behind the focus on Rosenau is necessary. On the one hand, despite the presence of other global governance theorists, Rosenau's work coincides with the publication of the CGG, and thus captures the main sentiments and concerns of the Report on Global Governance in the mid 1990s when global governance emerged as a key concern in policy-making circles. On the other hand, Rosenau's work is concerned with the economic features of global governance, which is the main focus of this book. I argue that a major contributing factor to the wooliness surrounding the debate on global governance is found in the frustratingly vague usage of the term. By narrowing the scope of our inquiry to the policy content of the CGG and its theoretical complement, represented by James Rosenau's work, we are able to fine-tune our critical discussion about global economic governance. A third section provides an overview of the structure of the book.

THE EMERGENCE OF GLOBAL GOVERNANCE

It must be kept in mind that the CGG's Report has not been the first attempt to promote a more humane, co-operative, and peaceful international order. In the late 1800s, for example, Cecil Rhodes and Alfred Milner constructed the Society of the Elect and the Association of Helpers (or Secret Society), while US President Woodrow Wilson sought to create the League of Nations (1919–20), albeit unsuccessfully due to the failure of the US Senate to ratify the charter (Secretariat of the League of Nations, 1935). Although global governance differs from its predecessors, it shares a similar characteristic, in that none of these attempts to embed a particular vision of international order appeared from thin air. Instead, they emerged from historically specific material and ideological circumstances (see Cox, 1987; Helleiner, 1994; Webber and Rigby, 1996; Pauly, 1996; 1997; Agnew and Corbridge, 1995). In what follows, I will provide an overview of the material and ideational context from which the CGG and its particular version of global governance emerged. In doing so I shall focus on the institutional framework designed to regulate international trade and monetary relations in the post-World War II era – namely, the Bretton Woods system (BWS). While this international monetary and financial system was not the only feature of this period, it was one of the most important for the shaping both the world and domestic economies. Moreover, a discussion of the BWS provides a solid platform from which we may explore the themes in the next four chapters.

The Bretton Woods system (1944–71)

The post-war era, also referred to as the 'golden age' (1944–71) was characterized by what the neo-Gramscian theorist Robert Cox refers to as a hegemonic period. This term describes the manner in which a dominant state and other social forces (such as powerful capitalists in the form of transnational corporations and financial institutions) sustain their position through the creation of and adherence to universalized principles that are accepted or acquiesced to by a sufficient proportion of subordinate states and social forces, through both consensual and coercive means. For Cox, hegemony implies both intellectual and moral leadership, which translates into stronger states making certain concessions to obtain the consent of the weaker (Cox, 1987; 1993b: 264). One way universal norms of a hegemonic state like the US are transmitted to other subordinate states is through international organizations, such as the United Nations, the IMF, and the World Bank.

The semblance of inclusion and co-operation encapsulated in the BWS provided vital scaffolding for global capital accumulation, which was marked by mass production and consumption, also known as Fordism (Gramsci, 1971; Lipietz, 1987; Webber and Rigby, 1996). When World War II came to an end in 1945, the US needed to undertake two tasks in order to avoid a post-war economic slump. First, it had to find export markets that would consume its excess surplus, such as Western Europe and Japan. And second, it needed to find raw materials with which to manufacture its goods, such as steel from Germany. It is within this context that the US and key allies, such as the UK, created an international economic regime that was based upon universal norms centred on trade liberalization, the rejection of communism, and the adherence to stable monetary regimes (Ruggie, 1982). In July 1944, representatives of 44 countries met at Bretton Woods, New Hampshire, to design a multilateral post-war system through which the trade and monetary relations of the non-communist world could be regulated in a stable manner. An overriding concern for the policy-makers who were present at Bretton Woods was to avoid a repeat of the Great Depression experienced in the 1930s (Kindleberger, 1986). The policy-makers believed that the length and severity of the Depression was exacerbated by rampant protectionism in the 1930s, and by a lack of commitment by individual states to the creation of a stable international monetary and trade regime to guide national policy (Agnew and Corbridge, 1995; Helleiner, 1994; Pauly, 1997).

Key policy-makers present at the Bretton Woods conference attempted to construct an international agreement that would promote international political and economic co-operation. Specifically, the BWS was a set of rules that would govern the economic relations between member countries through a *fixed exchange rate system* (also known as the 'fixed-but-adjustable rate system'). Under this system, the US defined the value of its dollar in terms of gold: one ounce of gold was to be equal to (or at par with) $35. The BWS established that world trade would be conducted in American dollars. The use of the American dollar as the world's trading and reserve currency also bolstered US hegemony, as member states were not only dependent on economic policy in the US, but also disciplined through it. Discipline in this context refers to the fact that governments of the member countries were compelled to pursue national economic policies and, although the connection is rarely made, social programmes, that supported and reproduced the international rules of exchange rates and trade. The threat of the withholding of funds was always latent, if countries deviated from the international rules – which, of course, centred on the dominant position of the US in the world economy. Disciplining, and thereby reproducing, economic dependency in the world market also entailed certain responsibilities on the part of the US. The US government, for instance, was required to maintain gold reserves to back up its dollar. Traders could therefore, at any time, exchange their American dollars for gold at the set price. Under the fixed exchange rate system, member countries agreed to keep the value of their money within 1 per cent of this par value (Cohen, 1986; Helleiner, 1994). If they thought that a change in the value of their currency would help their economy, they discussed this issue with other members in the forum of the IMF, and obtained their consent before doing so. The underlying motivation behind this mechanism was to keep currencies stable and predictable. Thus, in contrast to today's economy, there was little motivation for currency speculation.[3]

The organizational structure of the IMF and World Bank also reflected the underlying power of the inter-state system, so as to ensure the reproduction of the status quo. A member government owns a number of shares that is determined by how much money it has paid into the IMF. Clearly, some shareholders are far more powerful than others. The US and other affluent countries have had a much higher proportion of shares, and thus higher representation in the IMF and the World Bank. For example, the populations of the Group of Seven (or G-7) industrialized countries and the rest of the European Union combined represent a mere 14 per cent of the world's total, yet these countries hold 56 per cent of the quotas, and thus of the voting rights in the IMF executive board. The size of a country's shares or quotas clearly establishes an internal pecking order among Fund members, since these quotas determine the voting power in the Fund. The original rationale behind this voting structure was to avoid the gridlock that is common to many international organizations, such as the UN. Nevertheless, to achieve significant changes or decisions through the IMF, such as a ratification of the Fund's Articles of Agreement (basically its constitution), an 85 per cent majority is required. Thus, any member or group of members capable of collecting 15 per cent of IMF shares possesses the ability to block decisions. In order for the required majority to be obtained, the US must agree to any modifications, since it holds about 18 per cent of the Fund's quotas. This highly unequal shareholder-based power structure, which continues to the present, not only translates into a serious democratic deficit for the IMF and World Bank. It also, importantly, implies a significant amount of power that the G-7 countries, especially the US, wield over the South.

While the IMF was created to prevent financial instability and the World Bank was devised to finance economic recovery, the General Agreement on Tariffs and Trade (GATT) was forged to prevent discriminatory trade practices, such as those that flourished in the 1930s, and which were largely seen as causing the Great Depression (1929–41). The basic goal of the GATT was not to regulate trade, as its successor the World Trade Organization (WTO) currently is empowered to do. Rather, the GATT was designed to facilitate freer trade on a multilateral basis. Freer trade has been facilitated through a series of international negotiations (known as 'rounds') over the past 50 years, each lasting several years. The number of states involved in these rounds has grown over this period as well. In 1947, 23 states participated, whereas the Uruguay round of trade negotiations (1986–94) included 107 states. In 2004, WTO membership was comprised of 147 states.

The GATT sought to centralize trade negotiations, as well as to ensure that trade liberalization would in turn be applied to all states. The core principle of the GATT is non-discrimination. This prevents the emergence of privileged trading blocs, which were believed to act in a protectionist or discriminatory manner against Third World states. To deter this type of discriminatory practice, the GATT devised the most-favoured-nation (MFN) clause.[4] MFN means that every time a member state (of the BWS) improves the benefits that it gives to one trading partner, it must grant the same best treatment to all other members, so that they remain equal.[5] This same principle forms the cornerstone of the WTO.

The post-Bretton Woods era (1971 to the present)

Towards the end of the 1960s, it became evident that this US-based world order was no longer working well. Not only was American hegemony in trouble; also, the world economy was facing a major downturn (Cox, 1993; Webber and Rigby, 1996; Agnew and Corbridge, 1995). It is useful to point out here that many analysts believe that this period marks the start of globalization (Ohmae, 1990; Reich, 1992; cf. Hirst and Thompson, 1999). We shall return to globalization later in the chapter; for now it is useful to explore three interrelated world events that led to the breakdown of the Bretton Woods system in the early 1970s: (1) the rise in the Euromarkets, (2) two significant hikes in the price of oil by the Organization of Petroleum Exporting Countries (OPEC),[6] and (3) the end of the fixed exchange rate arrangements. It is important to examine these events because they shed light on the demise of the BWS. They also represent the roots of the 1980s debt crisis, which plagued over 20 countries of the Third World. First, the Euromarkets, or Eurodollar markets, began to emerge as a major force within the world economy. Very broadly, Euromarkets are offshore markets where Eurocurrencies are traded. The largest Euromarket is in London. A Eurodollar deposit is nothing more than American dollars deposited in a bank outside the US. Banks were attracted to these foreign currency deposits due to the perceived profit opportunities arising from the comparative regulatory freedom accorded to such activity. American banks in particular found the offshore market irresistible because it allowed them to bypass many limitations set by US government, such as domestic reserve requirements, interest-rate limitations, and capital controls regulating financial flows. Unlike during the post-Bretton Woods era, capital controls were a key feature of the BWS, as it was generally believed that sustained and stable growth could only be achieved if states were masters over finance (Helleiner, 1994).

Second, the growth and power of the Euromarkets have been closely tied to further acceleration in the internationalization of banking activity, especially in the aftermath of skyrocketing oil prices in 1973–74, and again in 1978–79. Two immediate consequences of the oil shocks were a rise in imbalances in the pattern of global payments, and the phenomenon referred to as 'petrodollars'. Because most countries were experiencing a downturn in their economies during this period, many, particularly in the developing world, found it difficult to make payments on the rising cost of petroleum. Simultaneously, the cartel known as OPEC purchased US dollars with their huge profits and reinvested them in the unregulated Euromarkets, where their investments would receive the highest return. Banks operating in the Euromarkets, and especially American banks, provided huge loans to cash-strapped governments in the developing world.

The third, and decisive, factor that led to the demise of the BWS was the recessionary climate experienced by most countries at this time, and which was particularly acute in the US. The effects of economic 'stagflation' (high unemployment mixed with high inflation rates) translated into growing balance of payments problems for the country. In response to mounting domestic pressures, the Nixon administration in the US turned inwards, taking a protectionist stance. In 1971, the US government suspended the dollar's gold convertibility. This move was motivated by the fact that there were simply not enough US gold reserves to meet international demand for gold. In 1973, the US government abandoned the fixed exchange rate system, and effectively did away with the BWS. From this point onwards, national currencies that belonged to the BWS would be determined by the forces of supply and demand (and speculation) in the global marketplace, otherwise known as a 'floating exchange rate system'. It should be emphasized that, despite the shift to the floating system, the US dollar continues to act as the world's trading and reserve currency.

After 1973, governments became increasingly reliant on global financial markets to sustain their countries' balance of payments. The US began experiencing trade and budget deficits, and by the 1980s the once solvent US shifted its status from that of a creditor to that of a debtor nation. Since this period, the US has sustained its dominance in the world largely through borrowing, which has increased successively over the past several decades. This has had, and will continue to have, important ramifications for the rest of the world, especially the South. A 2004 report by the IMF suggests that 'the United States is running up a foreign debt of such record-breaking proportions that it threatens the financial stability of the global economy'. The report goes on to warn that

> the net financial obligations of the United States to the rest of the world could equal 40 percent of its total economy within a few years – 'an unprecedented level of external debt for a large industrial country' that it said could play havoc with the value of the dollar and international exchange rates ('IMF Report says US Deficits Threaten World Economy', *New York Times*, January 7, 2004).

The growing deficits also imply that the US must suck in huge amounts of foreign investment, in terms of both foreign direct investment (FDI)[7] and foreign portfolio investment (FPI).[8] Indeed, the biggest investors in US government bonds, also referred to as Treasury bonds, are the Japanese. We examine various aspects of this weakness of the US economy in the next four chapters.

Unlike the BWS, which was predicated on more insulated forms of national control over economic policy-formation, the post-Bretton Woods era is marked by the increased power of markets over states – what is generally referred to as neoliberalism. In very broad terms, neoliberalism refers to the diehard and naïve belief that the constant liberalization of financial markets and trade will lead to some sort of magical self-healing and self-adjustment of the economy, in which all societies will benefit. The so-called 'neoliberal revolution' was spearheaded by the United States' President Reagan (1981–89) and the British Prime Minister, Margaret Thatcher (1979–90), both of whom busily enacted policies that would strengthen the power of capitalists by, for example, mandating the removal of all trade tariffs and barriers to financial flows, the privatization of all state-run services including utilities, while diluting the bargaining power of labour unions in their struggles for wage increases and social benefits by weakening the labour laws to encourage greater 'wage flexibility', or what Greg Albo refers to as 'competitive austerity' (Albo, 1994).

The new policy orientation of neoliberalism was also reflected in the international development agenda pursued by the IMF and the World Bank in the 1980s – what has become known as the Washington consensus. This neoliberal model suggests that the liberalization of trade, privatisation of government-owned industries, and deregulation of financial markets will lead to greater prosperity and sustainable economic development. The immediate implication for the inter-state system is that nation-states compete with each other for capital flows in the form of FDI and FPI. Signalling creditworthiness and demonstrating the investment potential and benefits of a country have become the overriding preoccupations of governments, in order to attract and retain capital investments. This competition for capital from international lenders has led in turn to the reordering of policy agendas. Government support for education, pensions, and social welfare has been reduced (and even, in some cases, eliminated), all in the name of remaining competitive and creditworthy in the global economy. As Robert Cox argues,

> [w]ith the demise of the Bretton Woods [system], a new [neoliberal] doctrine has achieved pre-eminence: states must become the instruments for adjusting national economic activities to the exigencies of the global economy – states are becoming transmission belts from the global into the national economic spheres. Adjustment to global competitiveness is the new categorical imperative (Cox, 1993: 260).

From a neo-Gramscian perspective, an argument could be made that the role of the US – alongside the World Bank and the IMF – is no longer hegemonic but rather dominant in the post-Bretton Woods era. That is to say, while the US is still the most powerful country, it has lost the consensus it enjoyed during the BWS, and thus exercises its power largely, albeit not exclusively, through coercive force. According to Cox, one of the underlying reasons for this is that the 'great masses' have become detached from their traditional ideologies, found in the BWS, such as state interventionism and welfare protectionism, and no longer accept as true what they used to believe (Cox, 1987). The increased manifestation of discontent with an Anglo-American-dominated neoliberal world is evident, as we saw above, through the numerous protests aimed at its core global institutions, such as the World Bank, the IMF, the WTO, the G-7, and so on. The question that emerges at this point is: How can we best understand the nature of the interstate system in this context? Drawing on the work of Italian Marxist, Antonio Gramsci, Cox suggests that the current situation may best be described as a 'crisis of hegemony'. The latter characterizes increasing expressions of contestation and discontent with the status quo, and the subsequent attempts to establish an alternate hegemony; or, more precisely, competing hegemonies. The rise of nationalist and religious movements in many parts of the Middle East in reaction to the 'war on terrorism', and elected socialist governments in Latin America over the past decade – for example, in Brazil, Venezuela, Boliva, Peru, and Argentina – are cases in point. From Cox's perspective, these cases represent threats by the 'great masses' to the neoliberal foundations upon which the dominant state rests, and are therefore greeted with increased coercion by both the US government and its allies (cf. Gramsci, 1971: 25–6; Cox, 1987). We discuss the crisis of hegemony in Chapter 2.

New openings: struggles for alternative hegemonies

Since the breakdown of the BWS and the subsequent crisis of US hegemony, there has been an intensification of conflict over the shape and scope of a new international trade and monetary order. According to Cox, there were three possibilities of structural transformation of the world order:

> a reconstruction of hegemony with a broadening of political management on the lines envisaged by the Trilateral Commission [involving Germany, the United States, and Japan]; increased fragmentation of the world economy around big-power-centred economic spheres; and the possible assertion of a Third-World-based counter-hegemony with the concerted demand for the New International Economic Order [NIEO] as a forerunner (Cox 1993a: 60–1).

The NIEO, which was formed in 1974, was the result of a convergence of two larger historical movements: the Non-Aligned Movement

(NAM) and the United Nations' Economic Commission for Latin America (ECLA).[9] The United Nations Conference on Trade and Development (UNCTAD) was established as a special body of the UN in 1964 by the Group of 77 developing countries (the G-77), despite protests from advanced industrialised countries. UNCTAD plays a vital role in politicizing and articulating the fact that Third World concerns should also be the broader concern of the international community. We explore this in more detail in Chapter 3.

During the 1970s, two important developments occurred under the aegis of UNCTAD, which served to challenge American hegemony in the South. The first was the establishment of the International Debt Commission (IDC) by the G-77 in 1979, in response to the growing levels of indebtedness of Third World countries. The G-77 wished to replace the informal manner of managing public debt with a formal institution, which could 'achieve a fair division of the workout costs between creditors and debtors, more consistent treatment across countries, and speedier recoveries' (Reiffel, 2002). Fearing a loss of control over the debt negotiation process by the IMF, as well as by both the Paris and London Clubs, the G-7 countries, led by the US, turned down the proposal to create an IDC. I discuss the IDC in Chapter 4.

The second development within the parameters of UNCTAD was the UN Centre on Transnational Corporations (UNCTC), created by the UN Economic and Social Council in 1974 in response to the growing presence of foreign corporations (mainly US companies) in the South. One of the key roles of the UNCTC involved drafting a code of conduct for First World transnational corporations (TNCs) operating in the Third World. The UNCTC was abandoned in 1995, and eventually replaced by the UN Global Compact, which is discussed in Chapter 3. Unlike the UNCTC, which aimed its policy proposals towards mandatory regulations in the South, the Global Compact caters to the interests of TNCs by framing its codes defining 'good corporate citizenship' in the South in purely voluntary terms. Again, some of the major limitations of establishing an alternative reality for the global South are found in the power structures underpinning the UN system. It is useful to point out here that the coercion undertaken by the dominant state may assume multiple forms, such as military and economic expressions of force over, for example, highly indebted Third World countries, like those situated in South Asia, Latin America, the Middle East, and sub-Saharan Africa. Examples of military force include the so-called 'war games' or 'US-Philippine joint military exercises' (code-named Kalayaan-Aguila 2002 or Mindanao Balikatan 02–1) being held in Basilan and Zamboanga. As Philippine scholar Roland G. Simbulan notes, 'Kalayaan-Aguila 2002 marks the largest US military intervention engaged in actual combat against "real, actual targets" on Philippine soil since the Philippine-American War (1899–1913)' (Simbulan, 2002). While an example of economic coercion over Highly Indebted Poor Countries is evident in President Bush's 'new compact for global development', otherwise known as the Millennium Challenge Account, which seeks to gain more control over Third World governments through the practice of extending grants as opposed to loans. I examine this strategy in greater detail in Chapter 5.

Aside from these specific developments, the 1970s and 1980s saw an increase in the number of international forums and Blue Ribbon Commissions over a wide range of issues – for example, the United Nations Development Fund for Women (UNIFEM)[10] in 1976; Global Taxation of financial flows by Nobel Laureate James Tobin in 1978; the Independent Commission on International Development in 1980, also known as the Brandt Commission;[11] the UN Convention on Ozone Depleting Substances in 1985; the World Commission on Environment and Development (more popularly known as the Brundtland Commission) in 1987, and the Global Forum on Human Survival in 1988. It must be kept in mind that aside from the good intentions behind these initiatives, the fate of these global commissions and forums ultimately rested on overcoming the dominance of the US and its allies – most notably international capitalists, who were the largest beneficiaries of the neoliberal revolution (van der Pijl, 1984; 1998; Holman, 1996; Robinson, 2004).

Both capitalist interests and the advanced industrialized states were also restructuring their power relations during this period. The meteoric rise of the German and Japanese economies, and growing uncertainty and mounting conflict in the post-Bretton Woods era, led to the formation of the Trilateral Commission in 1973. Established by private citizens of Japan, the European Union and North America (the US and Canada), the Commission was set up to encourage closer co-operation among the core democratic industrialized areas of the world. The main objective behind its formation was to overcome the considerable friction among governments, so as to work towards resolving key common problems. The Trilateral Commission emerged from a growing sentiment in the international community that the US no longer wielded a hegemonic position, and thus should adopt a shared form of leadership with Europe and Japan in order to navigate effectively new challenges at the international level (Gill, 1991).[12] During this same period, the powerful G-7 was established. The G-7, which was originally comprised of France, Germany, Italy, Japan, the UK, and the US (Canada joined later, in 1976), held its first summit in 1975 in Rambouillet, France. Since this time, the G-7 (or now including Russia, G-8), which involves heads of state or government of the major industrial countries, has been meeting on an annual basis to deal with the major economic and political issues facing its domestic societies, and the international community as a whole, such as macroeconomic management, international trade, and relations with developing countries (Baker, 2005).[13]

The 'New World Order' and the CGG

What is new today is that the interdependence of nations is wider and deeper. What is also new is the role of people and the shift of focus from states to people. An aspect of this change is the growth of international civil society.
Commission on Global Governance, *Our Global Neighbourhood*, 1995: xiv.

The fall of the Berlin Wall in 1989 not only represented the collapse of the Soviet Union, and thus the end of the East–West tensions that had characterized much of the post-1945 era (Saull, 2001), but also signalled the triumph of neoliberal-led capitalism over other forms of organizing modes of production and exchange – most notably communism. The collapse of the Berlin Wall was believed by many to mark the start of a 'New World Order' – a phrase coined by George Bush Sr in his celebrated State of the Union speech in January 1991. While Bush Sr's New World Order was clearly predicated on continued US dominance, it also had the unintended consequence of legitimating the need for a more inclusive and multilateral form of leadership, particularly one that could address both the North–South and North–North issues that were discussed earlier in this chapter. As we will see, this new multilateral order was to be based on the existing power structures of the post-Bretton Woods era, such as the IMF and the World Bank, and, more importantly, US dominance.

In the attempts to develop a new multilateral order, Willy Brandt, former Chancellor of Germany (1969–74), invited members from his own Commission on International Development in 1980 (also known as the Brandt Commission) to meet with members of other Commissions, such as Olof Palme's Commission on Disarmament and Security (1982), and Gro Harlem Brundtland's Commission on Environment and Development, as well as Julius Nyerere's South Commission, established in 1987 (CGG, 1995: xv). This led to a meeting of minds in Sweden in 1991 and the presentation of a document entitled 'Common Responsibility in the 1990s: The Stockholm Initiative on Global Security and Governance' (or simply the Stockholm Initiative). As a follow-up to the Stockholm Initiative, Brandt, Brundtland, and Nyerere invited Ingvar Carlsson, former prime minister of Sweden, and Sir Shridath Ramphal, former Secretary-General of the British Commonwealth, to co-chair a Commission on Global Governance in 1992. The CGG also received support from an important figure in international circles at the time: Dr Boutros Boutros-Ghali, who was Secretary-General of the UN from 1992 to 1997.[14] The CGG published its final Report on Global Governance in 1995.

It is worth emphasizing that, according to the CGG, the perceived need for global governance is not only a result of the geo-politics of the New World Order, but also of transformations brought about by globalization. For the CGG, globalization has led to a series of changes, such as financial and trade liberalization, which have in turn been tied to the emergence of powerful non-state actors, such as TNCs[15] (Kindleberger, 1969; Hymer, 1976; Cohen et al., 1979; Vernon, 1971; 1977; Stopford et al., 1992), institutional investors, such as pension and mutual funds (Cerny, 1993; Strange, 1998; Harmes, 2002), offshore markets (Palan, 2003), emerging global-level private authorities regulating both states and much of transnational economic and social life, such as credit-rating agencies and cartels in various industries (Sinclair, 2003; Underhill, 1997; Murphy, 2000: 794), and technological advances in communications and transportation. According to the CGG, technological progress and the presence of powerful global economic actors have led to erosion in the authority of nation-states (Sassen, 1996; 1998; Strange 1996; Ohmae 1995; Archibugi et al., 1997). It is further assumed that technological progress and the weakening of the power of nation-states have led to the rise of important linkages between various civil society organizations able to exert their influence beyond national levels of government to form global linkages and institutions – or what some more optimistically refer to as global civil society or cosmopolitan democracy (Archibugi and Held, 1995; Archibugi 1998; cf. Colás, 2002; Drainville, 2004). Indeed, the CGG seems to echo this sanguinity surrounding the debates on cosmopolitan democracy, stressing that emerging forms of global governance are not characterized by a predominant power, either within the private or the public sphere, on the world stage. It follows that the only way to complement this positive trend is to strengthen the most important institutional feature of global governance – namely, the UN. In the words of the CGG, 'It is our firm conclusion that the United Nations must continue to play a central role in global governance' (CGG, 1995: 6; cf. Rittberger, 2001). We now turn to an examination of the underlying premises of this particular worldview.

ASSESSING GLOBAL ECONOMIC GOVERNANCE: THEORETICAL UNDERPINNINGS

If we cast a wide net over global economic governance, we discover a rich and diverse set of debates, such as regime theory (Ruggie, 1992; 1993; 2004), 'new multilateralism' (Cox, 1997; Gill, 1997; Schechter, 1999; Sakamoto, 1994), complex multilateralism (O'Brien et al., 2000), cosmopolitan democracy (Held, 2003; 2004; Held and McGrew, 2002; Held and Archibugi, 2005), and even world government (Murphy, 1994). When we search for specific theoretical assumptions that underpin *Our Global Neighbourhood*, the literature thins out considerably. James Rosenau's work (Rosenau, 1992; 1995; 1997) is an exception to the rule. Rosenau's theorizations of global economic governance are of particular import to our discussion, as his work analytically deepens and expands upon the CGG's findings. This is not to say that the other authors mentioned above do not provide important insight into the global governance debate. However, to avoid the vagueness inherent in many mainstream accounts of global governance, it is useful to strive to maintain a narrow and well defined focus, so as to interrogate more clearly some of the common-sense assumptions underpinning this term. Moreover, the three main criticisms that I levy against Rosenau's work are readily applicable to mainstream accounts of global governance.

Like the CGG, Rosenau is concerned with searching for 'order in disorder, for coherence in contradiction, and for continuity in change' in the post-1989 era (Rosenau, 1995: 13). Moreover, both Rosenau and the members of the CGG firmly believe that globalization has brought about irreversible social, political, and economic changes. Relatedly, there is a strong assumption that, due to the plethora of new actors and new economic and political challenges in the globalized, post-Cold War era, 'global life late in the twentieth century is more complex than ever before in history' (Rosenau, 1995: 16). Rosenau and the CGG, as well as many other global governance theorists (Ruggie, 2004; Held, 2003; Held and Archibugi, 2005; Slaughter, 2004; but cf. Rosenberg, 2000) assume that globalization has drastically altered the political and social fabric of the world order; according to Rosenau, the 'very high levels of interdependence and vulnerability stimulated by technological change now necessitate new forms of global political authority and even governance' (Rosenau, 1995: 19; cf. Held 2003; Ruggie 2004). The implications of this assumption are vast. From their vantage point, globalization is a fluid and omniscient force. It follows from this that the attempts to create some semblance of order, coherence, and continuity (global governance) flow through all 'systems of rule at all levels of human activity – from the family to the international organisation'. The need for this broad formulation is simple, according to Rosenau: '[I]n an ever more interdependent world where what happens in one corner and level [has repercussions for others], it seems a mistake to adhere to a narrow definition in which only formal institutions at the national and international levels are considered relevant' (Rosenau, 1995: 13). Mirroring this, the CGG highlights the growing significance of public–private partnerships as 'networks of institutions and processes ... that enable global actors to pool information, knowledge, and capacities to develop joint policies and practices on issues of common concern' (CGG, 1995: 15; Held and McGrew, 2002). This situation, Rosenau posits, has been the result of a shift away from thinking about governance solely in terms of command-type relationships, goals, policies, and directives, usually associated with the activities of governments. Such activities, which dominated the 'pre-globalization' era (the Cold War period) involve hierarchical or even authoritarian rule, which Rosenau distinguishes by the term 'command mechanisms' (Rosenau, 1995: 14; 1997). This position also resonates in many other mainstream readings of global governance. For example, Held and McGrew argue that 'the end of the Cold War contributed to the dwindling legitimacy accorded to hierarchical or hegemonic modes of regulating world order. These modes are contested by a diverse range of transnational pressure groups, social movements, and protest movements' (Held and McGrew, 2003: 8).

In the era of globalization, governance no longer exclusively entails the activities of governments. Indeed, governance may also include 'the many other channels through which "commands" flow in the form of goals framed, directives issued, and policies pursued' (Rosenau, 1995: 14; cf. Ruggie 2002; 2004). Rosenau's goal in thinking seriously about global governance is to understand the ways in which the practices and institutions of governance can and do evolve in such a manner as to be minimally dependent on hierarchical, command-based arrangements (Rousenau, 1992). This complements the CGG's concern that new governance mechanisms must strive to be more inclusive and participatory than in the past. For the CGG, what is required is a multifaceted strategy for global governance (CGG, 1995: 5). Rosenau suggests that there already exist variegated strategies in our globalizing world. To identify and describe these emerging relations and structures, he alters his analytical lens slightly by replacing command mechanisms with what he terms 'control or steering mechanisms' (Rosenau, 1992). Unlike their command counterparts, steering mechanisms do not presume the presence of hierarchy, thus allowing theorists to understand the process of governance as a way in which an organization or society steers itself. Rosenau's framework allows for this type of nascent strategy as it seeks to conceptualize the way various organizations and societies choose to steer or to control their activities in terms of a complex process that shapes, and is shaped by, macro-processes – such as the European Union, the World Social Forum, the World Bank, the North American Free Trade Agreement, Greenpeace, and the International Committee of the Red Cross – and micro-processes, such as local co-operatives and NGOs, as well as other forms of support networks located at sub-national, national, and global levels. As Rosenau suggests,

[g]lobal governance is the sum of myriad – literally millions of – control mechanisms driven by different histories, goals, structures, and processes. Perhaps every mechanism shares a history, culture, and structure with a few others, but there are no characteristic or attributes common to all mechanisms (Rosenau, 1995: 16).

If we pursue Rosenau's line of thinking, control mechanisms range from a mixture of private volunteer and profit-making organizations, to social movements, to transnational institutionalized control mechanisms, such as credit-rating agencies, and sub-national institutionalised mechanisms like crime syndicates (Rosenau, 1995). Thus, according to this view, 'spheres of authority', which, for Rosenau, include political, economic, and social dimensions, have been relocated from the arena of nation-states to non-state areas of competence or a mixture of private and public partnerships that operate at the local, global, and transnational spaces (Rosenau, 1997; Murphy, 2000; Sinclair and King, 2001; Ruggie, 2004; Held and Archibugi, 2005). Rosenau also points out state-sponsored mechanisms, such as those related to what has become known as the 'new regionalism'. For Rosenau, new regionalism, such as in the formation of the North American Free Trade Agreement (NAFTA), is a macro-phenomenon that is a central feature of global governance (Rosenau, 1995). Unlike the 'old regionalism', which was present during the Cold War, the new regionalism 'consists of more spontaneous processes from within that unfold largely on a bottom-up basis as the constituent states find common cause in a deepening interdependence' (Rosenau, 1995: 27; Hettne, 1999; 2000; cf. Phillips, 2004).

STRUCTURE OF THE BOOK

Drawing on the above discussion, Chapter 2 identifies three common-sense assumptions that run through the general understanding of global governance. First, global governance is seen as a by-product of globalization, which has decreased the power of nation-states. Second, there appears to be an absence of hierarchical power relations in global governance. And third, embracing the common values imbued in global governance is beneficial for the development of the South. To expose and transcend these common-sense assumptions, I construct an alternative theoretical lens that is firmly rooted in an historical-materialist approach. This frame for understanding is comprised of two main parts. The first deals with the need to move away from using globalization as the basis for explaining the rise and nature of global governance, and to view it as a moment of the wider neoliberal-led forms of capitalist restructuring. This restructuring does not occur in outer space but in and between nation-states, as well as through international organizations such as the IMF and the World Bank. The second part entails a more sophisticated understanding of the capitalist state, and in particular its role in the global restructuring of capitalism. Moreover, these restructuring processes, which are fraught with contradictions and conflicts, are heavily shaped, although not determined, by the neo-Gramscian notion of American dominance, or what Stephen Gill refers to as US supremacy (Cox, 1987; Gill, 2005). These terms capture the increased forms of economic and physical coercion undertaken by both the

US and ruling capitalist classes in other national social formations, under the rubric of neoliberal restructuring.

When the various strands of the chapter are pulled together, we will have an analytical platform from which we may explore three dimensions of global governance. Through this exercise, I hope to offer the reader three different windows through which to view and understand the various capitalist dimensions of global governance. Each window is represented by one of the following three chapters, and has been designed so as to allow us to gain a three-dimensional perspective of the capitalist nature of global governance, which includes the struggles and contradictions inherent in neoliberal restructuring.

In Chapter 3, I construct the first window through which we can observe how state and non-state actors (NGOs and TNCs) interact to balance societal needs in the Third World against capitalist restructuring strategies. Specifically, we explore historically two key international strategies of corporate social responsibility (CSR) in the post-war period: (1) the Code of Transnational Corporations set up by the UNCTC in 1974, and (2) its predecessor, the Global Compact, launched by the UN in 2000. Unlike most discussions of these two strategies of CSR, which tend to produce the same three common-sense assumptions underpinning global governance, this chapter seeks to go beyond the differences between the Code and the Global Compact by situating both strategies historically within the larger contradictions and struggles of global capitalism, as well as American dominance.

In Chapter 4, we peer through a second window that will allow us to grasp yet another dimension of global governance. Indeed, to date, there has been no attempt in the wider global governance debates to evaluate critically the manner in which transnational debt has been managed since the outset of the Bretton Woods system in 1944. Why has the implicit and *ad hoc* nature of transnational debt architecture been reproduced in the post-war period, despite its obvious shortcomings? Who benefits from this arrangement? In what follows, I tackle these questions by arguing that the informal arrangement governing transnational debt architecture not only helps augment the power of credit to serve as an effective form of social discipline, but that it is also profoundly contradictory in nature. Through an historical survey, spanning from the beginning of the Bretton Woods system to the 2001 Argentine default, the chapter demonstrates that the informal and *ad hoc* characteristic of the transnational debt architecture, coupled with the mounting power of global financial capitals over debtor states, has led to growing levels of volatility and increasing forms of fragility in the international credit system.

In Chapter 5 we encounter our third and final window through which to examine a highly controversial development agenda proposed by President George W. Bush in March 2002 – namely, the Millennium Challenge Account (MCA), or what many members of the Bush administration have referred to as a 'revolutionary development initiative'. Despite its impact on normalizing, and thus legitimating, the tendency towards the privatization of aid and militarization of development (physical coercion), there has been very little critical work on the MCA, and, in particular, the ramifications of this development agenda with regard to global economic governance. This chapter sets out to fill this gap by attempting to understand the MCA historically as a moment of global capitalism and American empire.

In Chapter 6, I revisit the main argument of the book, draw analytical and political conclusions regarding this study of global governance, and discuss areas for future research with regard to radical political economy or historical-materialist understandings of world politics.

2
Transcending Common Sense: Towards an Historical-Materialist Critique of Global Governance

There are good reasons to be critical of mainstream approaches to global governance owing to their neglect of the unequal, exclusionary, and imperialist tendencies that are intrinsic to this seemingly inclusive term. This weakness has at least two important and interrelated consequences. On the one hand, there is an absence of any explanation regarding the changing nature of American empire and capitalist power in the world, especially with regard to developing countries. On the other hand, global governance acts to normalize, neutralize, and legitimate neoliberal-led forms of domination that facilitate global capitalist restructuring and expansion based upon ever-greater degrees of exploitation. The effects of the latter may be witnessed in, for example, the greater economic and social vulnerability of workers through competitive austerity, the destruction of the environment, and hyper-commodification of human relationships. The aim of this chapter is to evaluate mainstream global governance assumptions from a radical political perspective (historical materialism) by, first, identifying three theoretical weaknesses tied to global governance, and, second, constructing a broad analytical frame of historical materialism through which we will be able to penetrate the smooth and even surface of global governance in order to examine its capitalist core.

COMMON-SENSE ASSUMPTIONS OF GLOBAL ECONOMIC GOVERNANCE AND NORTH–SOUTH RELATIONS

According to Italian Socialist Antonio Gramsci (1891–1937), the dominance of one social class over others in capitalist societies may be termed 'capitalist (or bourgeois) hegemony'. This notion represents not only political and economic control of the ruling classes, but also the ability of the dominant class to project its own way of viewing the world, so that subordinated classes accept it as 'common sense' and 'natural' (Gramsci, 1971). In the same vein, we can identify at least three common-sense assumptions underpinning the above understanding of global governance. First, the *raison d'être* for global governance is rooted in the arrival of globalization. For Rosenau and the CGG, globalization denotes an inevitable, external force that has acted to decrease the power of nation-states. Second, states and businesses, as well as local and international NGOs, co-exist on a level playing field; thus there is no hierarchy of power relations in global economic governance. And, third, the embrace of the 'common values' allegedly imbued in global governance is viewed as beneficial for the Third World. In other words, global economic governance has important implications for development. I would like to challenge these common-sense assumptions with the following counter-points. First, global governance is not only based on an ahistorical and highly structuralist account of globalization, but also on a one-dimensional understanding of the state. Second, there is no conceptualization of power – in terms of either material wealth or political authority – in global economic governance. And, third, the above conceptualizations of global governance are marred with ethnocentric understandings of what has been referred to as 'developmentalism'. In the remainder of this section, I elaborate on these points.

With regard to the first common-sense assumption, global governance, as espoused by Rosenau and the CGG, adheres to an ahistorical and highly structuralist understanding (i.e. devoid of any human agency, such as decisions taken by policy-makers) of globalization. For Rosenau and the CGG, globalization deals with the perceived effects of this phenomenon and its main root cause: technological innovation. While no one can deny that developments in, for instance, information technology have transformed our lives, particularly through what Harvey refers to as a time–space compression (Harvey, 1989), this explanation tells us little about the relations of power behind the decisions to promote the information revolution. For instance, the US military-industrial complex, which had strong ties to the technological industries in the US, played a large role in the development of Silicon Valley. The latter was built in the 1960s and 1970s using government money, particularly those funds stemming from the US Department of Defense (see Johnson, 2004). Moreover, neither Rosenau nor the CGG pose questions as to why international financial markets, as one of the key features of their understanding of 'globalization', have exploded tenfold compared with global trade and services – i.e. the productive sector. What is the link between active decisions to liberalize financial flows and the growth in power of Wall Street (Gowan, 1999; Soederberg, 2004)? What role have the IMF and the World Bank, or more specifically their neoliberal-inspired structural adjustment policies, played in augmenting the power of financial markets and TNCs in the South? Who made these decisions, and why? Most importantly, who benefits? The inability to explain how globalization came about, aside from the advent of certain technical advances, leads to a fatalistic belief that new occurrences on the world stage, which eventually lead to great transformations of social, political and economic life, are not constructed by human beings, but rather simply happen to them. This view leads to another: globalization is perceived as an inevitable and unstoppable process. It follows that the only option available to governments, NGOs, and societies in general, is to work together and thereby construct global economic governance in order to achieve a more just, democratic, and equitable world shaped by the uncontrollable forces of globalization (Held, 2003; Ruggie, 2004).

The CGG and Rosenau fall short of offering an historical account of the phenomenon that lies at the heart of their conceptualization of global governance. The novelty of globalization is thereby over-inflated. There have been a number of scholars who have sought to challenge the globalization thesis by way of an historically informed empirical and theoretical inquiry into the very claims made by the CGG and Rosenau (Altvater and Mahnkopf, 1996; 2002; Hirsch, 1990; Arrighi, 1994; Arrighi and Silver, 1999; Sklair, 2002; Radice, 1975; Panitch, 1994; Bonefeld and Holloway, 1995; Bonefeld and Psychopedis, 2000; Bond, 2003; Robinson, 2004; Drainville, 2004). In their oft-cited book, *Globalization in Question*, Paul Hirst and Grahame Thompson posit that globalization is largely a myth (Hirst and Thompson, 1996; 1999).[1] By making the distinction between globalization and internationalization, these authors conclude that, despite the technological innovations and the ascendancy of financial markets, we are not witnessing the development of a new economic structure, but rather a transition towards greater international trade and investment within an existing set of economic relations, or what they refer to as 'internationalization'. This state of affairs, according to Hirst and Thompson, is still fundamentally characterized by exchange between relatively distinct national economies, where many outcomes, such as the competitive performance of firms and sectors, are substantially determined by processes occurring at the national level (see Ruigruk and van Tulder, 1995). These authors also suggest that the myth of globalization has had important ramifications for the role of nation-states in the wider internationalization process. For instance, the globalization myth, or what some rightly term the 'hyper-globalist' view, has permitted analysts, journalists and policy-makers to side-step the importance of national-level processes in shaping our world. This in turn acts to legitimate new ways of thinking about social, political, and economic organizations, institutions, and structures, such as the exigency of the UN and what Rosenau refers to as private–public control or steering mechanisms in managing globalization. I will now turn to a closer examination of the state in this first assumption.

For Rosenau and the CGG, the state is viewed as a thing or structure that can easily be whittled away by various social forces in order to open up room for competing forms of steering mechanism. Although the CGG and Rosenau never clearly define what is meant by this main unit of their analysis, given the ease with which the power of nation-states is easily rivalled by economic actors, international organizations, and NGOs, we may be able to deduce that both Rosenau and the CGG adhere to a pluralist understanding of the state. Briefly, pluralism denotes a political system that is comprised of individuals, groups and organizations that compete to have their interests acknowledged and represented by the state. It is worth highlighting that pluralism assumes a level playing field among these various groups, organizations, individuals, and so forth – irrespective, for example, of their varying degrees of wealth, education, or professional connections with state officials (Schmitter, 1975; cf. Dahl, 1956). Accordingly, for the CGG and Rosenau, the state mediates between different interests in a manner assumed to serve 'the common good' (democratic ideals, private property, the rule of law), which is not necessarily tied to the will of the majority (see Siebert, 2003; Held, 2003). At an international level, the CGG's push for common values and goals across national, cultural, religious, and socio-economic spaces is a direct derivative of the liberal assumption of the 'common good'. This is also reflected in Rosenau's approach, where nascent control mechanisms and the variegated interests, goals and needs tied to them are seen to co-exist harmoniously with the (liberal democratic) common good. The latter is necessary to keep some semblance of order, coherence, and continuity in Rosenau's system. This stance seems to resonate with Held's understanding of cosmopolitanism, or what he more recently refers to as a 'social democratic' approach to global governance (Held, 2004). For Held, the powerfully complex forms of economic globalization require ongoing discussions in public life, so as to institutionalize the 'public use of reason' in non-coerced national and transnational forms of public dialogue and debate. Through this exercise, Held suggests that adequate levels of equality, liberty, rights, and vital interests will be ensured (Held, 2003: 313). Both Held and Rosenau fail not only to grasp the integral connection between capitalist society and state forms, but also do not understand the inherent structural contradictions that affect, and in turn are affected by, struggles and conflicts based around issues of power in all of its expressions – wealth, political, and social power of one group/class or government over another. I will pick up on this discussion of the social democratic nature of global economic governance when I discuss strategies of corporate social responsibility in the next chapter.

How this common good is recreated, and the tensions and struggles over competing versions of reality therein, are not considered by either Rosenau or the CGG. There also seems to be a crude sort of zero-sum game between the state and civil society at play in this analysis. If private organizations and societies, for instance, somehow become empowered through the forces of globalization, they would be able to compete, and eventually replace some of the traditional responsibilities of the state – i.e. shift from control to steering mechanisms, and thereby diminish its power. Some further implications of the first common-sense assumption that globalization has led to the withering away of the powers of the state lie in the failure to grasp historically the important, albeit constantly changing, role all states play in supporting greater internationalization of capital through coercive means. This serves particular (capitalist) interests, as opposed to 'the common good' (see Gramsci, 1971; Poulantzas, 2000; Holloway, 1995; Clarke, 1988; Hirsch, 1974; 1992; Panitch, 2000; Robinson, 2004). By analytically whittling away the roles and powers of states, global governance enthusiasts not only fail to grasp the changing nature of the *form* of state power, but also normalize and neutralize these coercive forms of state – most notably the current neoliberal expression. It is important to note that neoliberalism does not assume a homogeneous form across political, social, and economic spaces. As Alfredo Saad-Filho and Deborah Johnston argue,

[n]eoliberalism straddles a wide range of social, political and economic phenomena at different levels of complexity. Some of these are highly

abstract, for example the growing power of finance or the debasement of democracy, while others are relatively concrete, such as privatization or the relationship between foreign states and local non-governmental organisations. Nevertheless, it is not difficult to recognise the beast when it trespasses into new territories, tramples upon the poor, undermines rights and entitlements, and defeats resistance, through a combination of domestic political, economic, legal, ideological and media pressures, backed up by international blackmail and military force if necessary (Saad-Filho and Johnston, 2005: 1–2; cf. Soederberg et al., 2005 for different national expressions of neoliberalism).

In fact, neoliberalism is never discussed, let alone mentioned, either in the CGG's Report, or in Rosenau's conceptualization of global governance (Rosenau, 1992; 1995). As Craig Murphy notes, Rosenau, like many global governance theorists, fail to evaluate critically not only the supremacy of the neoliberal agenda both within and across states, but also how global governance has been complicit with the dominance of neoliberalism (Murphy, 2000: 796; cf. Osborne and Gaebler, 1992; Donahue and Nye, 2002). The reason for this is that neoliberalism is not seen as a problem, but rather as a neutral set of policies and processes emanating from a democratic state, brought about by natural economic progression of the market embodied in globalization (cf. Held and McGrew, 2003; Ruggie, 2004). With its emphasis on less state intervention in the marketplace, neoliberalism may be viewed, in Rosenau's framework, as an integral element in assisting in the shift from command to control mechanisms. A critical evaluation of the role neoliberalism has played in shaping people's lives over the past quarter of a century is also side-stepped – especially its effects on the increasing levels of impoverishment in the world witnessed, for example, in the stunning growth in urban slum populations (Global Urban Observatory, 2001, quoted in Davis, 2004) and the mammoth growth in the informal working class in the South (Altvater, 2002; Altvater and Mahnkopf, 2002). As Mike Davis observes,

the gap between poor and rich countries increased, just as it had done for the previous 20 years and, in most countries, income inequality increased, or, at best, stabilised. Global inequality, as measured by World Bank economists, reached an incredible Gini coefficient level of 0.67 by the end of the century. This was mathematically equivalent to a situation where the poorest two-thirds of the world receive zero income; and the top third, everything (Davis, 2004: 23; cf. UN-HABITAT 2003).[2]

The second common-sense assumption of global governance is that civil society, whether conceived at the local, national, or global level, is a neutral space devoid of power relations, which in turn allows for a highly optimistic view that anything is possible regardless of one's identity, material existence, or spatial location. Robert Latham articulates this problem as follows:

> Governance, unlike *power* for instance, has not been a central term of contestation and analysis in political science or the social sciences more generally. Its meaning has basically been taken for granted. It is taken to be what decision-makers, administrators, or steering committees generate as they manage or administer the activities of their organisations or those of the people and things for which they assume responsibility (Latham, 1999: 25).

For the CGG and Rosenau, global governance appears as a smooth surface in which inequality, exploitation, and class struggle are noticeably absent. One reason for this is global governance's conceptualization that civil society, like the state, is pluralist, as opposed to capitalist, in nature. Another is that its defenders refuse to nail down precisely where civil society begins and where it ends. Ellen Meiksins Wood captures the slippery nature of civil society when she observes that the term

> has come to represent a separate sphere of human relations and activity, differentiated from the state but neither public nor private or perhaps both at once, embodying not only a whole range of social interactions apart from the private sphere of the household and the public sphere of the state, but more specifically a network of distinctly *economic* relations, the sphere of the market-place, the arena of production, distribution, and exchange (Wood, 1990: 61).

As will become clearer, by contextualizing global governance within the wider contradictions and struggles associated with global capitalism, we are better placed to observe and explain relations of power that are not only unequal but also inherently exploitative in nature. This condition places important limits on the assumptions of mainstream understandings of global governance that states and societies are able to choose their own destiny by simply working hard to exert their particular interests through the most appropriate steering or control mechanisms, and thereby change the social structures around them. The construction of an analytical framework later in the chapter enables us to grasp these relations of power historically, so that we can evaluate the actual progress of struggles. We will also be able to identify various limitations in relations of domination, or as Marx once put it: '[people] make their own history, but they do not make it just as they please; they do not make it under circumstances chosen by themselves, but under circumstances directly encountered, given and transmitted from the past' (Marx, 1986: 97).

The third and final common-sense assumption underpinning global governance is its ethnocentric and paternalistic understanding of development, or what some scholars have critically referred to as 'developmentalism' (see Escobar, 1995; 2004; McMichael, 2004; Leys, 1996; Said, 1979; Berger, 2004; Robinson, 2002). Broadly speaking, this term describes an ideologically driven attempt by political and economic leaders, as well as some large international NGOs, in industrialized countries to save or rescue poor countries from poverty, technological backwardness, overpopulation, and primitive, non-democratic forms of social organization, so that they may achieve 'human progress'. Developmentalism thus refers to a social construction that not only views the global South as infantile and inferior to the industrialized world, but also regards these North–South relations in an ahistorical manner. That is to say, there appears to be a gross neglect of the effects of imperial and colonial rule in the Third World, in which 'developed' countries exploited the land and labour of the South by imposing foreign forms of accumulation (I discuss this later in terms of 'primitive accumulation'), Eurocentric values and beliefs, including political systems, and the redrawing of new geo-political boundaries. Although Rosenau pays little attention to the Third World in his theorizations of global governance, other than in acknowledging the presence of nascent control mechanisms emanating from the southern hemisphere, there is an implicit assumption that the processes of global governance will lead to some form of humanitarian assistance to combat HIV/AIDS, child poverty and labour, illiteracy and malnutrition – all of which are expressed in the UN's Millennium Development Goals (see Chapter 5). What is far too easily done by both the CGG and Rosenau is the promotion of capitalist society as the only desirable form of social organization, not to mention its highly unequal and exploitative relations.

There is a particular Anglo-American form of neoliberal-led capitalism that is promulgated by the most powerful aid agencies in the world: the US Agency for International Development (USAID), and the international financial institutions (IFIs) such as the World Bank and the IMF, and the freshly minted Millennium Challenge Corporation, discussed in Chapter 5. On the other hand, the CGG fervently attempts to defend the detrimental effects of the IMF's past conditionalities as a major source of poverty and immiseration among millions of people in the South. For the CGG, 'the problems now often lie with the workings of the global international economic system as a whole rather than the IMF'. However, the solutions lie in 'an enlargement of the IMF's capacity to provide balance-of-payments support to finance cyclical deficits and shocks' (CGG, 1995: 184–5).

The immediate consequence of this position is the uncritical fashion in which IFIs are embraced by both Rosenau and the CGG. The shift from command to control mechanisms represents a relocation of authority through the introduction of a variety of organisations and societal interests. In other words, the institutional terrain of the pre-globalization era is thought to become more accountable and transparent through the growing involvement of members of civil society.

> The growing range of actors involved makes the challenge of governance more complex. Policy makers have to serve, engage, and mobilise a much wider variety of institutions – and hence to cope with a broader range of interests, values, and operating styles. Although institutional diversity may complicate the process, it could also greatly increase the capacity of the governance system to meet the complex demands placed on it (CGG, 1995: 34).

Again, the pluralist assumption is at work here that civil society is somehow a separate sphere of human activity from wider capitalist social relations, which integrally involve the state. This in turn allows the CGG to reproduce the status quo with regard to the IFIs, and Rosenau to embrace the transnational institutionalized control mechanisms and credit-rating agencies, such as Standard & Poor's and Moody's, viewed as competing institutions of specialized knowledge, rather than as institutions imbued with the power relations of neoliberalism. While Rosenau is careful to mention that there is far from a consensus regarding these new partnerships, he is unable to explain the underlying causes that have brought these new private–

public partnerships together in this particular configuration, and more importantly, identify the underlying relations of domination and exploitation tied to them. To accomplish this task, Rosenau's analysis would have needed to discuss the increasingly important role played by capitalists in the financing of 'development', primarily through FPI and FDI (the 'privatisation of aid') since the mid 1980s (see Chapters 3 and 5). In contrast to Rosenau, our framework suggests that there are specific capital interests which have important stakes in shaping the nature and degree of surveillance and disciplinary strategies in the global South, e.g., structural adjustment programmes, or transparency requirements under the IMF and World Bank's Reports on Observances of Standards and Codes (ROSC) programme, or regular reporting of credit-rating agencies. It must be highlighted that states play an important role in facilitating these strategies by legitimating neoliberal forms of political domination both over societies and within international organizations, such as the World Bank, the IMF, and the WTO. One such form of domination is the recreation of the illusion that state intervention reflects the 'common good' of 'civil society' as opposed to specific capitalist interests. What the CGG and Rosenau both ignore is that multilateral institutions and civil society do not float in mid-air, but are integral moments of the inter-state system that characterizes global capitalism, and thus reflect its power relations, tensions and contradictions. This is not to say that the IMF and World Bank are either instruments of powerful countries, such as the US government (see Gowan 1999), or autonomous actors (see Woods, 2003), but it does imply that their respective relationships to their capitalist foundations must be acknowledged and addressed (Murphy, 1994; 2000; Cox, 1987; Drainville, 2004; Taylor 2005).

Another feature that is absent from the discussions of the role of the IMF and the World Bank in the global governance debates concerning how best to achieve human and material progress, and thereby a sense of direction and significance for individuals living in the Third World, is the historical unfolding of relations of power within global capitalism. The implications of an uncritical understanding of 'development', coupled with the pluralist perspective of the IFIs, leads to the normalization, and thus acceptance, of neoliberal-led forms of political management in the South under the aegis of the Washington consensus. This not only symbolizes the 'common good', but also embraces the position that the root cause of the 'backwardness' of the Third World is the implementation of 'bad governance' policies, such as profligate government spending, protectionism, and currency manipulation (see Williamson, 1990; Fine et al., 2001; World Bank, 2002a). In other words, the reproduction of developmentalism inherent in global governance serves to normalize relations of power not only between advanced industrialized countries and the South, but also the relations of domination within Third World countries.[3] This, in turn, results in the further legitimation of capitalism as a natural, inevitable and desirable form of social organization. There is therefore no alternative but to go along with its expansion, based on the increased exploitation of labour and the environment, and the commodification of all areas of social life.

To begin to grasp the inner nature of global governance it is necessary not only to pierce its skin, but also to cut through to the bone. To accomplish these tasks, we need to understand historically the wider contradictions and relations of power from which global governance emerged. I will now turn to a conceptual map enabling us to approach global governance within an historical-materialist framework.

TOWARDS AN HISTORICAL-MATERIALIST UNDERSTANDING OF GLOBAL ECONOMIC GOVERNANCE

Beyond the common sense of global economic governance: neoliberalism in crisis?

Before addressing the two main components of our analytical frame, it is helpful to explain briefly the neo-Gramscian notion of 'common sense', and how it relates to our analysis. For Gramsci, common sense is not something permanent and immobile, but constantly transforms itself as 'ideology' and 'actual social experience' enter into confrontation (Showstack Sassoon, 1980; Gramsci, 1971; Cox, 1987). The Gramscian notion of ideology refers to shared ideas or beliefs (common sense) that serve to justify the interests of dominant classes by legitimating the latter's power in society, and thereby distorting the real situation in which people find themselves (Gramsci, 1971; Boggs, 1976; Cox, 1987). The pervasiveness and sheer dominance of neoliberalism, and its main common sense (natural) belief that market actors are inherently more rational than states, provides a good example of an ideology. It should be kept in mind that ideology can also assume a concrete form, such as IMF structural adjustment programmes or the UN's Global Compact (see Chapter 3).

Let's return to the above statement regarding the confrontation between people's actual social experience and ideology by looking at the role of neoliberalism in the South. For over three decades, Third World countries have been instructed by the IMF and the World Bank that sound macroeconomic fundamentals[4] (which, among other things, include balanced budgets, low inflation, high interest rates, stable currencies, the openness of the economy in terms of trade and finance, and the creation of market-friendly policies aimed at allowing foreign investors to enter freely) will lead to stable forms of economic growth, and thus an overall improvement in standards of living.

The neoliberal ideology underpinning this common-sense assumption, however, has clashed with the actual social experiences of the majority of the population situated in the Third World. While neoliberalism may have proved beneficial for the upper classes, and some middle classes, in the developing world the austerity programmes tied to the neoliberal-inspired structural adjustment programmes (SAPs), have had devastating consequences for many individuals and families situated in the lower echelons of these societies. Neoliberal common sense, for instance, would have it that the austerity programmes – which have involved, among other things, the slashing of social and welfare programmes, high interest rates, the privatization of state-owned industries, appropriation of land held by peasants for agri-business, and the removal of subsidies for food – are necessary to signal to the IFIs and other public and private donors, as well as potential investors that debtor countries have achieved, or at the very least are working towards achieving some measure of 'progress'.

The record has shown, however, that most people living in developing countries, other than India and China, have not experienced a material improvement in their lives, despite the fact that developing countries have continually attempted to adhere to the neoliberal tenets found in SAPs, such as privatization, liberalization, and deregulation. This will become more apparent as we proceed with our deconstruction of global governance throughout the book. For our purposes here, we can draw on two examples to illustrate our point. The first fact that reveals the laggard nature of economic growth in the South is the sheer volume of remittances from migrant workers to their families in the Third World.[5] According to a 2004 World Bank study, remittances amounted to $93 billion in 2003. The study observes that '[t]his is more than poor countries receive from aid or capital markets. The real number may be twice as high – making remittances greater than foreign direct investment and in some countries more valuable than exports' ('Economic Focus: Monetary Lifeline', *The Economist*, July 31, 2004). A second example of the growing confrontation between neoliberal ideology and actual social experience concerns one of the IMF's pin-up economies, Argentina. As has been well documented, at the end of 2001 Argentina had been transformed from one of the wealthiest countries in Latin America to the country with the world's biggest sovereign default. The common-sense assumption that neoliberal policies would lead to sustained economic growth and prosperity in Argentina were shattered.

Seen from this perspective, common-sense assumptions tied to neoliberal ideology – such as the assumption that the private operation of key sectors and services like water and healthcare will be far more efficient than when managed by governments – have come into direct confrontation with the real social experiences of many people in the South. The upshot of this has been the aggravation of the crisis of hegemony, which has existed since the fall of the BWS. Take, for example, the fact that both the IMF and the World Bank came under scrutiny at home too, as many think-tanks, politicians, and NGOs began to question the wisdom of the Washington consensus, therefore deepening the crisis of hegemony that characterizes American dominance. The subsequent birth of the post-Washington consensus, with its focus on good governance and inclusionary politics in the mid 1990s, and President Bush's Millennium Challenge Account (see Chapter 5) in 2003, may be viewed as attempts by the dominant classes to reform and revive neoliberal ideology, so as to legitimate capital accumulation strategies. These are based upon not only the ever-widening spatial reach of TNCs and global finance, but also the constant deepening of their exploitative activities, which we explore more fully in Chapters 3 and 4, respectively.

Over the past three decades, neoliberal ideology and its underlying common-sense assumptions have been fraught with contradictions, and therefore have constantly undergone transformations. I contend that global governance should be understood as a moment of this wider attempt to reproduce the status quo by freezing the contradictions associated with the crisis of hegemony. The main task of an historical-materialist approach[6] is to expose the contradictions in global governance in order to demystify the normal or common-sense nature of its neoliberal assumptions. It is hoped that we also reveal relations of inequality, exploitation, exclusion, and domination that lie at the core of global governance. The immediate consequence of such an exercise is to provide legitimation for competing versions of reality, which can form the basis of transformative political action towards a more equitable society. To this end, it is essential that we construct an alternative framework whereby we can we root our analysis of global governance within the contradictions and uneven development of capitalism, including a more sophisticated understanding of the role played by states.

Before continuing with this section, a proviso is in order. In what follows, I am not attempting to construct a comprehensive theoretical framework that will allow us to make sense of every moment and dimension of the CGG's and Rosenau's conceptualizations of global governance. This would be an overly ambitious project, given the variegated nuances and multiple levels of analysis involved in the concept of global governance. Instead, I offer a particular version of historical materialism, which draws loosely on Marx, neo-Gramscian analysis and Marxist state theory, that will enable us to expose the capitalist nature of global governance, as well as its role in recreating the conditions for the continuation of the crisis of hegemony. My theoretical approach is comprised of two main interlocking assumptions. First, there is a need to transcend the simplistic notion that global governance has been brought about through globalization. We should instead strive to contextualize global governance historically, within the wider contradictions of global capitalism, such as the chronic tendency to enter crisis. Second, unlike the CGG and Rosenau, all states continue to play an integral role in guaranteeing and recreating the conditions necessary for the restructuring of global capitalism, particularly along the lines of neoliberalism. Since this restructuring does not take place on a level playing field, some states – most notably the US – are not only more powerful than others, but also attempt to exercise their dominance over other states in order to recreate and expand their power in global capitalism. This dominance is understood here by the term 'American imperialism'. Taken together, both assumptions help us understand the shifting nature of the common-sense assumptions of neoliberalism, and, in effect, the foundations of global economic governance.

In the remainder of this section, I attempt to flesh out these three components of our alternative theoretical lens for deconstructing global economic governance by discussing, first, the nature of the social relations of capitalist production; second, the inherent tendency to crisis, and subsequent need for capitalist restructuring; and third, the role of capitalist states in relation to restructuring activities, and the nature of American imperialism in this process.

The social relations of capitalist production

Before examining some of the contradictions inherent in capitalism, it is useful to introduce one of the basic concepts of a Marxist or historical-materialist approach – namely, the social relations of production. Marxists reject not only the separation between society and economy, but also the very term 'economy', as understood by modern economists as an aggregation of individuals, households, and firms. The reason for this is that Marxists believe the manner in which societies are organized is historically contingent on what they refer to as a dominant mode of production. In the Middle Ages, for example, feudal societies (or fiefdoms) were organized around a particular mode of production. The King awarded land grants or fiefs to his most important nobles, barons, and bishops, in return for their contribution of soldiers for the King's armies. These noblemen or lords possessed the means of production – namely, a large amount of land – and had the rights to a particular amount of labour provided by serfs or peasants who lived on the estate. At the lowest end of society were the peasants or serfs. In exchange for the permission to live and work the land, the lord offered his peasants protection. The relations of domination between lords and the peasantry, which were fraught with tensions and contradictions, were not a natural state of existence. Thus, the coercive force, found in, for example, the military, was necessary to reproduce the unequal and exploitative relations between lords and peasants. As John Roemer observes:

> Feudalism was a coercive system; force against the peasantry was needed to extract the corvée and demesne labour [unpaid labour] that, under feudal rights, were owed to the lord. Such coercion was necessary, because the peasant family had access to its own means of reproduction, by virtue of its tenure on the family plot ... Hence, it was necessary for the lord to use *extraeconomic coercion* to extract serf labour for the manor ... (Roemer, 1988: 29; author's emphasis).

Within the context of a feudal mode of production, wealth and power were defined by the land. The more wealth each kingdom wished to amass, the more land its army needed to seize. Since land is not a boundless resource, this mode of production soon reached its limits. The transition to a new mode of production – capitalism – was long and bloody. Unlike its predecessor, the capitalist mode of production is based on private property relations and involves the production and exchange of commodities with the sole aim of increasing the value of capital initially invested. Profit is the amount of capital remaining after the expenses incurred in the production of a commodity have been paid. Unlike that of feudalism, the goal of capitalism is to amass continually more and more profits: what Marxists refer to as capital accumulation through surplus-value. The latter, like the corvée, is a form of unpaid labour. The appropriation of surplus does not necessarily represent exploitation, however. As we have seen, feudal societies also produced a surplus. 'The important point is that the exploitative injustice of capitalist production lies not in the disposition of the surplus per se ... but rather with the fact that those who perform the surplus are [labourers] who are excluded from the decision-making over its disposition' (Brennan 2005: 48).

There are many contradictions in the capitalist mode of production that are linked to exploitative relations between capitalists and workers, which in turn affect the capital accumulation process. Before turning to these contradictions, however, it is important to describe the two unequal social classes that not only comprise capitalist society, but also are inherently exploitative and thereby conflictual in nature: (1) the bourgeoisie, or capitalists, who own the means of production, such as a factory, and (2) the working class, who do not own any means of production. Workers own only their labour-power, which they must sell to the capitalist if they wish to earn a wage. The various and nationally historic configurations of these two social classes comprise what Marxists refer to as the social relations of capitalist production (or what I sometimes refer to in this book as 'relations of power'). I discuss this concept in detail below for two reasons – both of which are integral to achieving a better grasp of my version of historical materialism. First and foremost, social relations of production are not only fraught with contradictions, but also need to be constantly reproduced through ideological and coercive means. Second, understanding this concept helps us to demystify the mainstream notion that the economy and society are somehow separate entities.

It is important to underscore that capitalist society, like its feudalist counterpart, neither emerged from thin air nor was its birth attributable to some 'natural' or 'inevitable' occurrence. Both forms of social relations of production and exchange were created by historical conditions and human agency (the capacity to act, make decisions, and enter into conflicts with others). Marx uses the term 'primitive accumulation' to explain how capital accumulation and its underlying capitalist social relations of production emerged. Primitive accumulation 'plays approximately the same role in political economy as original sin does in theology' (Marx, 1990: 873). He further argues that primitive accumulation is 'nothing else than the historical process of divorcing the producer from the means of production' (Marx, 1990: 874–5). This separation, and thus the organization of labour as wage-labour, and the subsequent formation of a social class, is a necessary condition for capital since, according to Marx, 'money and commodities are no more capital than the means of production and subsistence are. They need to be transformed into capital [that is, relations from which surplus-value may be extracted]' (Marx, 1990: 874). This is also true of labour-power, which must be transformed into a commodity by setting workers free in the double sense of the word. Workers neither form part of the means of production themselves, as do serfs, nor do they own the means of production, as would be the case with self-employed peasant proprietors (Marx, 1990; Marx and Engels, 1964). Thus, by ensuring the 'freedom' of the workers, who own nothing but their labour-power, which they must sell to capitalists in order to survive, and of the capitalists, who own the means of production, the two opposing classes are forged, and therefore fulfil the fundamental conditions of capitalist production.

Occurring in Western Europe roughly between the sixteenth and early nineteenth centuries, primitive accumulation took place by predation, fraud, and violence, which forced peasants from the land and made them dependent on wage-labour primarily in the cities (Marx, 1990, Part 8; cf. Perelman, 2000). Although primitive accumulation was generally completed in Western Europe and North America in the nineteenth century, it is still an ongoing trend in many areas of the Third World. The approximately 3 billion people still producing and living in peasant societies in Asia, Africa, and Latin America (Amin, 2003) comprise, at least from the perspective of capitalists, a reserve army of future workers that can eventually be exposed, with the assistance of international organizations (the IMF, the World Bank, the WTO) and national governments, to conditions of super-exploitation: sweatshops in export promotion zones, for example.[7]

Crisis and restructuring in global capitalism

Given the highly conflictual nature of the unequal and exploitative relations that comprise capitalist society, crises are an inherent feature of capital accumulation. To overcome crises, capitalists need to restructure the social relations of production (capital–labour relations) by, for example, creating new products, introducing new machinery to reduce labour costs, disciplining the workforce to avoid paying higher wages, or seeking new labour and consumer markets abroad. It is to the topics of crisis and restructuring that we now turn. In the following two sections, it should be kept in mind that we are tracing the foundations of the crisis of hegemony.

Primitive accumulation was necessary to expand capitalist markets so as to overcome periodic barriers to capital accumulation, such as the chronic tendency of capital to accumulate beyond what can be reinvested profitably in the production and exchange of commodities (Clarke, 1988; Marx, 1981, Chapter 3; Harvey, 1999). Periods of overaccumulation are characterized by surpluses of capital and labour that are left unutilized or underutilized (Harvey, 1999; 2003a; 2003b; Clarke, 1988; Hirsch, 1974; 1992; Bonefeld, 1995; Holloway, 1995). The mammoth size of financial markets in relation to the so-called real economy (the production and trade of goods and services), rising levels of unemployment, and the numerous and creative attempts by retailers to off-load items by deferring payments or the principal sum of the goods (or both) are hallmarks of a crisis of overaccumulation. If system-wide devaluations of capital and labour-power are not to follow, then restructuring strategies must be found to absorb these surpluses. David Harvey suggests that restructuring strategies have tended historically to take two basic forms, reflecting what he refers to as spatial and temporal fixes, or a combination of the two – 'spatio-temporal fixes'. According to Harvey, 'temporal fixes' refers to displacements through investment in long-term capital projects or social expenditures (through activities such as research and development) that defer the re-entry of the excess of capital well into the future. 'Spatial fixes' describes the opening up of new markets, new production capacities and new resource, social and labour possibilities in different cities, regions, or countries (Harvey 2003a: 64). A good example of a spatio-temporal fix is provided by the neoliberal structural adjustment policies of the IMF and World Bank, which, by stressing the virtues of market-led reform, have paved the way for capitalists from the advanced industrial countries to exploit labour and the environment of the developing world through foreign direct investment in a Third World corporation, or foreign portfolio investment involving the purchase of a developing country's state-owned companies (see Chapter 3) and short-term government bonds (see Chapter 4).

Because of the chronic tendency towards the overaccumulation of capital, there has always been a constant need for capitalists to restructure, through expansion or temporal deferment. Capitalism is thus not something that is confined to national boundaries, and then, like leavened bread, has expanded to other national spaces. As Marx and Engels make clear in the *Communist Manifesto* (1848), given the inner contradiction of capitalism, it has always been inherently global and conflictual in nature:

> The bourgeoisie cannot exist without constantly revolutionising the instruments of production, and thereby the relations of production, and with them the whole relations of society ... The need of a constantly expanding market for its products chases the bourgeoisie over the whole surface of the globe. It must nestle everywhere, settle everywhere, establish connections everywhere. The bourgeoisie has through its exploitation of the world market given a cosmopolitan character to production and consumption in every country ... All old-established national industries have been destroyed or are daily being destroyed. They are dislodged by new industries, whose introduction becomes a life and death question for all civilised nations, by industries that no longer work up indigenous raw material, but raw material drawn from the remotest zones; industries whose products are consumed, not only at home, but in every quarter of the globe. In place of the old wants, satisfied by the productions of the country, we find new wants, requiring for their satisfaction the products of distant lands and climates. In place of the old local and national seclusion and self-sufficiency, we have intercourse in every direction, universal inter-dependence of nations (Marx and Engels, 1964: 63; Marx, 1981; cf. Luxemburg, 2003; von Braunmühl, 1978).

Before continuing, it is important to mention three provisos with regard to capitalist restructuring. First, the expansion of capital is neither a thing nor merely an economic process, but a development of social relations. The expression of this expansion in the form of colonialism and imperialism has much to do with primitive accumulation – the annihilation of self-earned private property or, which is the same thing, the expropriation of the labourer. Interestingly, as Harvey points out, the bourgeoisie was 'forced to acknowledge in its programme of colonisation what it sought to conceal at home: that wage labour and capital are both based on the forcible separation of the labourer from control over the means of production. This is the secret of 'primitive' or 'original' capital accumulation (Harvey 2001: 371–2). Second, restructuring efforts do not immediately translate into success in terms of creating new profitable venues for capital. Harvey, like many other Marxists, contends that global capitalism has been plagued by a crisis of overaccumulation since the early 1970s, the period corresponding to the fall of the BWS and the rise of so-called globalization (cf. Altvater, 2002). In other words, the various forms of restructuring of capital, along the lines of spatio-temporal fixes, have largely failed since the 1970s to deal effectively with overaccumulation of capital (Harvey, 2003a: 64). With the advent of neoliberalism in the late 1970s, restructuring tendencies began to assume a more austere expression. We will explore some of these capitalist strategies in the following chapters.

Third, restructuring strategies are inherently contradictory processes that cannot be carried out by capitalists themselves. It is not only the inevitable confrontation and struggles between capital and labour that require mediation by a seemingly neutral force, but also conflicts between competing capitalists – for example, between financial and industrial capitalists. The necessity of state intervention results from the fact that the capitalist process of reproduction structurally presupposes social functions that cannot be fulfilled directly by individual capitalists (Hirsch, 1974; 1992). The capitalist state and its ideological and coercive functions are integral moments of the social relations of production, and of the reproduction of these relations. The ability of the state to intervene legitimately into the social relations of production is embodied in its apparent neutrality, derived largely from bourgeois law, which grants it the superficial appearance of separation from the relations of production in the bourgeois constructions of 'civil society' and the market (Carruthers and Babb, 2000). The state's monopoly over the legitimate use of force (Weber, 1946: 78), such as the military, prisons, and police, is also important in its role as mediator and guarantor of the social reproduction of capital. Given the centrality of state actions to the restructuring of the social relations of capital to overcome the barriers brought about by the crisis of overaccumulation, it is important that we turn to the second aspect of our historical-materialist framework regarding the role of states and imperialism.

The American state and new imperialism

Since it is a moment of the wider contradictions and ongoing conflicts tied to capitalist restructuring, American imperialism assumes different expressions during different periods, such as the internationalist policies pursued during the Clinton administration (1993–2001), which the CGG mistakenly saw as an environment that could foster a UN-centred world of international co-operation. Currently we are faced with a more isolationist and protectionist posture under the Bush II administration (2001 to the present). What is important to keep in mind here is that despite the very real policy differences of the American state in global capitalism – whether multilateral or unilateral, Republican or Democratic – imperialist tendencies have remained at the core of its economic and military interventions into other nation-states, especially the global South, during the post-war period.

It is very important to highlight that Marx never developed a theory of imperialism, although the theories of imperialism that have emerged after Marx have drawn from Marx's work. There is a plethora of competing theories of imperialism spanning traditions of Marxism, neo-Marxism, Keynesianism, neoclassicism, and so on (Harvey, 2001). That said, in this section I will try to provide an understanding of imperialism at it relates specifically to our objective of deconstructing global economic governance as represented by the CGG and Rosenau.

I would like to take a brief detour here to spell out as clearly as possible my understanding of imperialism and American empire. For me, an understanding of imperialism and its source, American empire, must be rooted in a Marxian understanding of the spatial and temporal expansion of capital accumulation. I view the American capitalist state as dominant, both in economic and military terms, in relation to other states and societies. However, given the global nature of capital accumulation since its inception, it would be a fallacy to interpret the US state as representing simply American interests. For example, capitalists from all parts of the globe have a stake in the recreation of US-led imperialism, which is embodied in the Anglo-American form of neoliberalism – the expression par excellence of the political strategy to cope with the restructuring of capital relations. The neoliberal strategies pursued by American empire are, like all interventions by bourgeois states, highly contradictory as well as highly contested. American-led imperialsim represents political and ideological attempts to recreate capitalist social relations while assisting increased capitalist exploitation of all aspects of social life (labour markets, the environment, credit relations, and so on). Given that these strategies are not only highly contradictory in nature, but also conflict-ridden, we cannot generalize about imperialism; nor can we simply grasp the American state in the abstract. To grasp imperialism and its connection to global governance, we must begin to recognize and explain its various moments by studying concrete policy strategies.

While Marx and Engels rightly suggest that the bourgeoisie has played the most revolutionary part in the constant expansion of capitalism, it is important to stress that capitalists have not accomplished this feat on their own (Marx and Engels, 1964). Unlike global governance theorists, I maintain that states continue to play a key role in mediating the contradictions of capitalist accumulation. The question that surfaces here is: What is the state, or, more specifically, the imperial state? I begin our discussion with a brief elaboration of what I mean by imperialism, or 'new imperialism'. The latter should not be confused with classical imperialism,[8] which was associated with the territorial expansion of particular states and an elimination of competition, with the presence of monopoly capitalism. Drawing broadly on the recent work of Marxists (Panitch and Gindin, 2003; Harvey, 1999; 2003a; 2003b), 'new imperialism' describes a set of contradictory and international class-led strategies aimed at the wider restructuring of the social relations of capitalism, with the aims not only of overcoming the barriers to capital valorization imposed by the crisis of overaccumulation, but also of recreating the status quo, involving the subjugation of developing countries by the advanced industrialised countries (or G-7), particularly the US. At the heart of this expansion is the need to recreate and legitimize primitive accumulation. The US plays a central role in influencing the overall strategies of imperialism, such as those discussed in the following three chapters: the self-regulatory nature of the Global Compact (Chapter 3), the market-based Collection Action Clauses imposed on debtor states (Chapter 4), and the Millennium Challenge Account (Chapter 5).

'American imperialism' refers to a historically specific expression of domination and exploitation by the US, and transnational capitalist interests tied to it, over other countries. Since it is a moment of global capitalism, American imperialism is both highly dynamic and contradictory in nature. On the one hand, the American imperial state (Panitch, 2000) must constantly recreate the conditions of its power by ensuring, among other things, that all states, particularly subordinate or poorer states, adhere to the international rules and laws in order to facilitate the reproduction of capitalist social relations. This legal regime has largely been formulated by the US, along with other powerful industrial countries, and embedded in the global trade architecture represented by the World Trade Organization, the global development architecture represented by the World Bank and the IMF, and the New International Financial Architecture primarily represented by the Financial Stability Forum and the G-20 (Soederberg, 2002; 2004). In this way the American imperial state takes charge of recreating the conditions of its power through ideological and coercive means (Panitch, 2000; Cox, 1987). On the other hand, since capitalism is inherently prone to crisis (Marx, 1981; Harvey, 1999), there is a need to deepen and expand continually various strategies of exploitation. Since the early 1980s, these global restructuring strategies may be described by the term 'neoliberalism'. I discuss this term in more detail below. For now it is useful to grasp that neoliberal strategies of global restructuring have been captured in David Harvey's notion of 'accumulation by dispossession' (Harvey, 2003a; 2003b). According to Harvey, 'accumulation by dispossession' represents the crux of what he deems 'new imperialism'. Present forms of accumulation by dispossession

> include the commodification and privatization of land and the forceful expulsion of peasant populations; the conversion of various forms of property rights (common, collective, state, etc.) into exclusive private property rights; the suppression of rights to the commons; the commodification of labour power and the suppression of alternative (indigenous) forms of production and consumption; colonial, neo-colonial, and imperial processes of appropriation of assets (including natural resources); the monetization of exchange and taxation, particularly of land; the slave trade; and usury, the national debt, and ultimately the credit system, as radical means of primitive accumulation (Harvey, 2003b: 145).

The US plays a key role in facilitating – and, along with those state and capitalist interests aligned with it, is also the main benefactor of – 'accumulation by dispossession'. Drawing on this term, I suggest that American imperialism shapes, and is shaped by, the tensions inherent in reproducing the conditions of its own power in the world market by imposing new forms of domination over subordinate states, while, at the same time, overcoming inherent barriers to capital accumulation by physically expanding and deepening strategies of dispossession. Again, in following our earlier discussion of capitalist social relations and crisis, it is important to highlight that these strategies and policies are conflictual and contradictory in nature, which means that they also possess economic, political, ideational, and historical dimensions.

While the above definition of imperialism implies that the US plays a central role in shaping the inter-state system, care should be taken to avoid a deterministic understanding, in which the American state and capitalists are the main perpetrators of imperialism (Gowan, 1999; cf. Panitch and Gindin, 2003). In what follows, I suggest that there are two main problems with this perspective. First and foremost, it assumes wrongly that the US state is comprised of a homogeneous set of American national capitalist interests. There is a strong presence of foreign capitalists operating in the US, incorporating both the manufacturing and the financial sectors. The US has attracted the highest levels of FDI in the world during the post-war era, although, according to an OECD report, it was overtaken by China in 2003 ('Off to the Market', *Guardian*, June 29, 2004). The central position of Wall Street in the global financial markets makes the US a large importer of FDI, which is important to the recreation US dominance, as financial inflows, especially from countries like Japan, help to feed its ever-growing budget deficit (Gowan, 1999). As discussed above, when it comes to their constant search for surplus-value, capitalists know no national boundaries or national sentiment (Marx and Engels, 1964). The American bourgeoisie, for example, would invest their capital solely in China rather than the US if it facilitated a higher rate of profit. It should also be mentioned that a substantial amount ($1.9 of the $7.9 trillion) of American debt is held by foreigners. While Japan ($702 billion) remains the largest purchaser of US debt, China has rapidly increased its holdings ($250 billion), by 150 per cent from 2001 to 2005 (US House of Representatives, 2005).

Second, this position assumes an instrumentalist view of the American state that is, that the US is able to impose its policies on other states, and that other states, such as those in the G-7, agree with these policies. While many Third World states are usually in no position to deny the US's particular policy preferences, the ruling classes in the developing world will attempt to bargain for the best terms, so as to ensure the recreation of their own power. More importantly, the instrumentalist stance assumes that, generally speaking, the ruling classes (bourgeoisie + state officials, including politicians and bureaucracy) in the Third World are fundamentally opposed to US-led foreign policy, such as neoliberal-inspired SAPs. This is, in most cases, simply not correct. It must be kept in mind that states, whether in the developing world or the advanced industrialized countries, are capitalist in nature. Those classes wielding power within these states in the South are thus as interested in restructuring strategies, such as neoliberalism or other forms of political domination that allow capitals to overcome barriers to accumulation, as in the cases of the US, Europe and Japan (see Panitch, 2000). By 'other forms of political domination', I mean the left-leaning administrations of Latin America, in which the ruling classes have sought to forge new alliances with the 'great masses', so as to reproduce capitalist relations in these countries, while at the same time restructuring these relations in such a way as to turn a profit. The Lula and Chavez administrations of Brazil and Venezuela, respectively, are cases in point. Neoliberal policies, and their emphasis on serving the interests of capitalists, assist any country in legitimizing policies aimed at decreasing the power of labour (collective bargaining by trade unions) and social protection, selling off public enterprises to foreigners, and liberalizing trade and financial sectors. In short, the neoliberal ideology and its common-sense assumptions help the ruling classes to create attractive business environments, which can successfully compete with other developing countries in attracting and retaining capital inflows in the form of FDI and/or FPI:

> The 'internal bourgeoisie' that has become central to the organisation of the power bloc of each of the imperialist countries has an interest in sustaining neoliberalism. They have a stake in the 'American model,' which needs to be seen not as a foreign import or imposition undermining a defenceless 'national bourgeoisie' (as many opponents of neoliberalism would have it), but rather as a policy matrix that meets the internal class interests of the power bloc within each state in this phase of imperialism (Albo, 2003: 106).

American imperialism is a multifaceted and conflict-led strategy of overcoming the barriers to the crisis of overaccumulation. We are now ready to tackle the definition of the *capitalist* (or, which is the same thing, *bourgeois*) state. In contrast to the above pluralist conceptualization of states championed by both Rosenau and the CGG, the capitalist state is not a thing that embodies the common good, but is a form of social relations intimately tied to the reproduction of capitalism. This relationship is a complex one. The state is, however, not simply an instrument of capitalist rule or an autonomous actor (see Poulantzas, 2000). As John Holloway argues, 'it cannot be assumed, in functionalist fashion, either that everything that the state does will necessarily be in the best interests of capital, nor that the state can achieve what is necessary to secure the reproduction of capitalist society' (Holloway, 1995: 121). The capitalist state exists neither in the singular nor in isolation from other, national states (von Braunmühl, 1978; Holloway, 1995). These are defined by the historical specificity of their social formations within the wider global capitalist inter-state system. Reflecting the uneven development of global capital accumulation, some national states are also more powerful than others. But this power, often discussed in terms of hegemony in international relations literature, is not due simply to inherent military and economic strengths (see Bull, 1977; Waltz, 1979; Morgenthau, 1978), but to specific configurations of class power and their relation to global forms of capital accumulation, as represented by the inter-state system (Holloway, 1995).

The concept of 'non-hegemony' or 'dominance', as employed by Robert Cox, is useful in understanding the nature of US power within global capitalism in the post-Bretton Woods era. As was noted earlier, Cox suggests that the notion of the 'dominant state' describes the condition of a non-hegemonic moment of capitalist class rule, marked by a crisis of hegemony. This is a situation in which no dominant class, or fraction of capital (such as finance or industry) has been able to establish hegemony. This is evident in a non-hegemonic or dominant state, which is characterized by the overriding use of coercion (both physical and economic) in the constant reorganisation of the social relations of production (including the state) along spatial and temporal lines, to recreate and preserve its dominance. As this restructuring continues, the confrontation heightens between social experiences in the Third World (subordinate states) and neoliberal ideology. In the face of this contradiction the dominant American state needs to secure its position in global capitalism by engaging in increased coercion and subjugation, by either excluding or co-opting developing states, so as to ensure that they do not exert influence over key bourgeois international institutions, notably the World Bank, the IMF, and the WTO. These acts of deterrence and exclusion are what Gramsci refers to as a 'passive revolution' (Cox, 1987; Showstack Sassoon, 1982 in Carnoy, 1984). Passive revolutions are best described as strategies, both coercive and consensual, that act to prevent 'the development of a revolutionary adversary by "decapitating" its revolutionary potential' (Showstack Sassoon, 1982: 133). According to Cox, the most dangerous moments of the passive revolution are located in the South because it is there that the contradictions of neoliberal capitalism are most acute. As Cox observes: 'In the world hegemonic model, hegemony is more intense and consistent at the core and more laden with contradictions at the periphery' (Cox, 1993: 61).

Seen from this perspective, the rhetoric inherent in the CGG's and Rosenau's portrayal of global governance, with its garb of inclusion, participation, equality, and pluralist relations among states that helps to conceal the neoliberal forms of exploitation and domination, is symptomatic of a passive revolution. But it is important to keep in mind that the policies pursued by the dominant state, or what I have elsewhere referred to as 'imposed US leadership' (Soederberg, 2002c; 2004; cf. Arrighi, 1994), are intimately tied to the wider contradictions of capital accumulation and the social relations that constitute this crisis. This has immediate ramifications for the form and extent of the passive revolution imposed on the Third World. This passive revolution, which is led by the dominant US state in the interests of the bourgeoisie (Americans and other nationals), is aimed first and foremost at assisting the restructuring of global capitalism, so that the bourgeoisie can reap higher and higher levels of surplus-value.

The dominant US state and its capitalist restructuring strategies, which include moments of global governance, are rife with contradictions. This in effect implies that there always remains a possibility that subordinate states, such as those in the Third World, will attempt to escape the golden straightjacket, and thereby reveal the weakness of the seeming omnipotence of globalization. But, on the other hand, this also implies that more coercive forms of disciplinary action and surveillance – in both economic and physical terms – are required, to prevent future escapes.

CONCLUSION

In this chapter I have argued that global governance, as represented by mainstream theorists and policy-makers, lacks an historical understanding of capitalist relations of power. The immediate consequences of this neglect are, first, that there is no explanation of the changing nature of American empire and capitalist power in the world. And, second, mainstream versions of global governance serve to normalize, neutralize, and legitimize increasingly austere forms of capitalist restructuring and expansion, especially in the South. These restructuring processes may be regarded as a deepening and broadening of neoliberalism.

Underpinning this thesis is the claim that mainstream understandings of global governance need to be challenged in three ways. First, global governance needs to be understood as a moment of global capitalism, with all its underlying contradictions and class conflicts. Second, we need to identify and challenge three common-sense assumptions that have accompanied the mainstream debates about global economic governance: (1) that globalization is an omnipotent external force that is inevitable, (2) that struggles take place on a level playing field, implying a pluralist understanding of the world, and (3) that global governance has positive consequences for the development of the South, as understood in terms of economic growth. The third manner in which I challenged global governance was to suggest the need to explore the North–South terrain of global economic governance by analysing three important, albeit neglected, areas: international strategies of corporate social responsibility, transnational debt, and emerging forms of development assistance. When viewed through the lens of a particular interpretation of historical materialism, these topics will constitute three different windows through which we can study global governance.

While this framework cannot hope to represent a comprehensive theory, it will guide our investigations into the above three topics so as to allow us to go beyond the superficial, mainstream understanding of global economic governance as represented specifically by the CGG's and Rosenau's work. My version of historical materialism rests upon three pillars. First, we need to transcend the claim, often made in mainstream political science and economics, that society and the economy are separate and distinct areas of human activity. To do so, I introduce the most fundamental concept of Marxism: the social relations of capitalist production. The utility of this perspective is that we begin to see the inherent inequality and exploitative nature of capitalist society, as well as its deeply embedded, conflict-ridden and contradictory characteristics. We also learn that capitalist social relations are neither natural nor inevitable, but have been historically created and recreated by coercive and ideological means. The second pillar is the tendency to crisis, and the subsequent need for capitalist society to restructure itself in order to overcome the barriers imposed by crisis. Since the late 1970s, the global restructuring of capitalism has taken the form of neoliberalism. The third and final pillar of our historical-materialist framework relates to the role of capitalist states in relation to the neoliberal restructuring activities, and in particular the role of American imperialism in this process. These three domains are inextricably linked, and build on each other to form our understanding of historical materialism.

3
Global Governance and Corporate Social Responsibility

The international community needs to enlist the support of transnational business in global governance and to encourage best practices, acknowledging the role the private sector can play in meeting the needs of the global neighbourhood. Wider acceptance of these responsibilities is likely if the business sector is drawn in to participate in the processes of governance.

Commission on Global Governance, *Our Global Neighbourhood*, 1995: 256.

Corporate social responsibility (CSR) entails a wide array of divergent and competing interests: corporations, states, local and international NGOs, and a multiplicity of stakeholders within wider society. Although there is no universal definition of CSR, it is possible, and desirable, to provide a general definition by drawing on the corporate[1] and non-profit sectors' understandings of CSR. According to the World Business Council's publication, *Corporate Social Responsibility: Making Good Business Sense*, CSR refers to the relationship between corporations and stakeholders, such as employees, the wider community, suppliers, creditors, shareholders, the environment, and so on, in which there is a 'commitment by business to behave ethically and contribute to economic development while improving the quality of life of the workforce and their families as well as of the local community and society at large' (Holme and Watts, 2000: 3). The World Business Council goes on to note that a good CSR strategy allows the private sector to integrate the economic, social and environmental imperatives of their activities in the wider spatial context within which firms operate. In this way, CSR provides the opportunity to demonstrate the human face of business. The 'Oxfam Community Aid Abroad' programme,[2] in contrast, offers a more comprehensive understanding of CSR. Oxfam's CSR rating service, for instance, includes the following issues regarding business activity in the South: (1) human rights (do company operations protect human rights?); (2) workplace relations (do employees enjoy fair and safe conditions free from discrimination?); and (3) community relations (do companies engage with and invest in communities affected by their operations?). Moreover, companies have been assessed not only on their policies, but also on implementation, reporting, and accountability systems[3] (see Hopkins, 1998; UNCTAD, 2001). Thus, the common theme running through these understandings of CSR is the belief that corporations should be accountable to a wide array of stakeholders and shareholders.

Despite its growing popularity, there has been surprisingly little critical scholarly attention paid to the historical-materialist aspects of global CSR strategies. In what follows, I will explore two key strategies: (1) the Code of Conduct (or, simply, 'the Code') for Transnational Corporate Activity in the South, which was established by the now defunct United Nations Centre on Transnational Corporations (UNCTC) in 1974, and (2) the Code's neoliberal successor, the Global Compact ('GC' or 'Compact'), which was launched by the United Nations in 2000. This chapter fills this gap by attempting to understanding the capitalist nature of these global CSR strategies through the application of the historical-materialist framework outlined in Chapter 2.

If we follow the CGG's and Rosenau's understanding of global governance, CSR would occur on a level playing-field, in which a variety of actors (state and non-state) coalesce within various spaces (global, national and local) to create, over time, 'control mechanisms' aimed at dealing with CSR. Unfortunately, scholarly debates about international CSR strategies have tended not only to avoid the wider theoretical debates about global governance, but also to discuss exclusively the Global Compact without adequately contextualizing its roots historically in the contradictions and relations of power in global capitalism (Kell and Ruggie, 1999; Ruggie, 2000; 2002; 2004; Hocking and Kelly, 2002; Thérien and Pouliot, 2004; cf. Bair, 2004). More importantly, these discussions have tended to reproduce the three common-sense assumptions tied to global governance discussed in the preceding chapter: (1) an ahistorical understanding of globalization that lacks a proper theory of the state, (2) the idea of a level playing-field (pluralism), and (3) an uncritical embracing of neoliberalism, especially as it pertains to the re-creation of the fictions tied to 'developmentalism' (Escobar, 1995; 2004; McMichael, 2004). There are at least two consequences stemming from the recreation of these common-sense assumptions. First, the debates have attempted to centre on the differences between the Code and the GC – particularly the distinction that while the Code was based on mandatory compliance between states and the UN, the GC rests on voluntary observance. Second, the discussions have neglected to ask some tough questions about both CSR strategies: What were the similarities of the Code and the GC? What were the underlying contradictions of capitalism from which these projects emerged? Who benefits? And to what extent do both the Code and the GC represent different reactions to the tension brought about by capitalist restructuring?

By drawing on the historical-materialist framework discussed in the previous chapter, we may pierce the surface of CSR and make sense of its inner nature. This task is accomplished by examining historically the two major international CSR strategies within the wider contradictions and conflicts of global capitalism, as well as the role of US dominance. I argue that, despite their superficial differences, both the Code and the GC have their roots within the wider contradictions and conflicts tied to global capitalist restructuring. Once we historically situate each CSR strategy within global capitalism, their similarities and differences become much clearer. In fact, both CSR strategies represent attempts to normalize, neutralize, and thus legitimize, the increasing power of TNCs over both nature and labour in the South. Like the post-Washington consensus or second-generation reforms discussed in Chapter 1, the GC is not simply an idea born in the mind of the UN Secretary-General; instead it is a highly contradictory and historically led attempt by the ruling classes in the North and the South, the US, and by extension international organizations such as the UN, to deal with the confrontation between neoliberal ideology and 'actual social experience' of the masses (lower echelons of society in the Third World such as peasants and wage-labourers) and the ongoing, indeed intensifying, exploitative activities of TNCs in the South. Since the Code and the GC are rooted in the global restructuring of capitalism and the contradictions therein, each strategy must be seen as a political means of appeasing growing criticisms and movements (investment strikes, consumer boycotts, and so on) aimed against the transgressions of TNCs against humanity and the environment. Indeed, the Code and the GC were necessary interventions to save the reputation of corporate brand names, so as to facilitate profit-maximisation in the face of the ongoing overaccumulation crisis through increased economic and environmental exploitation.

This chapter falls into five main sections. To grasp the wider historical-materialist backdrop within which the Compact emerged, we explore the shifting nature of TNCs in the South during the post-Bretton Woods era, as well as some important developments surrounding this transformation, such as the attempt by Third World states to establish a New International Economic Order, the United Nations Centre on TNCs, and the UN's Code of Conduct on TNCs. We can then seek to examine the limitations, and eventual demise of the Code in the late 1980s by identifying some contradictions underpinning this strategy. I then examine the broader struggles over CSR in the South, as well as attempts to freeze these conflicts through the creation of the World Trade Organization. After this, we are ready not only to turn our attention to the Compact, but also to view it as a passive revolution that emerged from larger historical contradictions of global capitalism. I conclude by summarizing the argument presented here, and its implications for our understanding of global governance.

THE CRISIS OF GLOBAL CAPITALISM AND THE RISE OF THE UN CENTRE ON TRANSNATIONAL CORPORATIONS

Crisis, capital, and north–south reconfigurations

As we saw in the previous chapter, globalization enthusiasts believe that the rise of transnational corporations[4] emerged from technological innovations and/or natural progress, and has substantially and irrevocably weakened the role of the state. This fatalist view has led many observers – particularly the World Bank, the IMF, and some UN bodies – to conclude that globalization is inevitable. I countered this claim by suggesting that globalization must be understood historically as a moment of the contradictions and struggles inherent to global capitalism. Thus, TNCs are not simply contingent institutions, but rather specific and historical manifestations of capitalist development (Jenkins, 1987; cf. Radice, 1975).

The fall of the Bretton Woods system in 1971 was underpinned by a crisis of capital overaccumulation. As a result of this tendency to crisis, excesses (or surpluses) of capital and labour are left unutilized or underutilized (Marx, 1981; Hirsch, 1974; Harvey, 1999; Clarke, 1988). It will be recalled from the previous chapter that the crisis of overaccumulation manifested itself at the international level by high levels of 'stagflation' (unemployment plus inflation), escalating labour disputes in the form of strikes and walk-outs, burgeoning trade and budget deficits, especially in the US, and growing tensions in the world economy, spurred on, among other things, by protectionist policies. The General Agreement on Tariffs and Trade, a *de facto* source of international trade regulation tied to the BWS, was unable to limit the beggar-thy-neighbour policies[5] pursued by states at this time. This period was also marked by the meteoric rise in power of TNCs.

From 1945 up to the 1970s, TNC activities in the South were concentrated in the extractive sector (mining, oil, forestry).[6] While Third World countries were adopting more export-oriented industrialization strategies, in the late 1960s and 1970s, it wasn't until the immediate post-Bretton Woods era, that TNCs began to increase dramatically their presence in the industrial sector – particularly in export processing zones (EPZs) of the global South. Very generally, EPZs are spatially restricted industrial estates, which constitute free trade enclaves in the customs and trade regime of the country. Within this space, foreign manufacturing firms, which produce mainly for export, benefit from certain tax and financial incentives, as well as an abundant supply of cheap labour. 'Between 1950 and 1984 the share of US FDI in the Third World which was employed in the manufacturing sector more than doubled from 15 to 37 percent' (Jenkins, 1987: 7; see Table 3.1 for comparison between pre- and post-Bretton Woods FDI figures). These strategies on the part of TNCs may be described as global capitalist restructuring. It will be recalled that restructuring strategies generally involve either a temporal or spatial fix, or both (Harvey, 1999; 2003a; 2003b). These restructuring activities (in the form, for example, of EPZs) may be understood as spatial fixes, in that they expand the geographical scope of the system of accumulation. Indeed, these restructuring strategies were deemed so novel that they began to spur on important debates about the new international division of labour (cf. Fröbel et al., 1980; cf. Jenkins, 1984). One important characteristic of these restructuring strategies was the concentration and centralization of capital, particularly productive capital.[7] As Jenkins documents, the output of the world's largest firms (almost all TNCs) outstripped the growth of world production throughout the 1960s and 1970s (see Table 3.2).

The main vehicle for the centralization process is foreign direct investment.[8] There are two main types of FDI: the TNC can either purchase an existing foreign company, or it can create a new company, also known as a 'greenfield investment'. The latter refers to an investment that can contribute to additional productive capacity in a country, but may also create new competition for existing

Table 3.1   US Direct Investment Position Abroad on an Historical-Cost Basis,[*] 1955–2003 ($millions)

Year	1950	1960	1970	1971[**]	1976	1982	1987	1992	1997	2003
All										
Countries	12,979	31,865	75,480	82,760	136,809	207,752	326,253	502,063	871,316	1,788,911
Developing										
Countries	6,146	11,128	19,192	20,719	29,313	66,480	107,329	181,497	345,799	633,415

[*]   An accounting principle requiring all financial statement items to be based on original cost.
[**]   The year of the collapse of the Bretton Woods system.

Source: US Department of Commerce, *Selected Data on US Direct Investment Abroad*, various years.

Table 3.2   Growth of the World's Largest Firms, 1962–82 (% per annum)

	1962–67	1967–72	1972–77	1977–82
GDP of Market Economics	8.3	10.7	14.3	9.4
Sales of Largest Firms	9.3	11.2	15.4	11.2

Source: *UN Yearbook of National Account Statistics*, various years, cited in Jenkins, 1987: 11.

local companies (UNCTAD, 2003). The continued centralization of capital serves to deepen capitalism's unequal development (see Frank, 1981; Emmanuel, 1972) and to increase the domination of transnational financial capital (for example, banks) and TNCs, and their increasingly intertwined activities aimed at overcoming the falling rate of profit through the acquisition of more profitable firms, also known as mergers and acquisitions (M&As), and diversification into sectors with higher profits (Andreff, 1984; cf. Marx, 1981). For Andreff, the great majority of direct cross-investments among the main capitalist countries have been carried out through buy-outs or share purchases in existing firms by TNCs or transnational banks, as opposed to greenfield investments (Audreff, 1984: 59 – see Chapter 4). I will discuss the impact of M&As later in this chapter. While the relationship between the TNCs, particularly with regard to their host countries in the Third World, whether parasitical or beneficial, has been, and continues to be, rigorously debated among both leftist and mainstream theorists (see, for example, Amin, 1974; Palloix, 1977; Cardoso and Faletto, 1979; Hymer, 1976; Cohen et al., 1979; Baran and Sweezy, 1966; Radice, 1975; Barnett and Müller, 1974; Vernon, 1971; Kindleberger, 1969; Hirst and Thompson, 1999; Carroll, 2004;

Ohmae, 1990), there was no doubt that TNCs were, and still are, becoming an important feature in global capitalism. The expansion of TNCs plainly illustrates the uneven nature of capital accumulation on a global scale. As we will see below, the bulk of TNCs' operations are concentrated within the advanced industrialized countries – especially Germany, Japan, and the US.

Struggles over the New International Economic Order and the UNCTC

Capitalist strategies aimed at overcoming the crisis of capitalism, both at home and abroad, were accompanied by social, economic, political, and ideological upheavals. During the 1970s, the decade in which the Bretton Woods system was dismantled, the US was plagued not only with high levels of stagflation, but also with legitimacy problems tied, among other things, to the scandals of the withdrawal of Vietnam and Watergate. As we will see, restructuring strategies occurred within the context of high levels of struggle and contestation during this period, especially with regard to the relationship between the US and the Third World. Attempts by the American state to assist capitalists in the expropriation of the labour in the South were taking place against the wider backdrop of the shift in US power in the world order from that of a hegemonic to that of a dominant state. The US's dominant status denotes the increasing use of physical and economic coercion required to reproduce its status on the international stage. Seen from this perspective, the American state, and all those capital interests (inside and outside the US) aligned with its strategies for dealing with overaccumulated capital, must constantly prevent subordinate states from exerting influence over international organisations, producing a passive revolution in which revolutionary struggles are decapitated (Cox, 1987; Gramsci, 1971). Concurrently, the 'dominant' American state (reflecting a crisis of hegemony) also opened up spaces to contest and challenge the status quo – specifically the increasing activities of TNCs in the South.

The Non-Aligned Movement and the Group of 77 merged to create the United Nations Conference on Trade and Development (UNCTAD) in 1964. Through this organization, Third World countries demanded fairer terms of trade and more liberal terms for financing development (Rothstein, 1979). At this point, the advanced industrialized countries remained firmly of the view that any forum for economic change should continue through the Bretton Woods institutions – the IMF and the World Bank – which, as have seen, were and are largely controlled by the G-7, and the US in particular. This strategy was significant because, as international organizations, the IMF and the World Bank reflected the underlying material power of social relations, and thus reproduced the dominance of the US and G-7 countries by (1) embodying the rules facilitating expansion of these leading industrialized countries, (2) legitimizing the norms of the world order, (3) co-opting elites from the South, and (4) absorbing counter-hegemonic ideas (Cox: 1993a: 62).

The demise of the BWS in 1971 opened up new spaces for struggles, including the possibility of forging a fairer world order in which developing countries would play a proactive role in their integration into global capitalism. The former Executive Secretary of the United Nations Economic Commission for Latin America (ECLA), and later the Secretary-General of UNCTAD, Raúl Prebisch, was a key spokesperson on the need for a new economic order. Prebisch argued that 'good development' could be achieved by avoiding the past mistakes of encouraging the Third World to conform to the institutional, production and socio-economic arrangements of the First World, as this tended to cause 'bad development', leading to increased dependency, particularly on TNCs, and to poverty and political instability. Prebisch opined that international trade only served to reinforce 'bad development'. For Prebisch, protectionism in trade and import-substitution strategies were acceptable measures, indeed necessary steps, if the global South was to enter a self-sustaining development path (Prebisch, 1967). This strategy, according to Prebisch, would in turn allow Third World countries to adopt 'good development' practices, such as technology transfer.[9] The latter serves to provide knowledge, skills, methods, and specialized equipment to Third World workers and companies; this, in turn, is supposed to lead to higher wages, and an increase in people's standard of living.[10] Such a protectionist stance was fitting for its times. The US was actively engaging in protectionist policies at this time. In 1971, for example, US President Nixon introduced tax legislation that discouraged US investment abroad by providing a tax credit for domestic investment, and that encouraged exports as opposed to FDI. A surcharge was also imposed on imports to the US. This move could be understood as an attempt to deal with a key contradiction tied to the restructuring strategy: while capitalists reaped higher profits abroad (cheap labour, lower taxation standards, and so on), workers at home were losing jobs.

Echoing these concerns of mainstream dependency theorists such as Prebisch, the Sixth Special Session of the UN General Assembly adopted, without a vote, a manifesto entitled 'Declaration and Programme of Action of the New International Order' in April 1974. In December of that same year, the General Assembly approved the Charter of Economic Rights and Duties of States – also known as the New International Economic Order (Bhagwati, 1977; Murphy, 1984). In that it sought to challenge the dominance of US rule in the world order (including the G-7), the NIEO represented, in Gramscian terms, a 'counter-hegemonic movement'. The NIEO consisted of 20 principles, which ranged 'from the inalienable right to "permanent sovereignty of every state over its natural resources and all economic properties ... including the right to nationalization or transfer of ownership to its nationals" to "the need for all states to put an end to the waste of natural resources, including food products"' (Bair, 2004: 6; see Box 3.1, below). In contrast to the dominant 'hyper-globalist' view of states embedded in the Commission of Global Governance and the Compact, the NIEO held that states should play a key role in ensuring the implementation of fair and equitable forms of economic growth, especially as it pertained to trade and technology transfer tied to FDI flows.

UNCTC Code of Conduct of TNCs

In the early 1970s, according to Craig Murphy, many Third World countries were advocating a binding international code of conduct for TNCs in order to ensure fair investment practices. Specifically, it was thought that a code of conduct would increase the power of Third World governments relative to that of firms based in the developed world (Murphy, 1984: 160). In 1973, one year before the NIEO was declared, the United Nations Economic and Social Council (also known as ECOSOC) commissioned a 'Group of Eminent Persons' to advise on matters related to TNCs and their impact on development. The Group recommended a permanent centre be established to study TNCs and related policy issues. In addition, they recommended the formation of a Commission on TNCs, to which the centre should report. To this end, the UN Centre on TNCs (UNCTC) was created in 1974, and was responsible for information-gathering, research and policy-analysis, technical assistance, and consensus-building to support the Commission. However, in 1977 the UNCTC turned its attention to a more controversial exercise: a Draft Code of Conduct for TNCs (see Box 3.1, below). Unlike the other codes that were emerging at this time, such as the OECD's *Declaration on International Investment and Multinational Enterprises* of 1976, which has also been deemed a 'pre-emptive western strike emphasizing business responsibility' (Robinson, quoted in Jenkins, 1987: 171), the Code was to move beyond voluntary guidelines.

Needless to say, both the NIEO and the Code were resisted by the US and other powerful industrialized countries. After two oil price hikes in the 1970s, and deteriorating domestic economic conditions in the industrialized world, the UNCTC and NIEO did not register as top agenda items for the US or other G-7 countries.

On one level, the UNCTC's Code reflected the suspicion of the mainstream understanding of the corporation as a 'moral person' or 'soulful corporation' (Donaldson, 1982; Monks and Minow, 2003; Baran and Sweezy, 1966; Bakan, 2004). An underlying premise here is that, because the modern corporation is marked by the separation between owners and managers (Berle and Means, 1932), it may move beyond mere goals of profit-maximization towards non-economic interests, such as a robust and human corporate culture, community and environmental responsibility, global business acumen, maximising customer satisfaction, and so forth. The notion of the corporation as a moral agent has a long history. In a paper delivered at the 1956 annual meeting of the American Economic Association, Carl Kaysen spoke of the 'wide-ranging scope of responsibility assumed by management' as one of the 'characteristic features of behaviour' of the modern corporation.

> No longer the agent of proprietorship seeking to maximize return on investment, management sees itself as responsible to stockholders, employees, customers, the general public, and, perhaps most important, the firm itself as an institution ... From one point of view, this behaviour can be termed responsible: there is no display of greed or graspingness; there is no attempt to push off onto workers or the community at large part of the social costs of the enterprise. The modern corporation is a soulful corporation (Quoted in Baran and Sweezy, 1966: 22–3).

There is a built-in paradox to this portrayal of TNCs as moral agents, however. TNCs must live up to their image as caring, responsible, and fair legal entities. The compulsion to do so is driven purely by economic factors, however. A corporation's reputation is not just a moral issue; it is a valuable asset in its own right, which can affect financial performance and provide a source of competitive advantage.

Box 3.1   **Principal Obligations of TNCs in the Draft United Nations Code of Conduct on Transnational Corporations**

The Code of Conduct lists the obligations of TNCs under the general heading 'Activities of Transnational Corporations', comprising three subheadings. Under the first, 'General and political', the following are found:

- respect for national sovereignty and observance of domestic laws, regulations and administrative practices;
- adherence to economic goals and development objectives, policies and priorities;
- review and renegotiation of contracts;
- adherence to socio-cultural objectives and values;
- respect for human rights and fundamental freedoms;
- non-collaboration by transnational corporations with racist minority regimes in southern Africa;
- non-interference in international political affairs;
- non-interference in intergovernmental relations;
- abstention from corrupt practices.

Under the subheading 'Economic, financial and social' are:

- the duty, by TNCs, to allocate their decision-making powers among their entities so as to enable them to contribute to the economic and social development of the countries in which they operate;
- observance of the balance of payments policies and financial transactions policies of such countries;
- avoidance of transfer pricing practices;
- avoidance of corporate structures and practices aimed to modify the tax base of the corporation contrary to national laws and regulations;
- observance of the principles concerning restrictive business practices and competition as contained in the Set of Multilaterally Agreed Equitable Principles and Rules for the Control of Restrictive Business Practices adopted by the General Assembly in resolution 35/63 of 5 December 1980;
- contribution to strengthening the technological capacities of developing countries in accordance with the practices and priorities of these countries;
- observance of national consumer protection laws and regulations and international standards;
- observance of environment protection laws and regulations and international standards;
- steps to protect the environment and make efforts to develop and apply adequate technologies for this purpose.

The third subheading concerns 'Disclosure of information', and urges TNCs to disclose to the public in the countries in which they operate, by appropriate means of communication, full and comprehensible information on the structure, policies, activities, and operations of the TNC as a whole.

Source: UNCTAD, 2001: 6–7.

It also can be lost overnight (Larkin, 2003). As we will see below, the image of a soulful corporation and the desire to strive towards profit-maximization, even in the face of crisis, come into conflict. The ability to see the limitations of the corporation as a moral agent was evident in the significance the Code attached to CSR.

Concern about CSR has not been confined to the South, however. Opposition to the apartheid regime in South Africa, for example, catapulted many investors, such as pension funds – especially public funds – to begin to engage in 'socially responsible investing' practices. This basically refers to giving up returns to achieve a social good[11] (Clowes, 2000: 160; Brancato, 1997). Many public employees in the US and pension funds, urged or ordered their money managers to divest their portfolios of the stocks of companies doing business in South Africa and to boycott the stocks of those companies in the future. Against this backdrop, the Investor Responsibility Research Center IRRC[12] was formed in 1972 with the support of Harvard University and the Carnegie Foundation (John and Thomson, 2003). Among other activities, the IRRC undertook research identifying the companies doing business in South Africa: those producing defence equipment, cigarettes, and alcoholic beverages; those accused of violating the Occupational Health and Safety Act; and those considered anti-union or discriminatory in some other way (John and Thomson, 2003; cf. Jenkins et al., 2002; Fung et al., 2001). As we will see, over the years social movements loosely organized around the theme of CSR have continued to grow, in terms of both economic strength and numbers (Sparkes, 2002).[13]

It is worth taking a detour here, before we examine the limits and ultimate demise of the UNCTC Code in the late 1980s. As we will see later in the discussion, the fall of the Code is widely understood in terms of internal stalemate within the G-77 countries, and the growing impatience of the US administration with this protectionist code in the era of neoliberalism. While both points are valid, there was a more fundamental factor at play – namely, the internal contradictions of capitalism, tied to the overaccumulation crisis and the reconfiguration of relations of power with regard to neoliberal restructuring strategies in the South. Recognizing this helps us make sense of the class-based nature of both the Code and its successor, the GC.

Theorizing TNCs and Third World States in the NIEO

It is important to understand the broader context from which the NIEO emerged, and more significantly, who sought to benefit from both the

NIEO and the UNCTC Code. From the mid 1960s to early 1990s, about half of the G-77 countries were under a military dictatorship, while the majority of the rest were ruled by various forms of authoritarianism, ranging, for example, from the Institutional Revolutionary Party (PRI) in Mexico (1929–2000) and Philippine President Ferdinand Marcos (1965–86) to the South African apartheid regime. As these countries' nationally specific modes of capital accumulation (i.e. import-substitution industrialization) began to enter the same crisis of overaccumulation experienced throughout the world market from the late 1960s onwards, ruling classes attempted to reproduce their dominance by delimiting the political activity, and thus power, of the subordinate classes (cf. Soederberg, 2002a; 2002b). Subsequent passive revolutions at the national level often took the form of military–bureaucratic and authoritarian regimes in the periphery. The ensuing debates about an NIEO reflect Cox's observation that the contradictions inherent in the non-hegemonic order of the post-Bretton Woods era were more acute in the South than the North. Craig Murphy observes that the Third World was divided on various issues regarding the NIEO, exemplified by the contrasts between the more radical resolutions of the non-aligned states, which focused on issues such as neocolonialism, democratization, collective self-reliance, and so forth (Murphy, 1984).

The mainstream camp embodied in the resolution on the International Development Strategy of the Second Development Decade that the General Assembly adopted in 1970 was more focused on encouraging industrial development in the Third World on national terms (Murphy, 1984: 91–6). A more critical way of viewing the NIEO is to understand it as a project aimed at institutionalizing the power of dominant classes in the South, whatever the political regime (democratic, authoritarian), as long as these classes continued to embrace capitalism. I want to argue here that another, more sinister, feature of the NIEO existed – namely, the attempt to serve and protect ruling class interests in the South, during an intensified crisis of capitalism, by forming a pact between Third World states and foreign capitalists. The UNCTC Code is a case in point. The Code sought to achieve more wriggle-room for the ruling classes of the Third World with regard to TNCs, while depoliticizing conflict in their societies by displacing the locus of struggle to the international realm: the UNCTAD.

Unlike advanced industrialized countries, developing countries possess relatively weak environmental, labour and human rights regulations. This, in turn, permits TNCs and their supply chains to lower their production costs (and thus increase their profit margins) by running roughshod over the environment and labour force (Harvey, 2003b; Arrighi, 2004). Moreover, the repressive military dictatorships or authoritarian regimes in the South during the 1970s and 1980s facilitated relatively easier forms of exploitation. Capitalist restructuring strategies are neither an automatic nor a smooth process, however. Political, social, ideological and economic conflicts emerge from intensified forms of capitalist restructuring strategies, based on greater degrees of exploitation. In this connection, we turn to the role states have played, and continue to play, in attracting, limiting, and regulating the nature of FDI within their national boundaries.

In the post-Bretton Woods era all states must attract and retain global capital – either in the form of FDI or FPI – by implementing 'good investment climates', which in turn act to place constraints on domestic policy-making, particularly in the realm of social and economic programmes (Underhill, 1997). With the steady decline of public aid flows to the South, the need to attract, on a competitive basis, and maintain private capital flows is particularly salient for Third World states. However, despite this need to suck in private capital flows, it is vital that we not view the relationship between Third World states and foreign capitalists in a deterministic and instrumentalist manner, as, for instance, Prebisch tended to do. Stephen Gill and David Law's understanding of the relation between states and capitalists is instructive here. For Gill and Law, capitalists (both foreign and domestic) increasingly wield 'structural power' – or, in Gramscian terms, economic coercion – over states. This may, for example, take the form of either an investment strike or capital flight.[14]

Transnational corporations routinely appraise the legal freedoms (e.g. to remit profits), production costs, labour relations, political stability, and financial concessions offered by many different countries. This is popularly known as 'political risk analysis.' They also examine the size and growth potential of a country's market. As a result, governments are increasingly constrained in their freedom of manoeuvre by the economic policies of other states, as well as the investment decisions of internationally mobile capital. Indeed, such appraisals are made on a daily or even hourly basis by market analysts and investors in the financial sectors (Gill and Law, 1993: 105).

Although this conceptualization of the power of TNCs is compelling, they are mistaken to argue that corporate power assumes the form of a zero-sum game with Third World states. Instead, I suggest that the structural power of TNCs has not rendered Third World states defenceless. One reason why TNCs are able to wield such power in all states, and in developing countries in particular, lies in the decisions by states to grant freedoms to corporations, such as immunity from international human rights law, the right to sue for libel, or to call the police if their property is threatened, and file for injunctions against protesters or workers (Monbiot, 2003; cf. Klein, 2000; Bakan, 2004). It is important to emphasize that the protection of capitalists' rights is sanctioned, legitimized, and reproduced not only by the states within which TNCs operate, but also by the international system of nation-states that underpins the decisions and policies implemented in the three most powerful international organizations – the WTO, the IMF, and the World Bank. As we will see, the strain between TNCs and Third World states during the 1970s had more to do with which interests would best be served by the presence of foreign capital in the nation-state. Drawing on Nicos Poulantzas' attempts to make sense of the growing presence of American capital in France during the 1970s, Leo Panitch contends that the concentration of power by transnational capital does not take power away from states:

> The current internationalisation of capital neither suppresses or by-passes nation states, either in the direction of a peaceful integration of capital's [*sic*] 'above' the state level (since every process of internationalisation is effected under the dominance of the capital of a given country), or in the direction of their extinction by an American super-state, as if American capital purely and simply directed the other imperialist bourgeoisies. This internationalisation, on the other hand, deeply affects the politics and institutional forms of these states by including them in a system of interconnections which is in no way confined to the play of external and mutual pressures between juxtaposed states and capitalists. These states themselves take charge of the interest of the dominant imperialist capital in its development within the 'national' social formation, i.e., in its complex relation of internationalisation to the domestic bourgeoisie that it dominates (Quoted in Panitch, 1994: 9).

All states are *capitalist* states. Thus, and despite their military or authoritarian expressions, states are required by capitalist interests to mediate, depoliticize and neutralize class struggle in order to guarantee the reproduction of capitalist society. This role becomes even more important in times of crisis, when the restructuring of the entire social relations of production is required by, for example, appeals to foreign investors (see Hirsch, 1974). Yet the growing presence of TNCs in the South has also led to mounting discontent, particularly from those segments of society that have been adversely affected by FDI, such as the peasantry, which accounts for a large part of the Third World, and national capitalists, who were long protected from foreign competition through state-sponsored subsidisation. In neo-Gramscian terms, there was a confrontation between the dominant ideologies and actual social experience. To grasp the eventual demise of the Code, it is useful to explore these contradictions more closely.

THE LIMITATIONS AND DEMISE OF THE CODE

Contradictions underpinning the Code

The tensions between the needs of the masses in the Third World and those of the TNCs would begin to mount, however. The 1970s saw various attempts by capitalists to increase their influence in the South. For example, the International Chamber of Commerce (ICC), a powerful lobby group representing the largest corporations at the time, introduced its *Guidelines for International Investment* in 1972. According to Jenkins, the gist of the guidelines is captured in the recommendation that 'the government of the host country should place no restrictions on the remittance of loan interest ... licence fees, royalties and similar payments' (Jenkins, 1987: 171). These growing demands placed on Third World states by TNCs also acted to curtail some of their powers to broker deals to ensure the recreation of the status quo, such as the subsidizing of domestic firms, increased levels of military spending, the placating of demands placed on the state by labour groups, the taxing of TNCs so as to extract desperately needed income, as well as ensuring that TNCs avoid transfer pricing, and so forth. A number of developing countries introduced legislation limiting the scope of TNC operations. Foreign capital, for example, was often excluded from sectors such as insurance and banking, public utilities, mining, iron and steel, and retailing. Several countries, including Brazil, Mexico, Pakistan, the Philippines, and Sri Lanka, required majority shareholdings in joint ventures with foreign firms, particularly in low-priority areas (UNCTC, quoted in Jenkins, 1987: 172). Seen from this angle, the NIEO, and the Code in particular, not only served to legitimize state intervention in the activities of TNCs in their host countries; also, because of its universal nature,

TNCs were hard-pressed to engage in disciplinary activities against a specific Third World country.

The UNCTC was to struggle with the Code for the next decade, despite constant prodding by ECOSOC to conclude the process. There were, however, a number of disagreements that arose during the course of negotiations. Some of these evolved around the issue of whether or not the Code should be legally binding, or simply voluntary. Others arose from the question of whether or not state-owned enterprises should be included under the definition of TNCs. Another important source of contention was the insistence by the advanced industrialized countries that TNCs should be guaranteed equality of treatment with national firms (Jenkins, 1987: 172). It would be simplistic to conclude that the eventual stillbirth of the Code in the late 1980s was simply due to deadlock over these issues (see Bair, 2004). A more fruitful approach – especially for shedding light on the emergence of the Compact – is to relate these impasses to the underlying power relations tied to the intergovernmental negotiations on which the success of the Code depended. That is to say, these struggles to reform the scope of TNCs in the South remained constrained by the basic dynamics of capitalist accumulation. A careful reading of the main issues and approaches upon which the participants diverged reflects differential power relations not only between states, bourgeoisie, and labour within each national social formation, but also between nation-states. As we will see, the majority of the FDI flowing to the South was heading to a mere eight countries (see Holloway, 1995; von Braunmühl, 1978).

Developing countries were also battling mounting tensions and conflicts that centred on promoting the internationalization of capital by inviting FDI into their territories, with all the trade-offs entailed in such a proposal – such as reducing the power of labour unions and reducing wages, privatization of strategic industries, and so forth – in the face of the economic turmoil of the 1970s and much of the 1980s, such as stagflation, at home. This manifested itself most clearly in the disputes over the provisions of paragraph 6 of the draft Code, requiring TNCs to respect national sovereignty. For instance:

> some delegates resisted the extension of the formulation to include the right of each state to exercise permanent sovereignty over its natural resources, wealth and economic activities, on the ground that they could only accept such a broad formulation if it were balanced by a reference to international

law or internationally acceptable standards on the treatment of transnational corporations (UNCTC, 1985: 84).

The eventual abandonment of the Code in the late 1980s, and the subsequent official disbandment of the UNCTC in 1995 by the UN General Assembly's resolution 49/130, were brought about by the usual tendencies towards deadlock within consensus-based organizations. More importantly, the demise of the Code, and therein the attempt to restrict the scope of TNCs within the Third World and hold them accountable to the societies within which they operate, was determined by the relations of power and wider contradictions in global capitalism – most notably the move to more intensified restructuring strategies, in the form of neoliberalism.

Neoliberal restructuring strategies and the demise of the Code

The early 1980s were largely characterized by the Third World debt crisis and a deep recessionary climate in the G-7 countries, especially the US. It was against this backdrop that the neoliberal revolution arose. The neoliberal climate afforded capitalists more leeway not simply in terms of the spatial dislocation of capital (Harvey, 1999; 2003a; 2003b); but more importantly, it facilitated the increased exploitation of, and dominance over, labour and the environment. Economic forms of coercion, transmitted by, for example, the IMF's structural adjustment programmes in the 1980s, and its emphasis on the privatization of state-owned industry and liberalization of trade and finance, helped to open markets for TNCs that had previously been considered 'off limits', such as water, electricity, telecommunications, transportation network, banking, and so on. This coercive power is most notable with the shift from official aid flows to private capital flows, largely FDI and FPI in the form of stocks and bonds, in the 1990s (World Bank, 2001). This modification in aid, which was facilitated by neoliberal reforms occurring in the First World, such as financial deregulation and trade liberalization, served to strengthen the power of TNCs in the South.

The main vehicle for neoliberal capitalist restructuring has been the structural adjustment policies of the IMF and World Bank, which effectively helped to pry open domestic markets in the South by discouraging protectionism in the areas of finance and trade (Harvey, 2003b: 181; Cox, 1993a; 1993b; see also 3.4 and 3.5). These bodies place a heavy emphasis on cultivating a good 'business environment' by adhering to the principles of the so-called Washington consensus, such as fiscal discipline, trade liberalization, privatization, and liberalization of inflows of FDI (Williamson, 2000; Naim, 1999; Stiglitz, 2002). The neoliberal flavour of the Washington consensus reflected the general stance of the official development agenda that dominated not only major international financial institutions, such as the IMF and the World Bank – and its regional satellites, the Inter-American Development Bank, the African Development Bank, and the Asian Development Bank – but also national aid agencies, such as USAID and the Canadian International Development Agency. Through the unequal relations between 'donor' and 'debtor' countries, these agencies were able to wield a degree of economic coercion over the ruling classes in the Third World. We discuss these relations of exploitation within the wider debt structures in the following chapter. The common-sense assumption that trade liberalization and FDI would lead to economic growth and prosperity (read: 'development') began to take hold in the South (see Bhagwati, 2004).

As Hirst and Thompson observe, there was a 'sudden increase in FDI flows in the mid 1980s, particularly to the industrial countries. Export growth was eclipsed by this expansion of FDI.' Indeed, according to these authors, some 80 per cent of US trade was conducted by TNCs, which was not an untypical proportion for the developed countries as a whole (Hirst and Thompson, 1999: 68–9). Within the Third World, FDI was concentrated in a small number of countries. As Rhys Jenkins observes, only two countries – Mexico and Brazil – accounted for over a quarter of the total stock of FDI in the South, and eight countries made up for over half; the share of FDI flows to

Table 3.3   Stock of FDI in the South by Major Countries, 1967 and 1983

	1967 $ billions	1967 %	1983 $ billions	1983 %
Brazil	3.7	11.3	24.6	17.5
Mexico	1.8	5.5	13.6	9.7
Singapore	0.2	0.6	7.9	5.6
Indonesia	0.2	0.6	6.8	4.9
Malaysia	0.7	2.1	6.2	4.4
Argentina	1.8	5.5	5.8	4.1
Venezuela	3.5	10.6	4.3	3.1
Hong Kong	0.3	0.9	4.2	3.0
8 countries	12.2	37.2	73.4	52.4
Rest of Third World	32.8	62.8	140.0	47.6

Source: UNCTC, cited in Jenkins, 1987: 14.

these eight countries has increased significantly since 1967 (see Table 3.4). Moreover, these eight countries fall into two categories: the so-called newly industrializing countries (NICs), which are characterized by a large and rapidly expanding industrial sector, and OPEC. This in turn has led to an increasing differentiation within the Third World between a small group of quickly growing countries and 'the rest of the South' (Jenkins, 1987: 13–14).

While it is clear from Tables 3.4 and 3.5 that the majority of FDI flows take place within the so-called 'Triad' (Western Europe, the US, and Japan), developing countries began to receive increasingly more FDI, especially from 1980 onwards (Hirst and Thompson, 1999; Sklair and Robbins, 2002; UNCTAD, 2003). The centralization of capital also continued throughout the 1980s, largely in the form of mergers and acquisitions (M&As). A result of the M&As boom was that, by 1995, the 100 largest TNCs not only controlled about one-fifth of total global foreign assets, but also accounted for $2 trillion of foreign sales (Hirst and Thompson, 1999: 69; UNCTAD, 2000).

Table 3.4   FDI Outward Stock, by Host Region and Economy (selected), 1980–2002 ($ millions)

Host Region and Economy	1980	1985	1990	1995	2000	2001	2002
World	563,997	743,267	1,762,963	2,901,059	5,991,756	6,318,861	6,866,362[*]
Developed Economies	499,391	665,090	1,629,259	2,583,824	5,154,968	5,487,592	5,987,746[*]
European Union	215,582	304,579	797,322	1,298,257	2,980,615	3,171,860	3,434,297[*]
North America	239,158	281,512	515,358	817,224	1,528,943	1,626,312	1,775,134
United States	215,375	238,369	430,521	699,015	1,293,431	1,381,674	1,501,415
Developing Economies	64,606	78,176	133,088	310,864	817,450	806,524	849,464
Africa	6,871	10,960	20,777	33,004	48,591	43,066	43,574
Latin America and the Caribbean	51,529	55,517	63,358	90,861	160,186	167,906	173,187
Asia and the Pacific	6,206	11,699	48,953	187,000	608,673	595,552	632,702
Central Asia	–	–	–	–	558	758	1,521
South, East and South-East Asia	4,746	9,519	41,259	179,462	594,356	576,590	610,816
Pacific	13	37	85	426	442	558	588
Central and Eastern Europe	–	–	616	6,372	19,339	24,746	29,152

[*]   Value does not include data for Belgium and Luxembourg.

Source: UNCTAD, 2003: 262–5.

Table 3.5 FDI Inward Stock, by Host Region and Economy, 1980–2002 ($ millions)

Host Region and Economy	1980	1985	1990	1995	2000	2001	2002
World	699,415	977,755	1,954,152	3,002,152	6,146,812	6,606,855	7,122,506*
Developed Economies	391,946	570,901	1,399,880	2,041,408	3,988,075	4,277,195	4,594,850*
European Union	217,476	268,253	748,669	1,136,387	2,240,506	2,418,136	2,623,903
North America	137,209	249,272	507,793	658,843	1,419,383	1,530,527	1,572,561
United States	83,046	184,615	394,911	535,553	1,214,254	1,321,063	1,351,093
Developing Economies	307,469	406,805	551,481	920,400	2,029,412	2,173,769	2,339,632
Africa	32,162	33,844	50,775	77,400	144,503	157,823	170,876
Latin America and the Caribbean	50,404	80,129	116,963	201,755	608,924	705,746	762,229
Asia and the Pacific	224,904	292,832	383,743	641,245	1,275,985	1,310,200	1,406,527
Central Asia	–	–	–	4,018	16,123	20,856	25,139
South, East and South-East Asia	216,139	253,969	340,285,	582,542	1,186,143	1,215,410	1,304,973
Pacific	1,196	1,207	2,263	3,022	3,740	3,899	4,039
Central and Eastern Europe	–	49	2,841	40,187	129,169	155,734	187,868

* Value does not include data for Belgium and Luxembourg.

Source: UNCTAD, 2003: 257–60.

Although Tables 3.4 and 3.5 help us to grasp the highly uneven nature of FDI flows along the North–South axis, they fail to capture the changing nature of FDI flows to the South. These transformations reflect not only the effects of global neoliberal restructuring strategies, but also factors working against the successful passage and implementation of the Code. In order to overcome the barriers imposed by the crisis of overaccumulation, such as falling rates of profit, TNCs, especially the largest and most powerful American corporations, require more freedoms to enter the South in order to find productive outlets for excess capital. The Code would impose far too many restrictions on strategies aimed at grabbing cheap assets in the South, so that overaccumulated capital could seize hold of such assets and immediately turn them to profitable use (Harvey, 2003b: 149). I will now briefly explore some of these strategies of dispossession employed during the 1980s and early 1990s.

The UNCTC's restrictions on the scope and depth of corporate activity were diametrically opposed to the neoliberal strategies actively pursued by TNCs and the International Financial Institutions. Cross-border M&As being a case in point. In 1996, nearly 50 per cent of global FDI flows were made up of cross-border M&As, as opposed to greenfield investments (UNCTAD, quoted in Hirst and Thompson, 1999; UNCTAD, 2000). If we follow Andreff's conclusions, discussed above, then M&As have dominated the investment scene since the 1970s. Unsurprisingly, while the sales of the world's 500 largest TNCs have grown spectacularly worldwide, employment in these global companies has remained virtually flat since the early 1970s, at about 26 million people (Greider, 1997: 21). Technology transfer is another area in which the Code was seeking to establish 'an obligation' by TNCs in their host countries (see Box 3.1). Yet TNCs stood firmly opposed to this initiative as technology transfer and its promise of higher wages for workers in the Third World, would imply higher production costs and future competition for TNCs. To protect their profit margins, TNCs have engaged in all sorts of methods to avoid taxation in the South.

Transfer pricing has become a common practice for TNCs. Before discussing transfer pricing in more detail, it is important to note that this mechanism is facilitated by the manner in which TNCs constantly search to reduce production costs – namely, intra-firm trading. It is estimated, for example, that more than 40 per cent of US exports and nearly 50 per cent of its imports are goods that travel through intra-firm channels – trade conducted within the boundaries of a single company, involving transfers across borders between different parts of the organization (Hirst and Thompson, 1999; Jenkins, 1987). Borrowing an illustration from William Greider: a US computer company ships and designs components to its (cheap labour) assembly plant in Malaysia, and then distributes the finalized hardware back to the US, and to other buyers in Asia and Europe (Greider, 1997). According to the 1996 *World Investment Report*, there are now 40,000 corporations in the world whose activities cross national boundaries; these firms ply overseas markets through some 250,000 foreign affiliates (UNCTAD, 1996).

'Intra-firm trade' describes strategies pursued by TNCs in order to maximize profits by avoiding both market mechanisms and national laws through an instrument of internal costing and accounting known as 'transfer pricing'. This is a widespread technique whereby TNCs set prices for transfers of goods, services, technology and loans between their worldwide affiliates that differ considerably from the prices that unrelated firms would have had to pay. The immediate significance of transfer pricing is that it becomes very difficult for both host and home countries (the country where the TNC is domiciled) to tax the corporation. By lowering prices in countries where tax rates are high and raising them in countries with a lower tax rate, for example, TNCs can reduce their overall tax burden, and thereby increase their overall profits. Through their accounting systems TNCs can also transfer these prices among their affiliates, shifting funds around the world to avoid taxation. Governments, which have no way to control transfer pricing, are therefore under pressure to lower taxes as a means of attracting investment or keeping a company's operation in their country. Tax revenue, which might be used for social programmes or other domestic needs (the construction of roads, schools, hospitals), is therefore lost. According to UNCTAD, one-third of world trade consists of intra-firm trade (UNCTAD, 1996).

Neoliberal restructuring strategies, in the form of FDI, are neither an automatic nor a smooth process. On the one hand, the steadily decreasing foreign aid to the South, debt obligations (see Chapter 4), and the policies attached to loans made by the IMF and World Bank, have acted as extremely coercive forces in swaying Third World states to accommodate the demands of foreign capitals, who wish to engage in dispossession strategies. On the other hand, the ruling classes of the Third World have mainly benefited from the adoption of neoliberal reforms, and thus act as an internal coercive force in the construction of competitive 'business investment sites', such as EPZs like the maquiladora sector in Mexico. The low levels of research and development (R&D) and lack of technology transfer associated with the prevalence of M&As and EPZs – all of which have been sanctioned by Third World governments – have thus aided in creating and perpetuating low wages in the South, and, in turn, higher levels of inequality between the North and the South. Many workers in developing countries receive extremely low pay, and are subject to poor working conditions, in both relative and absolute terms (Hartman et al., 2003: 28; see also Rodrik, 1997; 1999; Moody, 1997; Cypher, 2001).

The growth in sweatshops and cheap labour havens helps explain the spectacular increase in the pay gap between top executives and production workers, which grew from 42:1 in 1980 to 419:1 in 1998 (excluding the value of stock options) ('49th Annual Executive Pay Survey', *Business Week*, April 19, 1999). To express the concentration of wealth in a way that also captures the stunning levels of inequality in our neoliberal world, Microsoft co-founders Bill Gates and Paul

Allen plus Berkshire Hathaway's Warren Buffet have a net worth larger than the combined GDP of the 41 poorest nations and their 550 million people ('Rich Comparison', *Wall Street Journal*, July 30, 1999). The biggest beneficiary of over three decades of centralization and concentration of capital has been, unsurprisingly, US-based TNCs. The latter represent more than half of the *Financial Times* 'Global 500' corporations, based on the market value of a company – i.e. the estimated value of a business that is obtained by multiplying the number of shares outstanding by the current prices of the share. Specifically, 16 of the top 20 TNCs in world (or 80 per cent) in 2004 were American (see Table 3.6). The US possesses four times as many constituents as its next rival, Japan ('US Still Far Ahead of Rival Regions', *Financial Times*, May 26, 2004).

Neoliberal restructuring strategies are fraught with contradictions. These paradoxes would not only emerge at the outset of the 1990s – when the world plunged, once again, into a deep recessionary phase – but also increase the friction between the Code and its emphasis on balancing the rights of host countries with the rights of foreign investors, and the general consensus that neoliberalism is the only alternative available for countries to achieve economic stability and prosperity. On the one hand, the former common-sense assumption during the BWS that state intervention in the economy was desirable was thought to be no longer valid in the era of globalization. On the other hand, the dominance of laissez-faire capitalism in both the Reagan (1981–89) and Bush (1989–93) administrations strengthened domestic forces in the US, such as the Heritage Foundation (see Chapter 4), that were adamantly opposed to the UNCTC specifically, and the UN generally. For the Heritage Foundation, the UNCTC was against business and the free market, while the UN was not very conducive to promoting US interests. From 1982 onwards, the Heritage Foundation launched a constant stream of criticism against the UNCTAD and the UNCTC. 'The United Nations has a long history of attacking the free enterprise system. A key element in this is the campaign against multinational corporations ... A leader in this attack is the New York-based Center on Transnational Corporations' (quoted in Bair, 2004: 11).

Due to this combination of external and internal forms of economic coercion, the G-77 eventually abandoned the Code in the late 1980s, while the UNCTC was rendered redundant in 1993 and officially dissolved in 1995. The UNCTC was eventually transformed into an UNCTAD programme, 'Investment, Technology and Enterprise

Table 3.6   Top 20 of the *Financial Times* Global 500 Rankings 2004 ($ millions)

Global Rank	Company	Country	Market Value	Sector	Turnover	Profit $
1	General Electric	US	299,336.4	Diversified Industrial	133,585.0	15,002
2	Microsoft	US	271,910.9	Software & Computer Services	32,187.0	9,993
3	Exxon Mobil	US	263,940.3	Oil & Gas	237,054.0	21,510
4	Pfizer	US	261,615.6	Pharmaceuticals & Biotechnology	45,188.0	3,910
5	Citigroup	US	259,190.8	Banks	94,713.0	17,853
6	Wal-Mart Stores	US	258,887.9	General Retailers	256,329.0	9,054
7	American International Group	US	183,696.1	Insurance	81,300.0	9,274
8	Intel	US	179,996.0	Information Technology Hardware	30,141.0	5,641
9	BP	UK	174,648.3	Oil & Gas	232,571.0	N/A
10	HSBC	UK	163,573.8	Banks	N/A	N/A
11	Cisco Systems	US	162,059.7	Information Technology	18,878.0	3,578
12	Vodafone Group	UK	159,192.2	Telecommunications Services	55,041.1	N/A
13	Royal Dutch/ Shell	Netherlands/ UK	158,813.1	Oil & Gas	201,932.0	N/A
14	IBM	US	157,009.1	Software & Computer Services	89,131.0	7,583
15	Johnson & Johnson	US	148,985.6	Pharmaceuticals & Biotechnology	41,862.0	7,197
16	Berkshire Hathaway	US	140,094.3	Insurance	63,859.0	8,151
17	Procter & Gamble	US	135,107.1	Personal Care & Household Products	43,377.0	5,186
18	Toyota Motor	Japan	128,667.0	Automobiles & Parts	151,377.1	N/A
19	Coca-Cola	US	119,231.1	Beverages	21,044.0	4,347
20	Bank of America	US	118,478.1	Banks	48,065.0	10,810

Sources: 'Global 500', *Financial Times*, May 21, 2004. Profits taken from *Fortune: Fortune 500*, April 5, 2004.

Development'. In stark contrast with the UNCTC, its successor strives to promote FDI in the South without conditions placed on its nature.[15] While lobbying by conservative elements in the US was an important factor, it was by no means the only reason for the downfall of the Code and the UNCTC. The ongoing crisis of overaccumulation necessitated not only the reproduction of neoliberal strategies in the form of FDI in the South, but also their intensification. The demise of the Code was a necessary step in this direction. This was then to complement ongoing capitalist–state strategies to increase bilateral and regional investment agreements, such as the Single European Market in 1992, and the North American Free Trade Agreement since 1994 (see Chapter 4).

The launching of the Uruguay Round of multilateral trade negotiations under GATT (1986–94) was another example of how states, at the behest of powerful TNCs, actively sought to facilitate neoliberal strategies by reducing barriers to trade and investment capital flows. The Uruguay Round, for instance, included new projects to negotiate international agreements on trade-related intellectual property rights (TRIPs) and trade-related investment measures (TRIMs). TRIPs facilitated deeper forms of neoliberalism by granting corporations increased rights to privatize and patent life-forms, including plant and other genetic resources of Third World countries. TRIMs render illegal certain measures that countries have employed to encourage TNCs to establish linkages with domestic firms. Both TRIPs and TRIMs fall under the authority of the WTO, which I will discuss below (see Jones, 2004; Wilkinson, 2000).

STRENGTHENING THE INSTITUTIONAL FRAMEWORK FOR INTENSIFIED NEOLIBERAL RESTRUCTURING STRATEGIES

Counter-hegemonic movements

The above capitalist and state-led strategies to fortify and legitimize neoliberalism in the South did not occur without resistance, however. As noted earlier, struggles around CSR issues, which began to take off during the South African apartheid regime, began to grow in terms of their network linkages, as well as multiply in number, to protest and demand more responsible action on the part of TNCs, especially with regard to labour, human rights, and the environment in their operations in the Third World (see Lipschutz, 2001; Lipschutz and Mayer, 1996; Keck and Sikkink, 1998; Pearson and Seyfang, 2001). Largely due to the effective and active roles of shareholder organizations, such as the Interfaith Center on Corporate Responsibility (ICCR), trade unions (UNITE!, AFL-CIO, IG Metall, LabourNet, LabourStart, and so on), and NGOs (the Campaign for Labor Rights, Sweatshop Watch, Child Labor Coalition, Clean Clothes Campaign, Amnesty International, Greenpeace, Human Rights Watch, CorpWatch, Global Unions, United Students Against Sweatshops,

Maquila Solidarity Network, and so on), a litany of charges levied against TNCs by non-profit NGOs empowered by the internet during the early 1990s continued to draw consumers' attention to horrific accounts of exploitation in the South. Examples are not difficult to find: sweatshop conditions within the supply-chains of major US clothing suppliers were unearthed; Royal Dutch Shell and Chevron, along with the Nigerian government, were charged for environmental transgressions, and their indirect role in endangering the livelihoods of the Ogoni and Ilaje people, indigenous groups who have been demanding more political autonomy and compensation for the destruction due to crude oil drilling in the once healthy ecosystem of Nigeria's Niger River delta, upon which these people depend for the maintenance of their traditional diet of wild rice, fish, and other river life. Pharmaceutical companies were implicated in over-pricing essential medicines in the Third World (see Klein, 2000; Korten, 1995; Bakan, 2004).

While groups from the developed world – i.e. middle-class institutional investors and consumers – dominate many of these counter-hegemonic networks and initiatives, there have been important victories in the South against corporate dispossession strategies. These 'David and Goliath' cases not only acted to discredit and harm the 'reputation' of brand names, but also challenged the common-sense assumptions linked to the corporation as a 'moral agent'. Let us look briefly at two cases: Aguas Argentinas, in Argentina, and the Coca-Cola battle in Kerala, India. Both examples deal directly with attempts by societies to reclaim power over the most basic of resources: water.

According to CorpWatch, a major NGO based in the US, the privatization policies promoted by the World Bank, the IMF and the US government have made 460 million people, globally, dependent on private water corporations for their daily supply, compared to 51 million in 1990 (Hacher, 2004). Because markets need to compete, they are more efficient than states, and, as the neoclassical rationale underpinning the Washington consensus has it, will thus provide consumers with a wider range of choices and better prices. Water privatization in the South has proved this assumption incorrect. The following case represents a classic example of neoliberal restructuring, and of the contradictions inherent in it. In Argentina, privatization was viewed as a vital strategy that could help save the country from an economic crisis in 1989 that had produced stagflation, and hyperinflation of almost 5,000 per cent. Under heavy pressure from the World Bank and the US government, a deal was struck in 1993 between Argentina's water authority and a consortium that includes the Suez group from France (the largest private water company in the world), Spain's Aguas de Barcelona, and the World Bank. This agreement established a new private entity, named Aguas Argentinas. According to the Ecology and Environment Foundation, Aguas Argentinas, which encompassed over 10 million people, represented 'the largest transfer of a water service and watershed into private control in the world'. As a result of this centralization of capital into a monopoly, residential water rates increased by 88.2 per cent between 1993 and 2002. It should be noted that there was no relationship between this rate and the consumer price index (inflation rate), which was hovering around 7.3 per cent during the same period. This price hike allowed the company to pocket net profits of 20 per cent – almost three times the average rate in other countries. In the United States, for example, water companies' profit margins increased between 6 and 12.5 percentage points in 1991, whereas in the United Kingdom a reasonable rate of profit for the sector is between 6 and 7 per cent, and 6 per cent is considered a very reasonable return on investment in France (Hacher, 2004).

Higher rates did not translate into better quality or quantity of service, however (see McDonald and Pape, 2002). In 1997, the company was found to have failed to honour 45 per cent of its contractual commitments for improvement and expansion of services, which resulted in enormous pollution. Prosecutors filed an indictment, in 2002, which was not directed at Aguas Argentinas but which stated that there were serious deficiencies in the fulfilment of Aguas Argentinas' concession contract (Santoro, 2004). In November, the country's Auditor-General criticized ETOSS (Ente Tripartito de Obras y Servicios Sanitarios) for the excessive delay in the application of penalties' and for delaying construction works promised in the concession contract. ETOSS is a government agency created to regulate Aguas Argentinas, but has proved to be rather ineffectual, largely because state officials have ignored its recommendations (Santoro, 2004).

In 2002 ETOSS, for example, levied $16 million in fines against Aguas Argentinas for missed commitments, but the company disputed the claims and has not paid the fines. The government later cancelled $10 million of the fines as part of a new contract (Santoro, 2004). Aguas Argentinas transports the sewage waste of 5,744,000 people, but according to a December 2003 study by the Argentine Auditor-General only 12 per cent of the total receives full sewage treatment. The rest, according to the Argentine Auditor-General, is dumped into the Rio de la Plata in the Berazetegui zone. Individuals and municipal authorities in Berazategui, together with the nearby municipalities of Quilmes and Berisso, recently sued Aguas Argentinas for the contamination of the river, asking for $300 million in compensation (Hacher, 2004).

The second case involves transgressions by Coca-Cola's bottling operation (Hindustan Coca-Cola Beverages Ltd) in Plachimada, which is in Kerala, India. After receiving complaints of the massive extraction of groundwater by Hindustan, and the consequent depletion and contamination of well water in Plachimada village, the Kerala State Health Department gathered data that confirms the charges against Hindustan. The villagers were promptly told by the medical officer of the Public Health Centre in the village not to drink the water from the wells near the Coca-Cola plant. Water samples from these wells, analysed at the Regional Analytical Laboratory at Kozhikode under the orders of the District Medical Officer, have revealed hardness, chlorides and concentration of total dissolved solids beyond tolerable levels for drinking water. However, instead of punishing the TNC for environmental abuse and endangering human life, the Kerala government proceeded to conduct studies that 'eulogise the company's inadequate harvesting system', according to Vinod Kumar of Maithri, a local NGO implementing the World Bank-aided drinking water and sanitation project in the neighbouring Mudalamada Panchayat (Surendranath, 2004; see also www.corpwatch.org).

Numerous protests against Coca-Cola's neoliberal strategies are emerging all over India. One protest, which has been led primarily by Dalits (formerly 'untouchables') and indigenous peoples in India, has continued for over a year. Aside from the above charges, Coca-Cola has illegally occupied a portion of the common property resources of the village, and was found guilty of evading payment of land revenue by a local court. Local police protected Coca-Cola's factory gates with about 200 officers, alongside 50 armed private security guards. In another community, Kudus village in Thane district, villagers have been forced to travel long distances in search of water, due to the water depletion in their area as a result of Coca-Cola's operations. More than 7,000 people, mostly women, protested against a proposed Coca-Cola factory in Sivaganga, Tamil Nadu. The protesters were justifiably worried that Coca-Cola's operations in the area would lead to scarcity and contamination of water. What all these counter-hegemonic movements have in common is the growing discontent with the arrangement whereby Coca-Cola receives subsidized water, land and tax breaks from their state, while they are left with contaminated water, or none at all (www.corpwatch.org).

At issue is the fact that TNCs should become accountable to societies in which they operate. States are also being increasingly called upon by their citizens to take legal action against foreign capitals operating within their borders, who threaten their quality of life. In short, it is becoming increasingly problematic for states of the developing world to extend corporate immunity to TNCs. This, in turn, has caused many problems with regard to reproducing the status quo in the global South. States have responded with increased economic coercion (investment strikes, the downgrading of public debt, and so on) to ensure that states in the developing world continue to guarantee the liberties enjoyed by TNCs.

Freezing contradictions: informal global networks of CSR

In response to the above counter-hegemonic movements, and the general backlash against corporate forms of neoliberal capitalist restructuring in the South, TNCs have been undertaking measures aimed at protecting one of the central factors in determining company sales and value: their reputation (Paine, 2003; Larkin, 2003; Seyfang and Pearson, 2001; Klein, 2000; Bakan, 2004). According to the managing director of a very large and powerful public relations company, Burston-Marsteller in New York, '[s]tudies show that 40 percent to 45 percent of a company's stock price is a reflection of shareholder confidence in the CEO [chief executive officer], his strategy and managing team' (Sparkes, 2002: 221). It is worth emphasizing that, according to CorpWatch, Burston-Marsteller 'is adept at creating a positive image for corporations involved in unethical business practices including human rights violations, environmental destruction and animal-testing. Many of these companies have faced public scrutiny and even convictions for their various activities.' Millions of dollars are spent annually on 'spinning a good company image'. TNCs are taking great pains to demonstrate that they are good corporate citizens. Various TNCs, for example, are beginning to implement company codes of conduct, which require contractors in the South to eradicate abusive working conditions.

The Fair Labour Association (FLA),[16] for example, was established to promote adherence to the International Labour Organization's Conventions[17] and improve working conditions worldwide. The FLA represents a multi-stakeholder coalition of companies, universities and NGOs. There are 175 US colleges and universities and twelve leading brand-name companies participating in the FLA, including Liz Claiborne, Adidas-Salomon, Nike, Patagonia, Puma, Reebok, and so on. At the same time, TNCs were posting websites dedicated to issues of CSR. Coca-Cola's global website[18] includes a section on 'citizenship'; Royal Dutch Shell's website[19] features a section dedicated to the 'environment and society', and a 'Shell Report' pertaining to issues of sustainable development, while McDonald's website[20] includes an entire page dedicated to corporate social responsibility. There have also been international initiatives by business to forge links with the environment and labour groups to address issues of monitoring and accountability. For example, in 1997 the Global Reporting Initiative (GRI)[21] was founded by the Coalition for Environmentally Responsible Economies (CERES).[22] The GRI became independent in 2002, and is an official collaborating centre of the United Nations Environment Programme (UNEP), and operates in conjunction with the Global Compact. There is also the Social Accountability SA8000 standard,[23] which certifies firms. Meanwhile, the Prince of Wales Business Leaders Forum,[24] which was formed in 1990, promotes more socially responsible business practices, and is working on indicators to measure social performance (Pearson and Seyfang, 2001).

Good intentions aside, there are at least three significant and interlocking limitations to these corporate efforts. First, there is an absence of hard-and-fast standards. As long as there are no common standards governing their reports, nor rigorous independent and public audits, the information provided by these corporations is at best incomplete, or, at worst, misleading. Second, the creation of common standards is insufficient without some sort of formalized enforcement and penalty mechanism. The latter can only be achieved through active state involvement – something contrary to the current neoliberal times. Third, CSR initiatives need to be complemented by regulatory mechanisms in the ongoing liberalization of trade and FDI flows under the aegis of the WTO. With this in mind, we now turn to a brief discussion of the WTO and its role in delimiting these struggles for greater corporate social justice.

Freezing contradictions legally through the state: enter the WTO

As we have seen, Robert Cox has suggested that US dominance is reproduced and legitimized, through international organizations such as the WTO, by, for example, (1) embodying rules that facilitate the expansion of hegemonic world orders, (2) ideologically legitimizing the norms of the world order, (3) co-opting the elites from peripheral countries, and (4) absorbing counter-hegemonic ideas (Cox, 1993a: 62; 1987). Given the legitimacy problems associated with TNC activity in the South in the face of the persistent crisis of overaccumulation, the WTO has served to legalize trade liberalization, while also making a sideswipe at the formal regulation of key CSR issues. This has resulted in the removal of harmful and sensitive issues from the area of grassroots struggle (see Shamir, 2004). Despite constant and vigorous lobbying by international labour organizations such as the International Confederation of Free Trade Unions (ICFTU) and the Trade Union Advisory Council (TUAC), the WTO has decided not to make a clear linkage between trade liberalization and the protection of worker's rights, either in the form of a social clause or a legal endorsement of core labour standards. The WTO has also resisted low-level co-operation with the ILO to explore labour and trade-related standards (Wilkinson, 2002: 198; 2000; O'Brien et al., 2000). Likewise, the legal framework of the WTO privileges trade liberalization over the environment. As Rorden Wilkinson explains, '[t]he move to patent so-called "innovations" [under TRIPs] in biotechnology, and the codification of these patents in international law have led many to suggest that the WTO is too quick to offer legal protection to scientific "advancements" that can have potentially damaging effects on human and animal life, as well as on the biosphere' (Wilkinson, 2002: 199–200; 2000).

The relationship between the WTO and NGOs was also circumscribed in the WTO's guidelines for the development of relations with NGOs.[25] For example, the sixth guideline explicitly states that, due to the 'special character of the WTO, which is both a legally binding intergovernmental treaty of rights and obligations among its Members and a forum for negotiations. As a result of extensive discussions, there is currently a broadly held view that it would not be possible for NGOs to be directly involved in the work of the WTO or its meetings' (WTO, 'Guidelines for arrangements on relations with NGOs', Document WT/L/162, July 18, 1996, quoted in Wilkinson, 2002: 202; cf. O'Brien et al., 2000). To be sure, the capitalist nature of the WTO, in its attempts to regulate FDI flows across national spaces in the interests of business and dominant states, should make us suspicious of the inclusive, transparent and accountable spirit of CSR networks. As many commentators have documented, the WTO operates in a shroud of secrecy, away from public scrutiny – G-7 interests are clearly over-represented in the WTO's decision-making forums, TNCs have a disproportionate degree of access, and therefore influence, in WTO decision-making, and 'the broad representation of interests in the WTO does not include those who suffer most from increased trade liberalization and accompanying changes in production processes' (Wilkinson, 2002: 200).

This section has highlighted the conflict-led and contradictory nature of capitalist strategies aimed at maximizing profits during a crisis of overaccumulation. The establishment of the WTO on January 1, 1995 may be understood as a state-led attempt to freeze the contradictions associated with the deepening and expansion of neoliberalism, in that the WTO acted as a buffer between member states and more radical NGOs. The WTO has sought to institutionalize, and thus depoliticize, the power of TNCs and their contentious relationship with radical NGOs. In such an institutional venue, which was marked by a formal and permanent inter-state organization aimed at both regulating trade and providing a forum for further reductions in barriers to trade, common standards regarding corporate social responsibility should have been addressed and ratified. Instead, any rigorous attempt to provide international protection of labour and environmental rights has been sidestepped. Likewise, alternative forms of economic exchange between countries, such as fair trade policies and greater South–South trade, have been removed from the agenda and declared unfeasible by the knowledge brokers (i.e. international trade lawyers, corporate interests, and heads of the G-7). This does not, however, imply that the WTO is an omnipotent and legitimate institution. Indeed, its democratic deficit is plainly observable by the 'great masses'.

In his address to the World Economic Forum in Davos, Switzerland, on January 31, 1999, the Secretary-General of the UN noted that

[g]lobalization is a fact of life. But I believe we have underestimated its fragility. The problem is this. The spread of markets outpaces the ability of societies and their political systems to adjust to them, let alone to guide the course they take. History teaches us that such an imbalance between the

economic, social and political realms can never be sustained for very long (Annan, 1999).

Put in more critical terms, the 'governance gap' to which Kofi Annan refers, and which has been, in part, aggravated by the WTO, desperately needs to be addressed, if the intensification of neoliberal-led capitalism, which is being carried out by TNCs in the South, is to retain legitimacy, particularly in the face of rising counter-hegemonic movements. The pinnacle of such movements was the WTO Seattle protest in December 1999 (a few months after the Global Compact was launched), which drew over 5,000 people from all over the world and all walks of life to show their disapproval of growing corporate power.

The solution to this problem was a Global Compact between the United Nations and business, comprised of shared values and principles, which was to give a human face to the global businesses operating in the South. We now turn to the UN's attempt to place a 'human face' on the increasing dispossession seen in the Third World.

GLOBAL COMPACT: LEARNING NETWORK OR PASSIVE REVOLUTION?

> Business must be encouraged to act responsibly in the global neighbourhood and contribute to its governance. There are signs that this community is beginning to respond to the opportunities to exercise such responsibility.
> Commission on Global Governance, *Our Global Neighbourhood*, 1995: 255.

In a speech delivered at the World Economic Forum[26] in January 1999, Kofi Annan, warned business leaders of an imminent backlash against globalization unless it was 'embedded in social values' and reflected the 'common objectives' of all segments of the world's population. Annan challenged the business community to join the United Nations in its aims at forging stronger social and environmental pillars to sustain the global economy in the form of a Global Compact (Ruggie, 2000). The Compact, which was launched in July 2000, comprises a 'coalition to make globalization work for all', involving corporations, including global entities such as Daimler Chrysler, Unilever, Deutsche Bank and Nike; and leaders of labour and civic groups such as the International Confederation of Free Trade Unions, Amnesty International, the Worldwide Fund for Nature, the World Conservation Union, and a consortium of NGOs from developing countries (Global Policy Forum, 2000). By the end of 2001, the GC had enlisted the support of approximately 400 companies in 30 countries. By 2004, the list had increased to about 1,200 companies, including many of the Global 500 corporations.

Given the Compact's scope and emphasis on forging new partnerships between both state and non-state actors, it has been heralded by many as global governance par excellence – or, as one observer put it, Annan's 'most creative reinvention' yet of the United Nations (*Christian Science Monitor*, quoted in Ruggie, 2001: 371). The main aim of the GC is to act as a 'learning network'. According to one of its key architects, John Ruggie,[27] a learning network constitutes an attempt to reach – through dialogue – a broad consensus on good corporate practices. The definition of good practices, 'together with illustrative case studies, are then publicised in an on-line learning bank, which will become a standard reference source on corporate social responsibility. The hope and expectation is that good practices will help drive out bad ones through the power of dialogue, transparency, advocacy, and competition' (Ruggie, 2001: 373).

The GC is not without its critics, however. Many NGOs, such as CorpWatch, NikeWatch, and Global Exchange, which view the voluntary nature of the Compact as a sign of its not going far enough in stamping out the raft of corporate crimes against human and animal rights, as well as transgressions against the environment (Transnational Resource and Action Centre, 2000). Moreover, these critics argue that the GC's website offers companies a free forum to polish their images without their inputs being qualified by critical comment or even questions (www.unglobalcompact.org/Portal). This has led to the charges that the Compact allows participating companies to 'bluewash' their image by wrapping themselves in the flag of the United Nations (Transnational Resource and Action Centre, quoted in Ruggie, 2001: 371). As other critics have astutely observed, '[t]hese same corporations most often oppose measures for corporate accountability, defined here as mechanisms for enforcing actual rules on companies' (Fisher and Ponniah, 2003: 59).

According to its website, the Compact seeks to advance responsible corporate citizenship so that business can be part of the solution to the challenges of globalization. It is assumed that a more sustainable and inclusive global economy can be achieved if business enters into a partnership with other social actors – governments, who defined the principles on which the initiative is based; companies, whose actions it seeks to influence; labour, in whose hands the concrete process of global production takes place; and civil society organizations, representing the wider community of stakeholders – including five UN agencies (the Office of the High Commissioner for Human Rights, the United Nations Environment Programme; the International Labour Organization, the United Nations Development Programme, and the United Nations Industrial Development Organization) (www. unglobalcompact.org).

Unlike the Code, the Compact is not a regulatory arrangement with a legally binding code of conduct, but rather a voluntary corporate citizenship initiative. According to its website, the GC has two objectives: (1) to ensure that the ten principles are integrated into the mainstream operations of businesses on a worldwide scale (see Box 3.2 below), and (2) to catalyse businesses to support UN goals, such as the Millennium Development Goals. To achieve these objectives, the Compact offers facilitation and engagement through several control mechanisms (Rosenau, 1995): 'Policy Dialogues', 'Learning', 'Local Structures' and 'Projects' (Ruggie, 2001; 2002; www. unglobalcompact.org). The UN's role in this Compact is to act as an authoritative convener and facilitator by asking firms to undertake the following three key commitments:

1. To advocate the GC in mission statements, annual reports, and similar public venues – on the premise that their doing so will raise the level of attention paid to, and responsibility for, these concerns within firms.
2. To post on the GC website at least once a year concrete steps to act on any or all of the principles, discussing both positive and negative lessons learned, thereby triggering a structured dialogue among the various participants about what is deemed to constitute good practice.
3. To join with the UN in partnership projects to benefit developing countries largely marginalized by globalization, particularly the least developed (see Ruggie, 2001: 372).

While the Compact's role as a learning network is praiseworthy, its attempts to achieve the better integration, on a voluntary basis, of the social needs of those hardest hit by neoliberal-led restructuring strategies is limited by the contradictory policies pursued by the global trade architecture being constructed by the WTO, whose forms of trade liberalization are not only top-down and exclusive in nature, but also aim to serve corporate interests of profit-maximization by making legal, and therefore attempting to legitimize to subordinate classes, neoliberal restructuring strategies. Another restriction of the GC lies in the fact that its creator, the UN, is itself an international organization and therefore imbued with the relations of power found in global capitalism (see Gowan, 2003). The UN, like the WTO, is a product of the hegemonic world order. In other words, the Compact, as a creation of the UN, acts to legitimize ideologically the neoliberal norms of the world order, such as self-regulation by powerful corporations, trade liberalization, and the superiority of market rationality over government intervention in the sphere of public goods like water, transport, health, education, and welfare services. The power relations in global capitalism involve not merely the inter-state system, but capitalists. It is therefore instructive to look more closely at the relationships between the Compact and its most powerful partner: the International Chamber of Commerce (ICC). With over 7,000 corporate members, the ICC represents one of the most powerful lobby groups in the world, counting some the largest transnational corporations in its membership list, including General Motors, Novartis, Bayer and Nestlé.

Given the sheer power of the ICC, it is interesting to note two important points made by its Secretary-General, Maria Livanos Cattaui, during an interview in 2001 with the *International Herald Tribune*. According to Cattaui, one of the main virtues of the GC is that it is about self-regulation, as opposed to heavy-handed government intervention, as represented by the UNCTC's Code on TNC activity in the South. Or, as Cattaui puts it,

> [t]he compact is – or should be – open-ended, free from 'command and control.' It can be a catalyst for good corporate citizenship and the spread of good business practices. It appeals to the competitive instincts of the market and will encourage companies always to raise their sights and go one better in upholding its principles. It mobilizes the virtues of private enterprise in fulfilment of the UN's goals ('Compact Must Avoid "Command and Control"', *International Herald Tribune*, January 25, 2001).

The avoidance of any monitoring and verification procedure suits the ICC in its attempts to use the Compact as a PR gimmick to legitimize the activities of its members. For instance, the ICC website consists of a collection of very brief reports on environmental and human rights initiatives by BP-Amoco, Fiat, Unilever and other corporations – some of which are not part of the Compact, such as Nestlé. As

Box 3.2   10 Principles of the Global Compact

Human Rights
The origin of Principles 1 and 2 is in the 1948 Universal Declaration of Human Rights (UDHR). The aim of this Declaration was to set basic minimum international standards for the protection of the rights and freedoms of the individual. The fundamental nature of these provisions means that they are now widely regarded as forming a foundation of international law. In particular, the principles of the UDHR are considered to be international customary law and do not require signature or ratification by the state to be recognized as a legal standard.[28]

- *Principle 1*: Businesses should support and respect the protection of internationally proclaimed human rights; and
- *Principle 2*: make sure that they are not complicit in human rights abuses.

Labour Standards
The four labour principles of the Global Compact are taken from the International Labour Organization's Declaration on Fundamental Principles and Rights at Work. This Declaration was adopted in 1998 by the International Labour Conference, an annual tripartite meeting that brings together governments, employers and workers from 177 countries. The Declaration calls upon all ILO member states to apply the principles in line with the original intent of the core Conventions on which it is based. A universal consensus now exists that all countries, regardless of level of economic development, cultural values, or ratifications of the relevant ILO Conventions, have an obligation to respect, promote, and realize these fundamental principles and rights.[29]

- *Principle 3*: Businesses should uphold the freedom of association and the effective recognition of the right to collective bargaining;
- *Principle 4*: the elimination of all forms of forced and compulsory labour;
- *Principle 5*: the effective abolition of child labour; and
- *Principle 6*: the elimination of discrimination in respect of employment and occupation.

Environment
The three environmental principles of the Global Compact are drawn from a Declaration of Principles and an International Action Plan (Agenda 21) that emerged from the United Nations Conference on Environment and Development (the Earth Summit) held in Rio de Janeiro in 1992. Chapter 30 of Agenda 21 stated that the policies and operations of business and industry can play a major role in reducing impacts on resource use and the environment. In particular, business can contribute through the promotion of cleaner production and responsible entrepreneurship.[30]

- *Principle 7*: Businesses should support a precautionary approach to environmental challenges;
- *Principle 8*: undertake initiatives to promote greater environmental responsibility; and

▶

> • *Principle 9*: encourage the development and diffusion of environmentally friendly technologies.
>
> **Anti-Corruption**
> • *Principle 10*: Businesses should work against all forms of corruption, including extortion and bribery.
>
> Source: United Nations 'Global Compact' (www.unglobalcompact.org/Portal/).

Raghavan notes, combined with the UN's secrecy about who is and who is not a member of the GC, this gives the impression that these highly controversial companies are part of the Compact. What's more, the ICC reports are presented as 'case studies' of 'how the private sector is fulfilling the Compact through corporate actions'.[31] The ICC invites companies to submit examples, but does not permit external comments from, for example, NGOs that are critical of the claims (Raghavan, 2001).

When asked about the ICC's position on civil society's participation in the GC, Cattaui replied that

[t]he danger is that too many players will be brought in, and we have seen hints that that might happen in some of the rhetoric coming out of the UN. If labour unions and so-called civil society nongovernmental organizations are seen as full partners in the Global Compact, its nature will certainly be different from the concept that a group of CEOs – all of them ICC members – welcomed wholeheartedly when they pledged their support in July 1999 ('Compact Must Avoid "Command and Control"', *International Herald Tribune*, January 25, 2001).

Indeed, the ICC has lobbied the Compact to help discourage attacks on growing corporate abuse of power around the world by more radical NGOs. For instance, NGOs draw constant attention to the ICC's long history of forcefully lobbying to weaken international environmental treaties, such as the Kyoto Protocol, the Convention on Biodiversity, and the Basel Convention against trade in toxic waste. In the place of the GC's Principles 7–9 (see Box 3.2), 'the ICC promotes a narrow corporate agenda, dominated by the commercial interests of some of the world's most environmentally irresponsible corporations – an agenda that often effectively undermines a precautionary approach and basic environmental responsibility, says the CEO report' (Raghavan, 2001).

Another role that international organizations play in reproducing and legitimizing dominant ideas is in their ability to absorb counter-hegemonic ideas. The manner in which the GC seeks to invite TNCs to participate in grafting a human face onto the social and economic ills brought about by neoliberalism, including the constant increase of corporate power, represents a passive revolution. It will be recalled that Gramsci developed this notion to explain how the ruling classes survived despite economic and political crises (Carnoy, 1984). The term 'passive revolution' refers to a top-down strategy aimed at preventing the development of a revolutionary adversary. The threat is not so much that those who oppose the constant increase of corporate power in the South cannot be silenced by coercion (economic or physical), but rather the effect that the constant upheaval will have on bourgeois states in the South, who are seeking to create good business civilizations.

What the Compact does, albeit inadvertently, is to accept certain demands from below – such as the need to enforce human rights, labour, and environmental protection through established state-sanctioned principles like the Universal Declaration of Human Rights – while also encouraging counter-hegemonic movements to restrict their struggle to the electronic terrain of the learning network. This in turn prevents the dominance of neoliberalism from being challenged, while TNCs are granted ever more freedom to pursue neoliberal strategies in the South.

It is important to stress that this view complements that of the Commission on Global Governance that control mechanisms can be both comprised of and occur beyond the purview of the state (see Chapter 2). Its significance lies in the acceptance that there is no alternative other than to embrace the structural power of capital and work within these new constraints – that is, by adopting the mode of governance that best promotes a healthy investment climate: neoliberalism. By denying the role of the state in the GC, and by moving away from regulatory mechanisms for TNCs operating in the Third World, the Compact's architects not only depoliticize struggle (counter-hegemonic movements) around the activities of TNCs by attempting to delimit the site of struggle to 'cyber-space' (the learning network), but also free bourgeois states of any responsibilities for their decisions to implement business-friendly environments at the expense of human and ecological interests. More to the point, the GC acts to legitimize and normalize the expropriation of the labourer, while seeking to neutralize and depoliticize struggle tied to the deepening and widening economic exploitation in the South by the 'moral' corporation. By denying the role of the state in the GC and thus moving away from the option of regulatory mechanisms to curb the behaviour of TNCs, the Compact's architects achieve two results. First, in the attempts to delimit the site of struggle to 'cyberspace' (e.g. the learning network), counter-hegemonic movements are not only depoliticized, but also encouraged to interact electronically with corporations, as opposed to face-to-face confrontation. Second, the self-regulatory characteristic of the GC not only encourages a dialogue between the UN, corporations and select civil society organisations, but also shifts the responsibility to the private sector and away from the bourgeois states. Thus the latter are exonerated from any responsibilities for their decisions to implement business-friendly environments at the expense of human and ecological costs.

This last section has attempted to transcend the superficial meaning of the Global Compact as a 'learning network', and to begin to make sense of its inner nature – that is, to view the GC as a moment of global capitalism and the contradictions therein. I have argued that the Compact represents a passive revolution aimed at placating counter-hegemonic movements, and thereby recreating and legitimizing increasing corporate transgressions against the environment and humanity under the aegis of neoliberalism.

CONCLUSION

In this chapter I have sought to provide the reader with the first of three windows through which to explore the capitalist nature of global governance. I looked at two main international strategies of CSR – the Code and the Global Compact – that have been implemented over the course of the post-Bretton Woods era. Through an historical materialist lens, we were able to understand the relations of power underpinning CSR projects, as well as how these strategies have emerged from the wider contradictions of global capitalism. Moreover, our historical-materialist framework assisted us in transcending the largely superficial differences between the Code and the GC, and thereby began to reveal both as class-based and contradictory moments of wider global capitalist restructuring. While many analysts have tended to focus on the differences between the Code and the GC, we have shown that both projects were attempts at resolving the confrontation between the dominant ideology of the ruling classes and the 'actual social experience' of those most affected by the increasing power of TNCs in the South.

While it is too soon to predict the impact of the GC, what we do know now is that it has not been able to absorb the growing backlash against neoliberal restructuring strategies centred on promoting the interests of capitalists, or more specifically the TNCs. There are at least two reasons why this paragon of global economic governance, and its common-sense assumption of 'embedded social values', has been rapidly waning in legitimacy. First, the General Agreement on Trade in Services (GATS), under the aegis of the WTO, opens more possibilities for neoliberalism, from water resources to banking, while the ongoing US bilateral agreements with Third World countries are based upon special interests, rather than on a concern for the well-being of poorer trading partners. The following remarks provide a case in point:

> In Morocco, prospects of the trade agreement were greeted by protests – an unusual occurrence in a country that is only slowly moving to democracy. The new agreement, many Moroccans fear, will make generic drugs needed in the fight against AIDS even less accessible in their country than they are in the United States. According to Morocco's Association de Lutte contre le SIDA, an AIDS agency, the agreement could increase the effective duration of patent protection from the normal length of 20 years to 30 years ('New Trade Pacts Betray the Poorest Partners', *New York Times*, July 10, 2004).

The old standby of pure brute force has also permitted neoliberal restructuring in the South. Many powerful corporations – such as Boeing, Lockheed Martin, Halliburton, General Electric, and Raytheon – have benefited handsomely through military contracts from the 'war on terrorism'.[32]

The second reason for the dwindling legitimacy of the GC relates to the inverse relationship between neoliberal restructuring and the crisis of hegemony. For instance, as neoliberal restructuring strategies continue to deepen their exploitative effects in the South, so too will inequality and poverty continue to persist in the face of super-profits reaped by TNCs. This situation will no doubt continue to foster the growth of counter-hegemonic movements, which strive to challenge the dominant neoliberal strategies pursued by both states and capitalists. After over two and a half decades, there is much evidence to suggest that the neoliberal promise that trade liberalization will eventually lead to improved economic circumstances for the developing world is indeed wrong. In fact, one-fifth of the world lives in extreme poverty (existing on less than $1 per day), while more than half of the population lives on less than $2 a day (UNDP, 2002; ILO, 2004).

the world's slums are growing, and growing, with the number of people living in such dire conditions now at the 1 billion mark – making up 32 per cent of the global urban population. The Report goes on to note that in developing regions, slum dwellers account for 43 per cent of the population, in contrast to about 6 per cent in more developed regions. In sub-Saharan Africa the proportion of urban residents in slums is highest, at 71.9 per cent, according to the report. Oceania had the lowest, at 24.1 per cent. South-central Asia accounted for 58 per cent, East Asia for 36.4 per cent, western Asia for 33.1 per cent, Latin America and the Caribbean for 31.9 per cent, north Africa for 28.2 per cent and Southeast Asia for 28 per cent (UN-HABITAT 2003).

Seen from this perspective, neoliberal restructuring may be characterized as an increase in socio-economic inequalities in the world, especially along the North–South axis, and the rise in power of corporations over all aspects of social life. It was suggested that the two global strategies of CSR discussed in this chapter – the Code and the CG – were not only rooted in the contradictions and struggles of neoliberal global restructuring, but also represented attempts to legitimize, as opposed to altering fundamentally, the status quo.

We now turn to the second window through which we attempt to view and understand the capitalist nature of global economic governance – namely, the contradictory and conflictual relations between creditors and debtors within the transnational debt architecture.

4
Managing Sovereign Default within the Transnational Debt Architecture

Within the last twenty years, there has been a globalization of private financial markets, which is in part a product of the confidence engendered by the post-war order. The ease of movement of large financial flows – which now far exceed trade in terms of their impact on currency markets – generates opportunities for a more efficient use of capital. But it also exposes individual countries, and the world as a whole, to greater instability. At the same time, major countries are less committed to intergovernmental economic co-operation.

Commission on Global Governance,
Our Global Neighbourhood, 1995: 179–80.

The tension between greater instability and less commitment to international economic co-operation, as the CGG notes here, is evident not only in the case of corporate social responsibility, but also in relation to debt. Aside from a few pages dedicated to the issue in *Our Global Neighbourhood*, global governance enthusiasts have tended to steer away from the issue of Third World debt. This neglect is puzzling given that, by its very nature, this debt speaks to the concerns of global governance. With its complex and multilayered dimensions, Third World debt not only moves across various levels of government (from IFIs to national state institutions), but also involves increasingly powerful private actors, such as mutual and pension funds. This chapter attempts to fill this gap in the global governance literature by examining critically and historically what I refer to as the 'transnational debt architecture'.

Although debates about Third World debt have been raging for decades, especially around the theme of debt cancellation in the poorest countries (for example in sub-Saharan Africa), it wasn't until Argentina, once a paragon of neoliberal success, entered into default at the end of 2001 that the issue of Third World debt grabbed the attention of international policy-makers. The Argentine case not only represented the largest default in history, in terms of both public and private debt, it also highlighted a continued problem associated with the existing transnational debt architecture: how to deal expediently and humanely with a bankrupt government. The seemingly endless lawsuits, stalemates and standoffs involving the Argentine government, its international commercial creditors, and the IMF suggest that this problem is nowhere near a resolution. This quagmire does not imply an absence of viable policy options, however.

Despite the fact that a variety of alternatives were intensely debated around the time of the default – albeit mainly restricted within the IMF, the US government, and private-sector creditors – the preferred solution that emerged from these discussions was what is known as the 'collection action clauses' (CACs) approach. Since the latter reveals much about the nature of the transnational debt architecture, it is useful to outline here what the CACs approach entailed. Briefly, this strategy involves provisions or contingency clauses[1] placed in sovereign bond issues and other debt instruments, such as bank loans. Unlike other proposals tabled at the official negotiations (Boorman, 2002), CACs are not only more decentralized, but also grant private-sector creditors, and their respective national judicial systems, far more control over their outstanding foreign public debts. This preferred solution is to mediate and resolve problems arising from sovereign debt in an informal manner. In other words, problems arising from public debt in the Third World should continue to be mediated through the market, as opposed to by multilateral organizations and statutory processes.

While the Argentine default has served to spark much-needed dialogue within official policy circles regarding transnational debt, the majority of these exchanges have remained within the narrow confines of technocratic and economic analyses (Cooper, 2002; Eichengreen, 2002; Krueger, 2002; Rogoff and Zettelmeyer, 2002; Lane and Phillips, 2002; cf. Fischer, 1999; Meltzer, 1984). These debates have neglected questions of power, preferring instead to view the post-war transnational debt architecture in terms of a rational evolutionary development, as opposed to a profoundly contradictory and class-led process. By historically contextualizing the management of the foreign government debt of emerging markets[2] within global capitalism, this chapter attempts to throw critical light on the inner nature of the transnational debt architecture by penetrating its smooth surface of a set of technical and legal relations between debtors and creditors. Why has the transnational debt architecture been managed in an informal and *ad hoc* framework since the 1950s, when governments were failing to pay interest and repay money borrowed from foreign creditors (Strange, 1986: 32–3)? What are the inherent contradictions within the debt architecture? How has the transnational debt architecture been reproduced? And who benefits from the status quo? Addressing these questions will help us throw a more critical light on the informal nature of global governance, which both the CGG and Rosenau largely take as qualities that are beneficial to the overall management of globalization (see Chapter 2).

In what follows, I suggest that the informal arrangement of transnational debt assists in recreating the conditions for capital accumulation by masking the increasingly exploitative relations of power that underpin it. As was discussed in the previous two chapters, the intensification of exploitation is intimately tied to neoliberal restructuring strategies aimed at dealing with the ongoing crisis of overaccumulation. I argue that the informal nature of the transnational debt architecture helps augment the power of credit to serve as an effective form of social discipline. This, in turn, permits donor states and capitals to coerce debtor states into accepting, implementing and internalizing neoliberal policies. The following historical survey of diverse moments of transnational debt reveals an inherent contradiction in this arrangement: the informal and *ad hoc* feature of the transnational debt architecture, coupled with the mounting power of global financial capitalists over debtor states, has led to growing levels of volatility and increasing fragility in the international credit system. This tension results in the fact that it has become increasingly more difficult to keep debtor countries within the bounds of the rules of the neoliberal-led global credit system. Up to now, the official international community has reacted to this paradox by intervening in such a manner as to establish the necessary political conditions needed to legitimize and support the further increase in capitalists' disciplinary and negotiation power over debtor states. This is evident in the recent decision by official international policy-makers to impose CACs, as opposed to a standardized, *de jure* mechanism to deal with future sovereign defaults. Solutions like the CACs only serve to heighten, rather than to diminish, the underlying contradiction of transnational debt. It is worth stressing that this paradox will remain throughout our analysis, although it assumes different, mystified forms at different times and places.

I develop this argument in four sections. The next section maps, analytically and historically, the contradictory terrain of the transnational debt architecture from the Bretton Woods system (1944–71) to the wake of the 1982 debt crises. It introduces a key solution to the above-mentioned contradiction, which I term the

'Golden Noose'. This heuristic device is composed of two main strands: securitized debt and neoliberalism. The next section explores the ongoing paradoxes of transnational debt, both despite and due to the presence of the Golden Noose. I consider one moment of the reappearance of the above contradiction: the growing tensions between social and financial risks. Next I briefly ponder the key official debates about the management of sovereign debt in the wake of the Argentine meltdown as a moment of the underlying contradiction in transnational debt. I conclude by demonstrating the need to go beyond the 'moral hazard' argument, which has dominated the debates about sovereign debt, in order to grasp the underlying power relations that have characterized not only the management of the Argentine default, but also, and more generally, the post-war governance of transnational debt.

THE POST-WAR TRANSNATIONAL DEBT ARCHITECTURE: A HISTORICAL OVERVIEW

The contradictions inherent in the modern system of foreign loans are the concrete expression of those which characterise the imperialist phase. Though foreign loans are indispensable for the emancipation of the rising capitalist states, they are yet the surest ties by which the old capitalist states maintain their influence, exercise financial control and exert pressure on the customs, foreign and commercial policy of the young capitalist states.

Rosa Luxemburg, *The Accumulation of Capital*, 2003: 401.

Managing credit in the Bretton Woods system

Up until World War I, countries that were either unable or unwilling to repay their loans were simply occupied militarily by the creditor nations. With the emergence of a Pax Americana (the US hegemonic state) and the BWS (1944–71), gunboat diplomacy was replaced by subtler methods of ensuring 'repayment morale' among debtor nations (Körner et al., 1984; cf. Luxemburg, 2003). What remained unchanged, however, were the underlying relations of power in the international credit system. As Susan Strange reminds us, the power to create credit implies the power to allow or to deny debtors the possibility of spending today and paying back tomorrow – the power to let debtor states exercise purchasing power, and thus influence markets for production (Strange, 1994). From 1944 onwards, this power was explicitly mediated by the two Bretton Woods institutions – namely, the IMF and the World Bank, and implicitly undergirded by US hegemony (Cox, 1987; Helleiner, 1994; Langley, 2002). This arrangement differed from previous ways of imposing repayment morale, in that states were not directly constrained by other sovereign states, but rather by the sanctions and incentives organized primarily by private-sector creditors and official multilateral lenders.

The disciplinary (coercive) features of this post-war international credit system were twofold. On the one hand, in exchange for IMF loans, countries dealing with payment arrears were to implement stabilization programmes, albeit less intrusive and comprehensive than the prescriptions of the Washington consensus. On the other, the 'repayment morale' was motivated by the debtor country's attempt to uphold its creditworthiness. This refers to an assessment by potential lenders of the capacity of the country to repay its external debt.[3] According to the Paris Club, 'being creditworthy is a key to success for developing countries, since this makes it possible for them to borrow larger amounts to finance growth development. In addition, a creditworthy debtor is in a position to borrow funds used to refinance existing loans' (www.clubdeparis.org). Until the demise of the Bretton Woods system in 1971, credit flows within the transnational debt architecture were largely dominated by bilateral loans (government-to-government) to the South. A caveat is in order here. Strictly speaking, foreign debt relations during this time were international as opposed to transnational in nature, as the former involved financial credits extended by governments to other governments (see Strange, 1998). I will continue to use the term 'transnational', however, for heuristic purposes to show the historical dynamics underpinning the present transnational debt architecture.

The absence of short-term debt flows to the Third World was due to the fact that the Bretton Woods credit system was premised on the Keynesian belief[4] that states should be masters over finance (Helleiner, 1994). Capital controls on short-term financial flows were put into place so as to discourage speculation and encourage enterprise. According to Keynes, 'enterprise was the activity of forecasting the prospective yields of assets over their whole life, whereas speculation is the activity of forecasting the psychology of the market' (quoted in Patomäki, 2001: 21; cf. Cohen, 2002).[5] As we will see later in this section, this central tenet of Bretton Woods was reversed after its demise in the early 1970s. This, in turn, affected the nature of the disciplinary relations underpinning the management of foreign public debt.

The capitalist nature of transnational debt: accumulation by dispossession

Despite the fact that official loans dominated sovereign debt relations in the Bretton Woods system, these public loans were not free, but were to be repaid with interest calculated on the market interest rates of industrialized countries. In other words, credit was not extended to the Third World out of good will, but instead in order to increase the value of interest-bearing capital tied to the donor states (see Marx, 1981; Harvey, 1999). This arrangement has been far from a win-win situation. While the official bilateral and multilateral creditors (principally the IMF and the World Bank) have, on several occasions, written off debts, on the whole, the granting of loans has proved a lucrative business, in which most of the risks are borne by the debtor state – or more specifically, the lower echelons of society. After all, it is the debtor state that is, in the event of a default, coerced by commercial lenders (i.e. banks), donor states, and the IFIs into selling off state assets (state-owned enterprises, even profitable ones), cutting government spending, and making its labour work harder and longer hours to produce exports at cut-throat prices in order to earn hard currency to meet its repayment schedule. Most mainstream analyses on debt (Meltzer, 1984; Lipson, 1981; 1986; Fischer, 1999; Krueger, 2002; Eichengreen, 2002) largely ignore the social dimension, and, more specifically, capitalist relations of power involved in the repayment of these legal obligations. Why do they continue to do so? According to Marx, it is in interest-bearing capital that the capital relationship reaches its most superficial and fetishized form.[6] Put simply, the latter term refers to the act of obscuring the human relationships in inanimate objects such as money: money is created, regulated, and sanctioned by human interactions and political institutions. Debt, too, is composed of human relationships (and thus power relations), but takes on a 'fetishized' appearance in the impersonal or legalistic relationship between creditor and debtor, as opposed to relations between human beings. 'M–M[1]' (money that produces more money), is viewed as self-valorizing, without the process that mediates the two moments: the exploitation of labour-power. In other words, money does not increase itself automatically, but requires the reproduction of the relations of capitalist production and the increased exploitation of labour and nature, in particular (Marx 1981: Chapter 21 and passim). Exploiting labour-power is not enough to repay foreign debt, however. The commodities produced by labour must be sold (traded) on the international markets in order to earn hard currencies to pay off their loans.[7] Yet when we look at the current account balances[8] of the middle-income countries (excluding China and the Russian Federation) over the past two decades, it becomes clear that what are considered by the World Bank as middle-income debtor states have largely been producing to pay for imports (or, in other words, other countries' exports) rather than exporting goods and services to repay their foreign debt obligations (see Table 4.1).

Table 4.1   Global Current Account Balances, 1981–2001[*] (percent of GDP)

	1981–90	1991	1996	1997	1998	1999	2000	2001
All Developing Countries (excluding China)	−1.8	−2.3	−2.0	−2.5	−3.1	−0.7	0.9	0.2
Middle-Income Countries	−1.3	−1.6	−1.3	−1.3	−1.8	0.0	1.2	0.6
East Asia and Pacific**	−1.4	0.5	−1.8	1.1	4.4	4.2	3.6	2.6
Indonesia	−3.1	−0.4	−3.4	−2.3	4.3	4.1	5.2	4.7
Europe and Central Asia	−0.5	−2.5	−1.3	−2.5	−2.7	−0.3	2.0	1.9
Turkey[†]	−1.3	−1.1	−1.3	−1.4	1.0	−0.7	−4.9	2.3
Poland	−1.4	−3.7	−2.3	−4.0	−4.4	−8.1	−6.3	−3.1
Latin America and Caribbean	−1.5	−2.8	−2.2	−3.3	−4.5	−3.2	−2.4	−2.9
Brazil	−1.1	−2.1	−3.0	−3.8	−4.3	−4.8	−4.1	−4.6
Mexico	−0.8	−3.7	−0.8	−1.9	−3.8	−2.9	−3.1	−2.9
Argentina	−2.2	−3.1	−2.5	−4.2	−4.9	−4.2	−3.1	−1.7
South Asia	−2.0	−1.5	−2.5	−1.1	−1.8	−1.0	−1.0	−0.5
India	−1.7	−1.2	−1.6	−0.7	−1.7	−0.7	−0.9	−0.7

[*]   World Bank data excludes China and the Russian Federation. Data compiled up to the year of the Argentine default.
[**]   Exports begin to pick up with the devaluation after the Asian crisis of 1997–98.
[†]   Turkey abandons currency-peg in 2001 after only 14 months into the three-year programme. Subsequent devaluation assists exports.

Source: World Bank, 2003: 197.

This table confirms what Marx and others have long argued: capitalism does not lead to economic prosperity and equality, as promised by neoclassical development economists (see Williamson, 1990), but instead will produce greater levels of social inequality, economic exploitation, and mounting social, economic and political instabilities (Harvey, 1999; 2003a; Clarke 1991; Bonefeld and Holloway, 1995; Arrighi, 1983; 1994; Taylor, 2004). This prompts us to ask: Why do creditors want to keep developing countries in the international credit system if debtor states can barely earn enough hard currency to honour their debts? The answer to this question lies in the wider contradictions of global capitalism. As was discussed in Chapter 2, when global capitalism encounters such obstacles to the valorization of capital, as it has since the late 1960s, surplus capital lies idle, with no profitable outlets in sight (Harvey, 1999; Clarke, 1988). To break these barriers to capital valorization, Harvey argues, capitalists must engage in predation, fraud, and violence by a wide range of means. As I noted in Chapter 2, Marx referred to primitive accumulation as the starting point of capitalist development. By this, Marx meant that primitive accumulation represented the enslavement of the worker, as this new form of accumulation marked of a new form of exploitation involving capitalists and wage-labourers. The social conditions of capitalist exploitation are not natural, but constructed through, for example, the creation of bourgeois laws of private property (Marx, 1976: 875). The conditions for capitalist exploitation thus need to be constantly reproduced through coercive and ideological processes, found both in the state and in the relations of domination between capitalists and labour. With the onset of a crisis of overaccumulation, the conditions for capitalist exploitation need to be not only recreated, but also intensified and expanded. Indeed, it is an ongoing process required to expand and deepen the reach of capital accumulation in order to overcome the barriers to the crisis of overaccumulation. Our attempts to grasp the processes involved in the reproduction and restructuring of capitalist relations across space and time – characterized by a deepening and widening of economic exploitation – might be assisted by drawing on David Harvey's term, 'accumulation by dispossession'. This term complements Harvey's understanding of 'spatio-temporal fixes'. Strategies of accumulation by dispossession do not replace the latter, but instead point to a more ruthless attempt at dealing with capital surplus (a symptom of a crisis of overaccumulation; see Arrighi, 2004). Harvey's notion of accumulation by dispossession suggests that capitalists must constantly seek to widen, deepen and intensify their exploitative activities in order to continue to accumulate in the face of stagnant effective demand (or, which is the same thing, a crisis of overaccumulation). According to Harvey, what accumulation of dispossession does is to realize a set of assets at very low costs. In this way, accumulation by dispossession represents class-led and highly contradictory and conflictual restructuring strategies that attempt to release 'a set of assets (including labour power) at very low (and in some cases zero) cost. Overaccumulated capital can seize hold of such assets and immediately turn them to profitable use' (Harvey, 2003b: 149). The establishment of export promotion zones, discussed in the previous chapter, is a case in point, as is the appropriation of assets, such as natural resources and state-owned companies, in the wake of a devaluation brought about by a financial crisis. Drawing on the work of Rosa Luxemburg, Lenin and Rudolf Hilferding, Harvey emphasizes that the credit system and finance capital were major levers of predation, fraud, and thievery.[9] The following quote is useful in grasping the significance of accumulation by dispossession to the wider credit system.

> The strong wave of financialisation that set in after 1973 has been every bit as spectacular for its speculative and predatory style. Stock promotions, Ponzi schemes, structured asset destruction through inflation, asset-stripping through mergers and acquisitions, and the promotion of levels of debt incumbency that reduce whole populations, even in the advanced capitalist countries, to debt peonage, to say nothing of corporate fraud and dispossession of assets (the raiding of pension funds and their decimation by stock and corporate collapses) by credit and stock manipulations – all of these are central features of what contemporary capitalism is about (Harvey, 2003b: 147).[10]

The dispossession of assets is an essential and ongoing feature of global neoliberalism and of the transnational debt architecture in particular. Idle capital in the global North constantly seeks profitable outlets by lending expensive capital to high-risk countries in the Third World. Because the developing world is considered a riskier borrower, capitalists can not only increase interest rates, but also demand a one-time risk premium payment for their troubles. Thus, the international credit system is an important sphere in which surplus capital, mostly from the North, can engage in predation, fraud, and thievery by lending to those countries with a relatively more disciplined labour force, valuable natural resources – all of which are possessed by emerging markets (Harvey, 2003a; 2003b; Bond, 2004a; 2004b). Capitalist states, especially the US, along with the IMF and World Bank, play an important role in securing the conditions necessary for the continuation of accumulation by dispossession. In contrast to the IMF, however, capitalist states possess a monopoly over coercive power, which, in turn, helps to enforce their judicial systems. The importance of this distinction will become clearer during our discussion of the Argentine default, below.

It is useful to stress that accumulation by dispossession is not simply an outside–inside process. By 'outside–inside process' I mean to suggest that strategies of accumulation by dispossession do not occur simply through the interaction with other (more powerful) countries (e.g., bilateral trade agreements with the United States or the World Trade Organization), or through capitalist strategies (e.g., TNCs operating in developing countries). The political elite and capitalist classes that comprise the bourgeois states in the developing world welcome those social forces that carry out strategies of accumulation by dispossession in their countries. Basing 'growth' on strategies of accumulation by dispossession is risky, to say the least. Crises will inevitably erupt. In these times the ruling classes must attempt to mediate not only the economic but also the social effects of such crises. The socialization of debt, which is the transformation of private debt into public debt, is a case in point. The responsibility of bailing out capitals (domestic and foreign) means that the burden of repayment gets shifted to society as a whole (socialization of debt). Interest payments ($M–M^1$) must take place through increased economic exploitation (lower real wages and longer hours), higher taxes, usually in the form of value-added tax, increases in the cost of basic foodstuffs, higher interest rates, and, indirectly, cuts in government spending on education, health, and welfare (Soederberg, 2000; 2001; Taylor, 2002). New forms of political domination, involving more coercive forms of social control, are required to support the ever-growing intensification of environmental and economic exploitation.

The post-Bretton Woods transnational debt architecture and accumulation by dispossession

The Bretton Woods system came to an end when President Nixon removed the US dollar from the gold standard in 1971, and began dismantling the Keynesian imperative of capital controls to delimit the movement of short-term, speculative financial flows across national borders (Helliener, 1994). The only major institutional change to the transnational debt architecture during the immediate post-Bretton Woods period was the creation of increased surveillance powers for the IMF. In 1977, international policy-makers forged what was to become one of the Fund's core responsibilities in the post-Bretton Woods era: surveillance duties (Article IV of the IMF Articles of Agreement).[11] Aside from keeping constant tabs on the economic and financial policies of member states, this surveillance function was to act as a good housekeeping seal of approval for private creditors (Pauly, 1997), and thereby further enshrine the power of transnational financial players in the debt architecture. Moreover, the 1977 surveillance decision fortified the previously existing informal and *ad hoc* nature of the transnational debt regime, most notably characterized by the Paris and London Clubs. The Paris Club was formed in 1956, when Argentina agreed to meet its public creditors in the French capital. In very broad terms, the Paris Club is an informal organization of donor countries, which does not provide concessionary funds for long-term relief; rather, it functions as a forum in which official creditors can negotiate whose payments of the principal loan will be postponed. It is important to point out that the debtor country's interest payments are never open to negotiation. Indeed, a precondition for the rescheduling of the timetable for repayment is that interest payments must be kept current. By the 1970s countries facing default were using what became known as the London Club. The latter served as an *ad hoc* forum in which private creditors could discuss the refinancing of loans to debtor states. Unlike rescheduling, which normally applies to official loans, refinancing replaces maturing debt with new obligations. Commercial banks prefer it because it avoids the impression that loan agreements have not been honoured, and, at least formally, upholds the sanctity of contracts (Lipson, 1981: 620). Co-ordination among private creditors (also known as 'collective action') did not pose much of a problem at this time, partly because there were only about 15 major banks involved in Third World lending, but also because the formation of syndicate lending encouraged a high degree of interdependence and co-operation among banks. Through its conditionalities and their effects on private lending patterns, the IMF played a vital syndicate leadership role (Lipson, 1981).

This arrangement facilitated new accumulation strategies of dispossession in the post-war era, one of which was 'overbanking'. With the demise of the Bretton Woods system and the subsequent removal of capital controls, new money gushed into the credit system in the form of 'petro-dollars'. 'Petro-dollars' refers to money that OPEC received as revenue from mainly developed countries during the two oil price hikes in the 1970s. Petro-dollars were swiftly recycled into loans. However, given the relatively low interest rates in the North, banks lent their money where they could earn the highest interest: cash-strapped developing countries. As a banker put it, 'a lack of first-class debtors led to the granting of loans to less solvent debtors, and the element of security was neglected in favour of the profit component' (Körner et al., 1984: 21–2; see also Helleiner, 1994; Kapstein, 1994). To assist their financial capitals in overcoming the barriers to capital valorization the US administration, following Britain's lead, began to transform Wall Street into a veritable offshore market, too. In 1979, US Comptroller of the Currency, John Heimann,[12] adjusted the accounting rules to allow US banks to increase their lending to the Third World, despite both the legal limit and the already high debt-to-GDP ratio in debtor states (Kapstein, 1994; Cohen, 1986). The so-called 'Heimann decision' resulted in irresponsible lending to already highly indebted countries in the South. 'As of 1979, the nine largest US banks had committed 113 per cent of their capital in loans to just six countries: Argentina, Brazil, Mexico, the Philippines, South Korea, and Taiwan. In fact, loans to Brazil and Mexico alone were equal to half of all US bank capital' (Lipson, 1981: 614).

In response to the growing levels of indebtedness in the Third World, UNCTAD and the G-77 put forward a proposal for an International Debt Commission (IDC) in 1979. The IDC was to be a permanent body that would replace both the Paris and London Clubs in dealing with the rescheduling and refinancing of Third World debt. The donors resisted such demands for more elaborate institutionalization, fearing that the supervision of rescheduling and refinancing might encourage more applications for debt relief, and, more importantly, shift the terms of bargaining in favour of debtor countries (Lipson, 1986). By October 1980, the G-77 had stopped pursuing this project, and debt negotiations were to remain informal and exclusionary. While this decision may be understood as a victory for donor countries and private creditors, when viewed against the backdrop of the ongoing crisis of overaccumulation within global capitalism, it also revealed an underlying contradiction in the transnational debt architecture. As Strange notes,

[t]he consequent uncertainty was a useful bargaining weapon in the hands of the creditors, and one which could be used with restraint or with ruthlessness according to the strategic importance of the country and the domestic character and prospects of its government. But the failure to set any clear rules also meant that as the financial system became more fragile and precarious in the 1970s and 1980s, the uncertainty over Mexican rescheduling, for instance, was apt to spill over on Brazil and its capacity to roll over its foreign debts ... (Strange, 1986: 33).

This fragility became evident when Chairman Volcker of the US Federal Reserve Bank decided to raise dramatically the interest rate, so as to deal with inflationary problems at home while drawing capital back to the US (see Helleiner, 1994). Since most loans were tied to the US interest rate, which serves as the *de facto* international benchmark, debtor countries could no longer manage their interest payments, as they were earning far less foreign exchange from exports than they needed to meet interest and principal repayments on their debts. This move resulted in the 1982 debt crisis, which forced 24 developing countries to reschedule and refinance their sovereign loans between 1982 and 1984.

The Golden Noose: neoliberalism and securitization

While the debt crisis effectively strengthened the bargaining and disciplinary power of international creditors over debtor states, it also highlighted an underlying contradiction: to recreate the power relations within the international credit system it is necessary to ensure that debtors are kept within the lending game. Indeed, avoiding the threat of delinking from the international credit system is also a primary concern of donor states and their capitals. As Strange observes, after the 1982 debt crisis the ruling classes of many developing countries decided neither to trade nor borrow from the global economy, thereby 'doing their best to be self-sufficient, autonomous and, as some argued, free'. She goes on to note that

> [a]nxiety to keep the debtors inside the financial structure despite their difficulties was all the greater if the debtor country was large, was a substantial importer of Western goods and was host to a large number of Western transnational corporations – none of whom were anxious to cope with a decoupled debtor country (Strange, 1994: 112).

The subsequent method of recreating the necessary conditions of accumulation by dispossession, while avoiding possible decoupling by the debtor countries, may be regarded as the Golden Noose of transnational debt: creditors, including both official and private lenders, must see to it that the noose is snug enough to weaken any resolve debtor countries might have with regard to decoupling, while coercing them to continue to engage in accumulation by dispossession (or socio-economic strangulation). In less sinister terms, the disciplinary and bargaining power of capital over debtor states must be administered in such a manner as to integrate debtor states into the global financial system, so that they become increasingly dependent not only upon loans from private and public creditors and the subsequent rescheduling and refinancing agreements, but also on the overall stability of the global capitalist system. We now turn to the two major strands that have been braided by dominant relations of power in global capitalism (the US, the G-7, the IFIs, and transnational financial capitalists) to create the Golden Noose of transnational debt: (a) securitization of debt, and (b) neoliberalism.

In the mid 1980s, banks began pulling out of the lending game to the developing world. At the same time, and in direct reaction to the ongoing crisis of overaccumulation, powerful financial capitals began pressuring their governments to engage in liberalization schemes to help overcome the shrinking profit margins of banks, due to increased competition by non-banks (insurance companies, pension and mutual funds, and so on) in what was quickly becoming a 'casino capitalism' (Strange, 1986), marked by the emergence of offshore markets driven primarily by speculation. The fusion of the once separate financial activities of commercial bank lending and stock market investing, and the creation of a firewall between lending and brokering (also known in the US as the Glass-Steagall Act of 1933) is referred to as 'disintermediation'. In 1999, the lending and brokering would be, once again, allowed to be integrated. The consequence of this political decision was that new, more mobile, less vulnerable, and high leveraged non-bank financial actors arrived on the lending scene. This, in turn, has led to the 'securitization' of debt – in other words, the transfer of capital through the sale of stocks and bonds, as opposed to bank loans; and short-term loans, rather than long-term loans, associated with official loans from donor countries and bank loans (Strange, 1998). In the attempts to keep the debtor countries within the international credit system while engaging in accumulation by dispossession, the US government sought to manage the defaults and write-downs (reductions in the value of loans) on bank debts through reschedulings (Paris Club) and multi-year restructuring agreements with the Fund. The last phase of this restructuring process was represented by the Baker Plan (1985) and its more substantial counterpart, the Brady Plan (1989; see IMF, 2003a).

The Baker Plan comprised loans to cover interest payments, with conditions that debtor countries privatize state enterprises, end subsidisation to local businesses, and open up the economy to foreign investment (Kapstein, 1994). However, by 1989 it was widely believed that most debtor nations were no closer to financial health than they had been in 1982. US Treasury Secretary Nicholas Brady convinced US banks to cut the actual value of their outstanding debt. Some of the write-offs were funded by the IMF and World Bank, while the remaining outstanding debts were rescheduled by converting them into what became known as Brady Bonds, which were sold on the secondary market[13] in order to allow private-sector creditors to diversify risk more widely throughout the financial community via debt-for-equity swaps. The latter allow banks to exchange large debts with the debtor nation for equity investments. These plans have had the effect of transferring wealth from debtors to creditors, multilateralizing huge debts incurred by US banks (Strange, 1994), assisting in the replacement of less volatile bank loans with foreign portfolio investment as the primary channel for international capital flows in the 1990s; but they did very little to bring down the levels of long-term debt (see Table 4.2) (D'Arista, 1999). These policies also led to a more complex and volatile structure of transnational debt. As noted above, during the Bretton Woods system transnational debt meant public loans, from both governments and multilateral lending agencies, such as the IMF. However, since the mid 1980s, these official sources of funding have been overshadowed by private loans from a diverse and powerful set of actors and institutions, such as pension and mutual funds. From this period onwards, transnational debt has not only meant financial credit extended by governments to other governments, but also, and more importantly, includes 'all forms of debt across state frontiers: all the liabilities incurred, and claims established, between institutions or individuals under one political jurisdiction, and institutions or individuals under another political jurisdiction' (Strange, 1998: 91–2).

The second strand comprising the Golden Noose was the introduction of neoliberal reforms that emanated from a shift from Keynesian-led economic policy formation to market-led restructuring in the donor states, and, in turn, accompanied all loans from the IFIs in the form of SAPs. These neoliberal policies quickly congealed into what many authors have referred to as the Washington consensus. Despite the immense diversity among developing countries, the SAPs were largely homogeneous in nature (see Stiglitz, 2002; M. Taylor, 2002; 2004). These policies included fiscal discipline, reordering public expenditure priorities, tax reform, liberalization of interest rates, competitive exchange rates, trade liberalization, privatization, deregulation, and property rights (Williamson, 1990). The policies, universally applied, had the effect of facilitating accumulation by dispossession by the international creditors.

Table 4.2 Long-Term Debt ($ billions)

	1970	1980	1990	2000
Debt Outstanding	62.6	451.6	1,179.3	1,998.7
Public and Publicly				
Guaranteed	47.3	381.1	1,113.8	1,490.4
Official Creditors	33.6	178.2	604.2	843.8
Multilateral	7.3	48.8	207.4	346.6
Bilateral	26.3	129.4	396.8	497.3
Private Creditors	13.6	202.8	509.6	646.6
Bonds	1.8	13.1	107.9	392.4
Private Non-Guaranteed	15.4	70.6	65.5	557.3
Bonds	0.0	0.0	0.8	124.5

Source: World Bank, 2002b: 189.

Broadly speaking, neoliberalism rests on the steadfast belief that political and social problems should be solved primarily through market-based mechanisms, as opposed to state intervention. The justification of this emerging development paradigm is based on two premises. First, it entails a particular reading of the cause of the debt crises: misguided macroeconomic policies on the part of debtor nations, as opposed to overlending by banks (see Kapstein, 1994). Developing countries were blamed for bringing about the debt crises through profligate spending, protecting national markets from competitive (and thus corrective) pressures exerted by foreign companies, excessive intervention into the economy – particularly in terms of the exchange rate – crowding out good investment and innovation through state ownership of key industries and resources, the presence of large and powerful unions, and so on. Second, neoliberalism is based upon the belief that, due to the profit motive, market participants are inherently more rational than governments. Taken together, these premises legitimate the greater scope of strategies of accumulation through the commodification of natural resources (water) and basic social services (health, welfare, public housing) (Mahnkopf and Altvater, 2002; Altvater, 2003). These premises also lend credence to the dominant idea in neoclassical economics that the only means that debtor states can repay their loans is to expose further their societies to the exigencies of the global marketplace by opening up their current and capital accounts.[14] The latter permits the free inflow and outflow of both long-term and short-term (hot money or speculative) financial flows.

The Golden Noose temporarily resolved the core contradiction of transnational debt by increasing the disciplinary power of capitals over debtor states. This same solution, however, would create new dilemmas for neoliberal strategies of accumulation by dispossession in the international credit system. The next section examines a key expression of the underlying contradiction: the growing tensions between financial and social risk. One of the main contributing factors to the growing strain between commercial creditors and debtor states has been the ongoing crisis of overaccumulation, and the consequent need for financial markets to strengthen their exploitative strategies of accumulation through lending practices. In the next section, we look at one way this is accomplished through the amplification of financial risk, which, in turn, not only creates higher returns, but also imposes detrimental social risks on debtor states and societies.

DIFFERENTIAL RISKS IN THE TRANSNATIONAL DEBT ARCHITECTURE

I used to think if there was reincarnation, I wanted to come back as the President or the Pope or a .400 baseball hitter. But now I want to come back as the bond market. You can intimidate everyone.

James Carville, former US President Clinton's campaign manager, quoted in Dani Rodrik, 'Why Financial Markets Misbehave', 2003: 189.

Differentiated risks

The two strands of the Golden Noose – securitized debt and neoliberal reforms – served to pry open emerging markets to allow capitals to overcome the barriers to accumulation in the ongoing crisis. As the crisis continued to deepen, so too did the IMF's fervent belief that free capital mobility led to enhanced growth and investment. Indeed, up to the 1997 East Asian Crisis, the Fund was lobbying to change its charter to force countries to liberalize capital markets (Cohen, 2002). Notwithstanding this strategy, the combination of financial liberalization in the donor countries (lifting of capital controls) and the Fund's informal insistence that countries open their capital accounts as part of their technical advice and conditionality, led to increased speculation in the developing world, particularly in the form of arbitrage. In the early 1990s, for example, there was a divergence between the interest rates to be earned in the North and those to be earned in the South. It was thus possible to borrow funds in New York at 5 or 6 per cent, and invest it in emerging markets at 12 or 14 per cent – or even higher. This game is called arbitrage, and while this means of deriving profit is far from new, the amounts of money involved and the rapidity with which it is played is novel (Strange, 1998). During the early 1990s, Argentina 'became the fourth largest recipient of foreign funds throughout the world. The influx climbed from \$3.2 billion in 1991, to \$11 billion in 1992, and to \$10.7 billion in 1993.' As the Argentine economy began to show superficial signs of improvement, largely due to this huge influx of capital flows, there was 'an overwhelming acceptance by the public of the drastic neoliberal reform measures' (Rock, 2002: 59).

This magical boom would only last until 1994, when the US effectively doubled its short-term interest rates from 3 to 6 per cent (Rock, 2002: 65–6; Weisbrot and Baker, 2002; IMF, 2003a). This situation prompts us to ask: What are the political and social ramifications when highly mobile institutional investors decide to exit in order to take advantage of higher rates or better investment conditions in another country? What happens to the disciplinary power of commercial creditors as speculative activities continue to amplify in order to overcome the barriers to capital valorization? And how do these neoliberal strategies of accumulation by dispossession affect the debtor states, particularly in terms of ensuring that they remain within the bounds of the international credit system?

As is well known, the disciplinary power of financial actors lies in their capacity to shape policy-making at the national level, largely due to their ability to withdraw and withhold credit quickly (Gill, 2003). In neoclassical economic theory, this relation between institutional investors and debtor states is typically viewed as a win-win situation (see Grabel, 1996; Haley, 1999; Shiller, 2000; Felix, 2002). Liberalized cross-border financial flows are supposed to encourage ostensibly reckless and wasteful governments to implement sound economic policy and market-led reforms. It is believed that this will lead to economic growth and prosperity in the South, while allowing institutional investors to reap high returns on their loans. It follows from this that capitals base their investment decisions (e.g. how many government bonds they will purchase) on what are considered to be rational calculations of financial risk. Financial risks include any policy or event that may threaten the ability of a creditor to realize interest on her loans (financial risk = loss × probability), such as non-compliance with the IMF's technical advice or an absence of sound macroeconomic fundamentals. Although there are many variations of financial risk – including currency risk, principal risk, country risk, credit risk, interest rate risk, liquidity risk, and so on – the general usage in finance theory refers to the variability of potential returns inherent in investment, speculative or trading activities: the greater the variability, the higher the risk.

Moving towards a deeper understanding of this phenomenon, Ulrich Beck reminds us that risks are more than some objective truth, but rather a type of virtual reality or real virtuality (Beck, 1992: 2001). Financial risks 'become real' when a group of highly leveraged (utilizing borrowed money) speculators attempts to profit from changes in macroeconomic variables, such as interest rates, currencies, and entire stock markets. If, for example, a group of powerful hedge funds seeks to profit from changes in the value of a currency in a developing country, the Central Bank of the developing country must undertake policies to defend the value of the currency by undertaking certain policies, e.g. increasing the interest rate. The ability of a Central Bank to defend its currency has very real consequences for the government and people of that country, should a few select lead steers (large financial actors) decide to run for the door, or, just as bad, bet against the currency, as in the case of Mexico in 1994, East Asia in 1997, Russia in 1998 (see Young, 2003). The meaning and power of financial risks, however, is based upon existing relations of power in capitalist society, and not simply on cultural perceptions, as espoused by Beck. That is to say, beneath their seemingly neutral, quantifiable, and objective meaning, financial risks are historically specific social constructs that are used to discipline debtors through very real threats of withholding desperately needed funds from impoverished states of the South.

It follows from this that the pseudo-scientific nature of financial risks acts not only to de-class the underlying capitalist strategies aimed at exploiting debtor states, but also to discredit other meanings of risk, especially social risk, such as increased levels of poverty, political instability, and, more generally, increased physical and economic coercion on the part of the state and capitals. The hegemonic position of financial risk, and thus risk defined in narrow economic terms, acts to dehumanize the social and political consequences of the constant amplification of risk in financial markets through increasingly speculative instruments and practices. Yet we need to ponder for a moment why financial risks are indeed ubiquitous in our society. The answer to this question lies in its connection to money. According to Marx, 'The essence of money is ... that the *mediating activity* or movement, the *human*, social act by which man's products mutually complement one another, is *estranged* from man and becomes the attribute of money, *a material thing outside of man.*' Simon Clarke elaborates as follows. 'Money ceases to be the means and becomes the end of exchange, while human needs are not recognised as the end, but become merely the means to the acquisition of money. Thus money becomes an independent social power ...' (Clarke, 1988: 86).

Seen from this angle, the recreation of financial risk as the only indicator upon which investment decisions should be based also acts to discipline debtor states to implement neoliberal reforms embodied in the SAPs, and constantly signal good creditworthiness by providing open capital accounts, low taxation and environmental standards, a well disciplined and cheap labour force, and so on. If social risks find their way into the official discourse at all, they are not seen as the consequence of capitalist strategy to overcome the crisis of overaccumulation, but instead as the results of not adhering to neoliberal policy. For debtor states, this tension expresses itself in deficits of political legitimacy for those in power; this in turn increases the possibility that a debtor state will remain within the bounds of the neoliberal-led international credit system. These two seemingly separate or independent moments of risk reveal that there is far from a win-win situation in the relationship between free capital mobility and debtor states. In the following two sections, I will show how the tensions between social and financial risks have been growing, and thereby testing the strength of the Golden Noose.

Financial risks

Strategies of accumulation by dispossession such as the securitization of debt constantly require not only greater space and shorter periods of time to invest their interest-bearing capital, but also increasing levels of risk to earn higher interest rates, or what Harvey refers to as a 'spatio-temporal fix' (Harvey, 1999; 2003a; 2003b). Regardless of the pseudo-scientific assumptions underpinning financial risk and their intricate and unintelligible calculus models, the majority of investment decisions in the post-Bretton Woods era have been driven by speculation ('reading the mind of the market'), not by enterprise (Soros, 1987). These speculative strategies have had a direct impact on the disciplinary power of creditors over debtor states. The incentives of dealers and money managers and the situation of investment decisions have strongly encouraged short-termism, which has, in effect, ruled out alternative orientations such as long-term investment in the productive sphere. In this process, the always-fragile confidence of investors is socially constructed, and is thus in constant need of reproduction (Patomäki, 2001). The temporal component of Harvey's spatio-temporal fix is evident in the short-term nature of lending is important not only in terms of quickly extracting profit and rapidly freeing money to be played in another market, but also in terms of continually exerting pressure on the debtor states to conform with neoliberal discipline – that is, to tighten the Golden Noose around the necks of debtor states.

The ongoing financial liberalization since the mid 1980s has also led to a higher concentration of very powerful financial actors. This situation has had important ramifications for how financial risk is constructed, not to mention the disciplinary power of these actors. The increasing presence of large financial actors and so-called lead steers, such as macro-hedge funds, are able to manipulate prices and orchestrate attacks that are intended to kick off a chain reaction leading to a drastic change in the price of an asset. As Adam Harmes explains, 'While the term "macro" implies "big," in this context it actually refers to a type of investment strategy rather than to the size of the fund. A macro strategy is one where the fund manager attempts to profit from changes in macroeconomic variables' (prices of stocks and bonds, currencies, interest rates, and so forth) (Harmes, 2001: 122). The bigger, better known and more leveraged they are, the easier price manipulation and orchestration of attacks can be (Patomäki, 2001: 95–6; Harmes, 2001; Bichler and Nitzan, 2003; Gowan, 1999; Palan, 2003; Mackenzie, 2004).

After several years of shying away from emerging markets after the 1997–98 East Asian debacle, the spatial element of Harvey's fix becomes evident, as capital flows are, once again, moving South. As *The Economist* reports, in 2002 'net private-capital flows to emerging markets were less than half their mid-1990s peak. But they have been rising, often to countries with a poor record of providing a decent return, or even of giving the money back that are now seen as must-have investments. This year, lending by foreign banks and bond investors, direct investment and share purchases have all increased' ('Fishing in Frothy Waters', *The Economist*, October 30, 2003). In another article *The Economist* observes that the size of banks bets is rising rapidly. This is because returns have fallen as fast as markets have risen ... So banks are having to bet more of their own money to continue generating huge profits. But the amount they have put on the table in recent months has become worryingly large ... Even the banks themselves admit that they are taking bigger risks to make bigger profits ('The Coming Storm', *The Economist*, February 21, 2004).

In its usual sober tone, the IMF attributes the recent investment boom to improving credit quality and earnings potential, associated with stronger economic growth. The Fund calls for caution as the 'low interest rate environment is also boosting the net present value of many assets. There remains, nevertheless, a risk that the momentum of flows into risky assets induced in part by low policy rates in the major financial centres will push valuations to levels that are not fully justified by the fundamentals' (IMF, 2003c: 1). Why are rational actors moving southwards when the investment conditions are far from sound? Accumulation by dispossession helps us to understand that the primary reason for this renewed interest in the South is rooted in capitalist strategies aimed at overcoming the manifestations of a deepening of the crisis of overaccumulation.

Social risks

The constant need to amplify financial risks, so as to overcome barriers to capital valorization, has had several important social implications for debtor states. The volatile nature of short-term and securitized loans to debtor states of the South involves a different type of disciplinary power over the policy-making functions of the state. Because commercial creditors have become so internationally mobile, and their power so concentrated, they have been able to universalize the criteria upon which the policies of debtor states are monitored and judged pertaining to their creditworthiness (their attractiveness as investment sites). Thus, the legal freedoms (remittance of profits), production costs, labour relations (disciplined workforce, absence or weak presence of unions), political stability, and financial concessions offered by one country will form the benchmark by which another country is judged (Gill and Law, 1993). This places enormous strain on both debtor states and their societies. Recall that due to low interest rates in the recession-hit advanced industrialized world, institutional investors are, once again, taking advantage of the relatively high rates in emerging markets by extending credit in the form of securities.[15] While high interest rates may fill gaps in spending for debtor states, as well as for their private sector, they also put fiscal solvency into doubt, as debt-servicing costs climb to a higher percentage of the country's gross domestic product[16] (GDP). This implies that more and more tax revenues go to pay foreign creditors, rather than being used as public expenditure on health and education (Rodrick, 2003). For example, the increasing interest payments on the debt drove Argentina's budget from surplus to deficit. Interest payments rose from $2.5 billion in 1991 to $9.5 billion in 2000, or from 1.2 to 3.4 per cent of GDP (Weisbrot and Baker, 2002). More than this, higher interest rates, which are what commercial creditors demand for taking higher risks (in addition to paying risk premium fees), involve commensurate levels of economic exploitation in order to extract the necessary surplus value from labour-power. While debtor states are not directly involved in the capital accumulation process, they are called on to facilitate this intensified exploitation by imposing new forms of political domination, such as by rolling back legislation designed to protect workers' rights and safety, and by further prying open its social relations of production to new forms of accumulation by dispossession by, for example, allowing for the further commodification of essential public services (Altvater and Mahnkopf, 2002; Young, 2003; Dinerstein, 2003). Indeed, there are strong parallels and social implications between the privatization of credit and the privatization of water, which were discussed in Chapter 3.

These new modes of political domination and more extreme forms of economic exploitation associated with, although not primarily caused by, increased financial risks also lead to legitimacy deficits, which act to impede rather than assist debtor states in recreating the conditions necessary to ensure that interest may be generated from productive activities. On the one hand, debtor states become increasingly more accountable to transnational capitals than to those whom they govern. On the other hand, the disciplinary power of financial capitals has also tightened around the necks of debtor states, in the sense that the latter's policy autonomy has been constrained, in terms of not only economic but also social policy-making (see Underhill, 1997). Thus, even if a government wished to provide a momentary break from neoliberal austerity programmes, any divergence from what is considered 'good policy' in the eyes of the commercial creditors would be punished by either capital flight or an investment strike, or both.

One of the main consequences of this has been that debtor states have suffered from a political legitimacy deficit, which has manifested itself in grass-roots and global forms of social mobilization and protests against neoliberal policies across the South. As Mary Ann Haley reminds us, since institutional investors are more concerned with political stability than with democracy, debtor nations are required to quell social conflict immediately if they are to maintain their creditworthiness (Haley, 1999). The contradiction of transnational debt reappears here: the disciplinary power of private creditors, and their attempts to carry out their strategy of accumulation by dispossession by, for example, increasing their speculative activities, and thus heightening both social and financial risks for Third World debtor countries, act to destabilize the very neoliberal policies that capitals require to reap the higher interest rates sought. The litany of crises in the emerging markets over the 1990s drove home this contradiction.

Bracing the noose: a neoliberal response

> The central problem in managing transnational debt today ... is that in too many cases, debtor states gamble for redemption through ever less credible policy measures instead of facing the uncertainty of approaching the country's private sector creditors. This places the official international community and the IMF in particular, in a difficult position in deciding whether to support those policies.
>
> J. Boorman, Special Advisor to the Managing Director of the IMF, 'Sovereign Debt Restructuring', conference speech, October 17, 2002.

To ensure that the debtor states remain within the bounds of the international credit system while they open their doors further to neoliberal strategies of accumulation by dispossession, donor states, and by extension the IFIs, have sought strategies that facilitate increased levels of financial risk-taking while upholding neoliberal reform principles. Some of these strategies involved the creation of the 'New International Financial Architecture' (NIFA), which involved institutions such as the G-20, the Financial Stability Forum, and the Reports on the Observances of Standards and Codes (Germain, 2001; Langley, 2004). As I have argued elsewhere, the NIFA was heavily influenced by US interests, especially in maintaining the norm of free capital mobility (Soederberg, 2002c; 2004). The centrality of the role of the US becomes more apparent when we consider the manner in which the Argentine default was managed. Within the larger context of the growing complexities of the transnational debt architecture, the definition of 'bad policy' shifted from misguided macroeconomic policies to poor financial regulation, due to corruption, lack of transparency, ineffective corporate governance, inappropriate regulation of the financial and banking sectors, and so on (IMF, 2003b; cf. de Soto, 2000). These strategies did not involve formal, standard-setting procedures to deal with sovereign debt, despite the fact that the financial risks had increased exponentially and the creditors themselves had changed, which in turn creates new collection action problems. According to the IMF, unlike the 1980s debt crises, where 85 per cent of a country's debt was represented by 15 banks with powerful incentives to co-operate, today's bondholders are much more numerous and may be anonymous. They generally do not have long-term relations with debtors or regulators, and their incentive to sue is greater, because they often do not have to share the proceeds of litigation (IMF, 2003a: 61). More importantly, the Fund goes on to suggest that this disorder could act to aggravate further the underlying contradiction of transnational debt, as this arrangement could lead to an unpredictable and inequitable allocation of payments.

The NIFA would not be able to resolve the underlying contradiction inherent in the transnational debt architecture, however. The weakness in the existing neoliberal-driven NIFA came to the fore in December 2001, when Argentina declared an inability to pay some $141 billion of its foreign debt. The official international community and the NIFA were ill equipped to deal with this crisis, to say the least.

THE REAPPEARANCE OF THE UNDERLYING CONTRADICTION IN TRANSNATIONAL DEBT: THE ARGENTINE DEFAULT

There have been various suggestions for streamlining, formalizing, and legalizing the procedures for dealing with sovereign debt problems.[17] Only two proposals, however, found their way into official policy discussions: the Sovereign Debt Restructuring Mechanism (SDRM) and collection action clauses (CACs). The IMF's Deputy Managing Director, Anne Krueger, put forward the SDRM in November 2001. As would noted above, this mechanism entailed a new international legal framework based on the features of domestic bankruptcy proceedings in the private sector. This statutory approach was aimed at creating a binding set of laws through which crisis-stricken countries could halt panics and keep investors from pulling their money out of the nation – effectively, buying time for political leaders to work out debts in an orderly fashion, much like Chapter 11 of US bankruptcy law.[18] The idea of the SDRM was driven partly by a perceived need to deal more effectively with sovereign debt so as to ensure that debtor countries are willing and able to implement neoliberal reforms, and partly by several years of lobbying by Jubilee 2000 for consideration of an arbitration mechanism that would fairly and independently determine which debts should be paid (Ambrose, 2003).

Largely because it underwent substantial and constant revisions in reaction to the critique by the US government and international financial community, Krueger's proposal was deemed by some to represent a 'moving target' (Akyuz, 2003). For instance, in the assistant managing director's original proposal, which, for the sake of convenience, we will refer to as SDRM-1, the IMF was to play a central role by determining which countries would be eligible to participate in the SDRM, and by ensuring that member countries adhere to the market-based procedures laid out in the larger framework. SDRM-1 was to allow countries in crisis to call a halt to debt payments while they negotiated with private sector lenders, under the jurisdiction of a new international judicial panel. During these negotiations the IMF would serve to protect the debtor country from litigation.

The conditions of repayment after a country declared bankruptcy would be negotiated among the creditors by 'supermajority', thereby overcoming the 'collective action' problem associated with a plethora of diverse and anonymous lenders. 'Supermajority' refers to a situation in which between 60 and 75 per cent of the creditors agree to the terms of restructuring, which would then be binding for the rest of the creditors and, of course, the debtor country. The proposed role of the IMF would be to oversee voting and adjudicate disputes in this process. As Krueger notes, 'the Fund's role would be essential to the success of such a system' (Miller, 2002: 4). For SDRM-1 to be realized, however, the IMF's Chapters of Agreement would have had to be subject to reform. And for any such radical change to occur, the US government, which wields veto power in the Fund, would have required its consent to these amendments.

Powerful financial interests were fervently opposed to SDRM-1, however. Some of the criticism included the role to be played by the IMF in the bankruptcy process; the worry that creditors' rights would be weaker than in the arrangement they currently enjoyed under domestic bankruptcy proceedings, and that the mere presence of SDRM-1 could distort the market value of debt instruments; and that this debt restructuring mechanism could encourage 'strategic defaults' – the suspensions of debt service by countries with the means to repay (IMF, 2003a: 64–6). One critic from the Brookings Institution in Washington, DC, Lex Rieffel, went so far as to suggest that SDRM was a reincarnation of the International Debt Commission (IDC), discussed earlier. According to Rieffel, the features shared between the IDC and the SDRM are as follows: (1) the creation of a supranational entity funded through some kind of international dues, tax or fees; (2) the placing of the intensely political process of sovereign negotiations in the hands of 'judges' who have no power to enforce their judgements against debtor countries; (3) the granting of power to the same judges to dilute the high standard of contract enforcement that underpins the US capital market, by far the deepest and most vibrant capital market today; and (4) the introduction of rigidities to the negotiation process ill-suited to the constantly evolving international financial marketplace (Rieffel, 2002).

The financial sector's discontent over the SDRM was also apparent in the following example. The directors of the world's most powerful private financial associations, such as the Emerging Markets Traders Association, the Institute for International Finance, the International Primary Market Association, the Bond Market Association, the Securities Industry Association, the International Securities Market Association, and the Emerging Market Creditors Association undertook a letter-writing campaign to the Acting Chairman of the IMF's International Monetary and Financial Committee (IMFC), UK Chancellor Gordon Brown, and then US Treasury Secretary Paul O'Neill. These letters urged Brown and O'Neill to help defeat the SDRM. The following quote, which is taken from a letter to O'Neill, makes this position readily apparent.

> We believe that a market-based approach to strengthening crisis management holds the only promise for success. Consequently, we have taken the lead in developing marketable collection action clauses ... that could command the support of both investors and issuers ... the active pursuit of an SDRM has eroded the support for these efforts (Chamberlin et al., 2002; cf. Chamberlin, 2003).

In response to mounting pressures from the international financial community, the US Treasury Under-Secretary, John Taylor, put forward an alternative approach – namely, CACs in bonds issued by sovereign governments. Essentially, the CACs approach would ensure that creditors remained in control of their loans to debtor nations in times of crisis. The CACs would contain provisions allowing a supermajority of bondholders to approve a process believed to make it easier to restructure debt by allowing a majority of creditors to impose a deal. Given the disparate nature of international creditors, a supermajority of creditors overcomes the problem of 'collection action', which occurs when individual creditors consider that their interests are best served by preventing what is termed a 'grab race' – where creditors try to get the best deal possible from the debtor government so as to enforce their claim as quickly as possible. It is widely believed among the financial community that grab races hinder other creditors, and thus may lead them in capturing the limited assets available (Boorman, 2002; Mussa, 2002). Another advantage of CACs is that, unlike SDRM-1, this market-based approach relies on the inclusion of various clauses in individual bond instruments (or bond and loan agreements) and, as a result, leaves jurisdiction to courts in the country or state under whose laws the debt instruments were issued (primarily the US and the UK). It is also the case, of course, that the current outstanding debt of sovereigns would remain untouched until maturing obligations were replaced with new issues containing CACs (Boorman, 2002). In response to these censures, Krueger revised her proposal, once again, by devising a more market-based version of SDRM, culminating in the creation of the SDRM-2 (Krueger, 2002). These efforts would prove to be in vain, however. During the 2003 annual meetings of the World Bank and IMF, the IMFC officially rejected SDRM-2 and welcomed the inclusion of CACs.[19]

CONCLUSION

One of the key issues underpinning these debates over sovereign debt was moral hazard.[20] The US Treasury Secretary and international financial interests argued that the knowledge that the IMF would act as an arbitrator, and in effect guarantor, of bad loans made a crisis more likely to occur.

> The idea is that creditors know that IMF financing helps crisis-prone countries stave off default and are therefore willing to lend to such countries at lower interest rate spreads than would prevail if the IMF did not exist. The IMF's presence thus weakens pressure on governments to pursue policies – such as sustainable fiscal policies and sound financial supervision and regulation – that could help prevent crises (Lane and Phillips, 2001).

Yet, from the above analysis, we are able to move beyond the narrow, economic confines of moral hazard debates. Strategies to deal with the underlying contradiction of transnational debt are class-led, and thus always highly conflictual, temporary, and contingent on historical circumstances. The discussions surrounding the Argentine default must be understood as a moment of the articulation of intensifying strain between social and financial risks, which itself emerges from the larger crisis of overaccumulation and the transnational debt architecture. Seen from this angle, the couching of tensions between social and financial risks in terms of moral hazard debates serves not only to reproduce the neoliberal assumption that any form of state intervention into markets will distort prices and cause general disequilibria, but also to cloak the relations of power and exploitation that lie beneath it.

When we move beyond the parameters of the moral hazard argument, two competing approaches emerge to the same problem – how best to discipline debtors. The common thread running through both strategies is the attempt to establish a particular mode of social discipline in the global South, which will ensure that developing countries adhere to neoliberal restructuring so as to support strategies of accumulation by dispossession, such as permitting financial markets to continue to increase risk (speculative activities) and thus derive ever-higher returns. The real debate, therefore, is about *who* was going to discipline debtor states to remain within the bounds of the international credit system (i.e. the IMF or creditors, and their respective national judicial systems), and *how* this was to be achieved. Both versions of SDRM provided a multilateral and statutory solution to the growing tensions between social and financial risks. The main thrust behind the SDRM was rooted in the Fund's *raison d'être* – namely, to ensure the stability of the global financial system by ensuring that debtor states continue to adhere to neoliberal reforms, so that they may generate the resources needed to service their outstanding debt. Yet there are social and political thresholds beyond which policies to force these results become unacceptable (Boorman, 2002). As a largely technocratic body, the IMF believes that it could act as a buffer between creditors and debtors so as to ensure that the latter implement credible policy measures required to honour their outstanding debt.

Following the tendency within the transnational debt architecture over the past several decades, the US government and powerful capital interests believed that the best way to deal with debtor states was to increase the disciplinary power of capital. While the IMF could be entrusted to act in the best interests of international finance, it was largely believed that the only method to solve the problem of the unwillingness and/or inability of debtor states to repay their loans was to expose these countries to the disciplinary actions of creditors and their respective governments – or, more specifically, the judicial system. The long and arduous standoff between the Argentine government and the IMF reveals the latter's lack of direct coercive power to discipline debtor states effectively to repay their loans, despite the IMF's preferred creditor status.

By these means, creditors can continue to accumulate while ensuring that debtor states become increasingly dependent on both donor countries and their capitals. In other words, only capitals and their states can guarantee to reproduce the necessary conditions for intensified neoliberal restructuring: accumulation by dispossession. In 2004, a US judge placed restrictions on the sale of some Argentine military property in the US, in the first such ruling in favour of creditors seeking to regain lost investments. Some of Argentina's bondholders, such as the Global Committee on Argentine Bondholders (GCAB), which represents some 70 major institutional investors, are enraged that the Argentine government is only offering 25 cents on the dollar on $88 billion of debt it defaulted on in January 2002. These investors are now attempting to seize Argentine assets to recoup their losses ('US Judge Freezes Argentine Assets in Debt Case', *Financial Times*, February 8, 2004). Of equal importance, the US government and international capitals are anxious to keep the IMF on the shortest leash possible, lest the possibility of the creation of a statutory means of managing transnational debt should emerge and thus dilute the disciplinary power of capitals over debtor states. This implies that the crisis of overaccumulation continues to deepen, and commercial creditors are quickly placing higher bets in the largely stagnant economies of the South.

The ability of capitalists to extract repayment through the coercive means of powerful donor states (legal systems backed up by a monopoly of violence) will prove to be as important as the disciplinary powers they exercise over the debtor governments. While it is impossible to predict when the next sovereign insolvency will occur under this arrangement, it is only a question of time. As this chapter made clear, the class-led attempts to resolve contradictions within the realm of the *ad hoc* and implicit transnational debt architecture will inevitably heighten, not diminish, these problems. With regard to the larger argument of the book, this chapter has sought to open a second window through which we can explore, more closely and critically, the capitalist features of global governance. It is now time to turn our attention to the third and final window through which we may observe the neoliberal features of global governance – especially as it pertains to the poorest of Third World countries, or what, following Samir Amin (1999), I refer to as 'excluded states'.

5
Global Governance and Development Assistance: The Case of America's Millennium Challenge Account

The security of people is enhanced when humanitarian agencies carry out action not only to provide relief but also to ensure the basic human rights and security of all victims of conflict or other human-caused and natural disasters. The need for such action will increase if ethnic conflicts continue to proliferate.

Commission on Global Governance, *Our Global Neighbourhood*, 1995: 86.

In September 2000, leaders of the industrialized world committed themselves to reducing poverty in the world by 2015, agreeing to work towards achieving eight Millennium Development Goals (MDGs) on poverty reduction, gender equality, maternal health, the environment, and so on.[1] The recognition of a global partnership, which underpinned the MDGs, was a reflection of the wider concept of global governance which may be described as 'steering or control mechanisms', initiated in multiple spaces of political organization with no single centre of global governance (Rosenau, 1995). As I have noted throughout, one of the main problems with this seemingly pluralist and multilateralist attempt at dealing with issues of human (in)security in the global South is that it fails to acknowledge the existence of the inherent contradictions and class-based power relations that define the global capitalist system. As we will see, this rosy gloss on global governance, and by extension the MDGs, has helped to mask not only American-led imperialism (or 'imposed leadership') in the South, but also the increasingly coercive neoliberal strategies tied to this dominance (Soederberg, 2004). As the crisis of capitalist overaccumulation began to deepen in the late 1990s, however, US support for a global partnership for development based on the ethos of global governance began to collapse.

This shift in policy orientation is clearly evident in George W. Bush's (2001 to the present) Millennium Challenge Account (MCA), or what the administration refers to as the 'new global development compact'.[2] By increasing its core development assistance over the next three years, the Bush administration hopes to replace existing loans to the poorest 79 countries with grants, so as to help governments 'who rule justly, invest in their people, and encourage economic freedom'.[3] Aid will be contingent on 16 broadly defined criteria – ranging from civil liberties to trade policy – that the recipient countries must meet as a precondition to receiving aid. For President Bush, the bottom line for the US, for its 'developing country partners, is how much development they are achieving' (Wayne, 2003: 5). In the words of an official at the Millennium Challenge Corporation, the institution that administers the MCA, this programme differs from other official development agencies in that it 'takes politics out' of aid, stressing the neutral and rational features of the MCA.[4]

The MCA reflects the ongoing transformation of American imperialism, which has become more explicit after the tragic events of September 11, 2001. This may be readily observed in the growing intensity with which the American state has sought to promote US values and rules as the most desirable and just in the world, most virulently articulated in both the Project for the New American Century and the 2002 American National Security Strategy (NSS).[5] According to President Bush, this strategy will be 'based on a distinctly American internationalism that reflects the union of our values and our national interests; the aim of which will be to help make the world not just safer but better. Our goals on the path to progress are clear: political and economic freedom, peaceful relations with other states, and respect for human dignity' (White House, 2002).

The NSS signals at least two important changes concerning the relations between the US government and the target of the MCA: 79 of the world's poorest countries, in which it is alleged that 'failed states' thrive. First, there is no room for moderates or non-alignment in America's war on terrorism – only for those either for or against the US. This stance, which has been captured by the term 'pre-emptive foreign policy', suggests that the US should maintain military strength beyond challenge, and use it to prevent acts of terrorism (Willetts, 1997; Lipschutz and Turcotte, 2005).[6] Second, it is believed that the route to achieving a more just and peaceful international environment in the post-Cold War world is in codifying American values and rules in the South ('Iraq and the Bush Doctrine', *Observer*, March 24, 2002). Despite its significance to the world's poorest regions, not to mention its ability to shed more light on the emerging nature of American empire in the post-9/11 world, there have been very few systematic attempts to assess critically this new development strategy. Why was the MCA created? What has motivated the world's stingiest donor (in relation to the size of its economy) in providing new forms of foreign aid for the world's poorest countries? Whose interests does the MCA serve? Who is involved in the creation of the criteria used to measure what President Bush refers to as 'greater responsibility from developing nations'.[7] Who gets to define what is meant by the three broad categories of the MCA: (1) ruling justly (good governance), (2) investing in people (health and education for all), and (3) 'economic freedom' (sound economic policies that foster enterprise and entrepreneurship) (USAID, 2002)? And what are the implications of these power relations for our understanding of global economic governance?

Our discussion of the MCA constitutes the third and final window through which we will examine and explain a neglected dimension of global governance. Before turning to the main argument of this chapter, it is helpful to say a few words regarding the analytical framework that guides this discussion. By drawing on an historical-materialist understanding of global capitalism, we are well positioned to tackle these questions, as we are to explain the changing nature of US imperialism as a moment of the wider restructuring of the relations of power. As noted in Chapter 1, the dominant American state recreates its power in the capitalist inter-state system largely by coercive means – in terms of both physical and economic force. It follows that as the crisis of global capitalism continues to deepen, these means will become more severs. To go beyond the novelty of the MCA, and thereby comprehend how and why this global development compact increasingly represents a moment of American imperialism, we need to grasp historically the material roots from which it emerged. The best way to accomplish this task is to examine the MCA in relation to the wider neoliberal development agenda: the Washington consensus.

I suggest that while the *form* of the MCA appears novel, its *content* continues to share the same objectives of preceding development agendas, most notably the neoliberal-led Washington consensus. It is helpful to unpack this argument briefly. The changing *form* of the MCA is best described by what I call 'pre-emptive development'. This term describes a set of coercive capitalist strategies aimed at seizing upon assets to the exclusion of other claimants. Unlike the traditional strategy of imposing conditionality, in which recipient countries were required to meet after loans were dispensed by the IMF and World

Bank, pre-emptive development entails the reverse: by using grants, as opposed to loans, creditor countries can withhold funds until all demands made by the donor country are met, largely through quantitative measurement. Despite the presence of pre-emptive forms of development, the *content* of the MCA reflects the same goals and interests that have been propagated by the Washington consensus over the past two decades: that the path to increased growth and prosperity lies in countries' willingness and ability to adopt policies that promote economic freedom and the rule of bourgeois law, such as private property, the commodification and privatization of land, and so on.

I develop this argument, first, by establishing the underlying power relations and contradictions from which the MCA emerged. It is necessary to historicize and contextualize the MCA, as it helps us move beyond the common-sense assumption that its emergence and subsequent *raison d'être* are exclusively tied to the tragic events of 9/11. The latter position not only legitimizes increased coercion of certain countries in the South – which includes, among other things, a trend toward the privatization and militarization of development – but also serves to obfuscate the underlying reasons for the creation of, and particular interests served by, the MCA. The second part of the chapter moves to a critical elaboration of the MCA, exploring what this agenda sets out to accomplish, how it is to achieve its aims, and which organizations are involved. In short, the application of the historical-materialist lens allows us to make sense of the shifting nature of political domination inherent in the MCA, and thereby helps shed more a critical light on global governance.

AMERICAN EMPIRE AND OFFICIAL DEVELOPMENT AGENDAS

American imperialism represents an historically specific expression of political domination over countries (developed and developing) not only by forces within the US, but also by other non-American capitalist interests that benefit from imperialist practices. As it is a moment of global capitalism, American imperialism is both highly dynamic and contradictory in nature. On the one hand, the American imperial state must constantly recreate the conditions of its power by ensuring, *inter alia*, that all states, particularly subordinate or poorer states, adhere to the international rules and laws in order to facilitate the reproduction of capitalist social relations (Panitch, 2000). This legal regime has been formulated largely by the US, along with other powerful industrial countries (the G-7), and embedded in the global trade architecture represented by the World Trade Organization, the global development architecture represented by the World Bank and the IMF, and the New International Financial Architecture (Soederberg, 2004). In this way the American imperial state takes charge of recreating the conditions of its power through ideological and coercive means (Panitch, 2000; Cox, 1987). On the other hand, since capitalism is inherently prone to crisis (Marx, 1981; Harvey, 1999; and see Chapter 2), there is a need continually to deepen and expand various strategies of exploitation. Since the early 1980s, these global restructuring strategies may be described by the term 'neoliberalism'. I discuss this term in more detail below. For now it is useful to grasp that neoliberal strategies of global restructuring have been captured by David Harvey's notion of 'accumulation by dispossession' (Harvey, 2003a; 2003b). According to Harvey, 'accumulation by dispossession' represents the crux of what he terms 'new imperialism', discussed in Chapters 2 and 4.

The US plays a key role in facilitating, and is also the main benefactor of, strategies of 'accumulation by dispossession'. I suggest that American imperialism shapes, and is shaped by, the tensions and contradictions inherent in reproducing the conditions of its own power in the world market by imposing new forms of domination over subordinate states, while at the same time overcoming inherent barriers to capital accumulation by physically expanding and deepening strategies of dispossession. In the next section I will look more closely at the inherent contradictions of a dominant strategy of accumulation by dispossession in the Third World – namely, the Washington consensus.

THE CAPITALIST NATURE OF OFFICIAL DEVELOPMENT AGENDAS

From the outset of the debt crises in the early 1980s to the late 1990s, the form of the official development agenda has been marked by the Washington consensus. This was premised on the steadfast belief that political and social problems should be solved primarily through market-based mechanisms and the rule of law, as opposed to state intervention. The principles of neoliberalism, which underpin the Washington consensus, quickly became guiding principles of the international financial institutions (IFIs) and one of the largest bilateral aid agencies, the United States Agency for International Development (USAID) (Fine, 2001: 134). Working under the assumption that states should relinquish all power, except for guaranteeing and enforcing the rule of law (private property rights, free repatriation of profits, and so on) to the rational forces of the marketplace over states, the official line of the Washington consensus sought to conceal processes of neoliberal restructuring by insisting that the implementation of sound economic policy and market-friendly reforms (privatization, liberalization, and deregulation) in the South would help these countries achieve economic stability and prosperity.

New York Times columnist Thomas Friedman's notion of the 'golden straitjacket' of globalization seems to capture the rationale of the Washington consensus (Friedman, 1999).[8] According to Friedman, the straitjacket will act to 'force contentious publics to understand the logic of globalization is that of peace (since war would interrupt globalization and therefore progress) and democracy (because new technologies increase individual autonomy and encourage initiative)' (Hoffman, 2002). What Friedman, like other neoliberals, fails to realize, however, is that the contradictions inherent in global capital accumulation inevitably create human insecurity. Neoliberal globalization consists in the prioritization of 'economic growth and market logics over all other goals and institutions of governance and enforces on all national polities, with varying degrees of coercion, privatization, trade liberalization, the deregulation of capital, and the erosion of the public sector and of democratic control' (Brodie, 2003). As we have seen in the previous chapters, the reproduction of neoliberal globalization is not a friction-free process, but is fraught with contradictions. As Elmar Altvater reminds us, global capital accumulation is an historical system defined by the fact that it makes structurally central and primary the endless accumulation of capital. This implies that the institutions and actors (IFIs, credit-rating agencies, TNCs, financial markets) that constitute its framework reward those who pursue the endless accumulation of capital and penalize those who don't. Moreover, these processes of profit-making, accumulation, and institutional regulation, which give a degree of security to the system, simultaneously produce insecurity at all levels of social and individual life (Altvater, 2002). The latter may be regarded as the security/insecurity paradox of neoliberal globalization, which is driven by an underlying crisis of overaccumulation.

Since neoliberalism is a moment of global capitalism, it too is infused with the security/insecurity paradox, which powerful social forces (transnational capital classes, capitalist states, trade unions, not-for-profit non-governmental organizations) within *and* outside the American state must strive to overcome. In the post-Bretton Woods era, American-led imperialism has attempted to resolve the security/insecurity paradox in relation to the South largely through economic and physical (military) coercion, such as the structural adjustment programmes (SAPs) of the IMF, and militarized post-war reconstruction efforts in, for example, Afghanistan, Bosnia, and Iraq, otherwise known as the 'non-integrating gap'. I will return to this notion below. It is the attempts to deal with the security/insecurity paradox that drive the changing form of American empire in relation to excluded states: as the US seeks to respond to perceived threats to its imperial dominance, we see a shift in the *form* of the official development agenda – or, which is the same thing, the reproduction of its *content* in an increasingly coercive manner.

One such manifestation of the security/insecurity paradox is the fact that capital has continually bypassed the poorest countries of the South, or what Samir Amin refers to as 'excluded states', most of which are situated in sub-Saharan Africa and South Asia (Amin, 1999). The ongoing attempts to liberalize financial markets have, for the most part, implied that excess short-term flows have seeped into 'emerging markets' when interest rates were advantageously high in relation to the G-7 countries, while bypassing the poorest countries. TNCs and their coveted FDI have tended to stream in the direction of the emerging markets. It follows that the political discontent emerging from these excluded states, particularly the immense peasant population, could also act to destabilize the neoliberal strategy in the South at large, through, for example, strategies of 'deglobalization' (see Bello, 2002). As Panitch and Gindin rightly point out, the most serious problems for US-led imperialism today are to be found in the so-called 'excluded states' or 'non-integrating gap'. To my mind, this term should not denote that countries are outside the scope of capitalism (Panitch and Gindin, 2003: 31). As we saw in Chapter 2, relations of capitalist production and exchange are not only fluid in nature, but also have existed for a long time in the form of a world market. Thus, no national economy, no matter how marginalized it appears to be economically and politically (i.e. anywhere from North Korea to Eritrea), stands outside capitalism, as it is affected by the relations of power and contradictions in the world, albeit to varying extents. That said, the 'non-integrating gap' captures the frustration involved in taming – both politically and economically – states and societies to be disciplined by the structural power of capital (see Chapter 3) and/or by international financial institutions. From this perspective, the unruly nature of the non-integrating gap could effectively challenge the neoliberal passive revolution aimed at recreating the dominance of the US, while carrying out global restructuring so as to attempt to overcome the crisis of overaccumulation.

CRISIS OF CONFIDENCE: CONSTRAINING EXCLUDED STATES WITHIN THE BOUNDS OF NEOLIBERAL GLOBALIZATION

While well-documented poverty rates and income polarization had created much discontent in the South regarding the neoliberal prescription of the IFIs, by the mid 1990s the growing levels of insecurity began to pose serious problems for the reproduction of neoliberal globalization.[9] The dangerous combination of the dwindling levels of public support for laissez-faire restructuring and austerity packages, on the one hand, and shrinking room for manoeuvre regarding national economic and social policy formation, on the other, had led to a crisis of neoliberal governance in the South. The common-sense assumption that unleashing the market would enhance the economic prosperity of the majority not only proved to be incorrect, but also led to the lack of popular support for neoliberal principles. The growing discontent in Argentina by the middle and working classes brought about by the largest sovereign default in history; or the peasant uprising in Cochabamba, Bolivia, against the privatization of water and gas; the peasant struggles of Cuzco, Peru, against the privatization of electricity – all are cases in point. The traditional response of the official development agenda to the deterioration of material conditions and the associated crisis of legitimacy in the South was to insist that developing countries further implement market-led restructuring: the more governments allow themselves to be disciplined by inherently rational economic actors, the more prosperity they will achieve. Several factors complicated this strategy, however, and led in turn to the reinvention of the Washington consensus in the late 1990s (also known as the Second Generation Reforms).

First, the growth-obsessed and one-size-fits-all nature of the SAPs were heavily criticized, not only by the anti-globalization movements during high-profile gatherings of the IFIs and the WTO in Seattle, Genoa, Prague, Washington, and so on, but also from both Keynesian and conservative pundits and think-tanks in Washington.[10] These criticisms became even more heightened with the litany of financial crises, and subsequent IMF-led bailouts, in the so-called 'emerging markets' – most of which were once showcases for the Fund (see Soederberg, 2002a; 2002b; 2004). Second, the coffers for public aid were quickly emptying. As Jose Antonio Ocampo says, 'bilateral aid fell in real terms throughout the decade, and in 1998 it was estimated to have reached 0.22 per cent of the GDP of industrialized countries, a significant fall with respect to the 0.35 per cent of GDP reached in the mid-1980s' (Ocampo, 2000: 43). Overall spending levels in the US, the world's largest bilateral donor, have slowly been declining since the 1960s. In fact, during the Clinton administration alone, discretionary spending on development aid (loosely defined as development, humanitarian, or economic aid) declined by $370 million, to $10.7 billion, in 2001.[11]

Third, in the post-Cold War era the overriding security threat for the US shifted. Specifically, the American concern with the external actions of states – the violation of international norms, such as those relating to terrorism or territorial aggression linked to the expansion of a competing mode of production: communism – moved to concern for a regime's domestic behaviour, such as how it treats its own people (Thomas, 2002; cf. UNDP, 1994). For the Clinton administration (1993–2001), the best way to combat these 'new wars' (Kaldor, 1999) was through multilateral tactics, largely in the form of global governance (Commission on Global Governance, 1995). Clinton's brand of global governance, also known as the strategy of 'engagement and enlargement', involved the (forced) transformation of all Third World countries (rogue states, failed states, and emerging markets) into states that were deemed democratic and pursued free market economics (Litwak, 2000: 49).

In a speech delivered to the 1998 IMF and World Bank Annual Meeting, and drawing on his overarching 'engagement and enlargement' strategy, President Clinton summed up both the concerns over the consequences of the crises and the means by which it may be averted. To paraphrase, unless Third World countries feel empowered with the tools to master economic change, they will feel the strong temptation to turn inwards, to close off their economies to the world. Now, more than ever, that would be a grave mistake. At a moment of financial crisis, a natural inclination is to close borders and retreat behind walls of protectionism. But it is precisely at moments like this we need to increase trade to spur greater growth (Clinton, 1998).

In summary, the new *form* of official development agenda had to overcome a major hindrance: on the one hand, recreating a neoliberal world system in light of a glaring absence of convincing evidence that market-oriented restructuring produces the benefits claimed by its promoters; on the other, further exposing the South, whether rogue states, failed states, or emerging markets, to the dictates of the marketplace (Kotz, 2003: 16). The most pressing issues that needed to be tackled in the reformulation of the neoliberal development agenda were the growing levels of poverty and social dislocation brought about by what were perceived by critics of the World Bank and the IMF as top-down, economistic, universalized SAPs (Fine, 2001; Pender, 2001).

FROM THE WASHINGTON CONSENSUS TO THE
EMPOWERING DEVELOPMENT AGENDA:
REFASHIONING NEOLIBERAL RESTRUCTURING

In response to the above contradictions a new *form* of the official development agenda arose, armed with new buzzwords such as, 'ownership' and 'social inclusion', to complement, not diminish, market discipline. According to the World Bank, inclusion 'treats poor people as co-producers, with authority and control over decisions and resources devolved to the lowest appropriate level', whereas ownership describes the process whereby the recipient country selects the policy mix and takes responsibility for its implementation and outcome (Graham and Masson, 2002). At base, the World Bank's new agenda – also referred to as the post-Washington consensus – reduces social problems tied to 'development' (viewed here as integrating poor countries into the world market through the adherence to neoliberal governance) to market imperfections, most notably economic instability. In doing so, the World Bank seeks to depoliticise the contradictions caused by structural adjustment by extending economic to non-economic analysis (most notably poverty). This is most blatantly obvious in the extension of its new-found ability to comprehend the social and the political, whilst empowering individuals to overcome conditions of poverty (Fine, 2001).

The World Bank underwent an overhaul not only in terms of its top-down, predominately economic focus to an allegedly more human-oriented stance (or 'empowering development'), but also balancing its stress on increasing productivity with fighting poverty. Since mid-1995, the World Bank has shifted its focus from financing infrastructure projects in the South to poverty alleviation programmes. The IMF also plays an important role in the fight against poverty. A concrete manifestation of this new focus has been the creation of a joint World Bank–IMF programme entitled the Poverty Reduction Strategy Papers (PRSP) (Taylor, 2004; IMF, 2003d). It should be noted that the PRSP are not about doing away with conditionality, but should instead be seen as direct responses to the above-mentioned threats to neoliberal-led globalization, which in turn are targeted at reconfiguring and deepening the domination of capitalist relations and American-led imperialism over the growing number of poor in the South. These recent transformations have not replaced the emphasis on market-led growth, however. Instead they are targeted at legitimizing, and thus reproducing, the coercive power of transnational capital in these countries (Gill and Law, 1993). On the other hand, these poverty alleviation programmes pursued by the Bank are accompanied by increased powers of surveillance and control over both public and private spheres in the South.

A case in point is the Poverty Reduction Growth Facility (PRGF). Keeping in line with these aims and the wider PRSP, the Fund has replaced its Enhanced Structural Adjustment Facility (ESAF) with the PRGF. According to the IMF, the latter differs from the former in the following manner. Through the PRGF, the IMF aims to integrate the objectives of poverty reduction and growth more fully into its operations in the poorest countries, or, more specifically, the Highly Indebted Poor Countries (HIPCs). Indeed, the PRGF was designed to give the IMF a more central and legitimate role in the 1996 'HIPC initiative', which was proposed by the IFIs in 1996. The PRGF places more emphasis on 'good governance' than its predecessor, which, we have seen, refers to the 'proper management' of liberalization policy along with public goods, achieving greater transparency, active public scrutiny, and so on (IMF, 2002b) – all of which is prescribed in the IFIs' international standards and codes (the Reports on the Observances of Standards and Codes), governing facets of a country's economy, such as corporate governance, transparency, and securities regulation (IMF, 2003e). This move not only gives the Bank's policies some financial teeth, but also allows for a more comprehensive and coherent surveillance programme, allowing the IFIs to monitor more effectively, and in greater detail, the countries' policy actions, the frequency of programme reviews, and the role of prior actions.[12] Empowering development was an attempt to 'embed' the values and norms of neoliberalism (market freedom and rule of law) in the rapidly deteriorating social, political, and economic life of the 'non-integrating' gap.

Nevertheless, empowering development would not be able to overcome the above-mentioned contradictions of neoliberal-led globalization in the excluded states, largely because of its inability to diminish the tensions of the security/insecurity paradox in the South, as well as new forms of insecurity in the US. In the following section I will examine the economic and military roots of the increasing unilateral and coercive nature of American dominance. This exercise will, in turn, assist us in understanding the factors underpinning the shift from neoliberal-led empowering to neoconservative forms of pre-emptive development.

NEW SECURITY AND ECONOMIC THREATS TO NEOLIBERAL GLOBALIZATION BEFORE AND AFTER 9/11

The bursting of the American bubble economy and the emergence of pre-emptive security policies

After experiencing what was considered by many to be the deepest recessionary period in the post-war era, during the early 1990s, in the second half of the decade the US economy began once again to serve as the main engine of growth to the world. During the period between 1995 and 2000, GDP growth accelerated, rising from 3.1 per cent to 4.1 per cent (Kotz, 2003: 21). The main impetus creating and sustaining American expansion was not, as officials claimed, neoliberal restructuring and the 'new economy', but rather a speculative bubble in the stock market (Shiller, 2000) which not only began growing at 4.9 per cent per year from 1997 to 2000, but also 'became the chief force propelling GDP growth, since it represented about two-thirds of GDP and it was then growing substantially faster than the GDP' (Kotz, 2003: 21). To get an idea of the dimensions of the bubble, Yale economist Robert Shiller observes that while '[t]he Dow Jones Industrial Average stood at around 3,600 in early 1994, by 1999, it had passed 11,000, more than tripling in five years, a total increase in stock market prices of over 200 per cent. At the start of 2000, the Dow passed 11,700.' Between 1994 and 1999, for example, '[t]he aggregate market value of the outstanding shares of US corporations rose from $5.5 trillion in 1994 to $17.1 trillion in 1999, an increase of $11.6 trillion' (Kotz, 2003: 26).

When the speculatively based expansion came to a screeching halt at the end of August 2000, it not only revealed the fragility of the economy's largely jobless growth. Given the increasing dependency of the Third World on the US economy, the sudden economic downturn in the US also served to accentuate the already high levels of insecurity in the South. In the aftermath of the bubble, the US continues to be marked by high levels of unemployment, and by corporate governance scandals; and despite the fact that the US Federal Reserve Bank forced interest rates down to levels not seen since 1958, low levels of both investment and consumer confidence continue to dampen the possibility of growth ('Bush Goes for Broke', *The Economist*, January 8, 2003).[13] In fact, since 2001 the Federal Reserve has cut interest rates 13 times which left its main rate at an historical low of 1 per cent.[14] Consumer, corporate, and government debt has not helped the situation. According to the Economic Policy Institute, a Washington-based think-tank, '[b]y 2001, total household debt exceeded total household disposable income by an all-time high of nearly 10 percent. Much of the run-up in debt occurred over the economic boom, as the ratio of debt to personal disposable income rose from 87.7 percent in 1992 to 109.0 percent in 2001' (Economic Policy Institute, 2002). The current 'housing bubble', which has bolstered the economy since the plunge in stock market prices, is intimately tied to this rise in debt (IMF, 2003f). Towards the end of March 2002, federal borrowing not only approached its legal ceiling of $5.95 trillion, but on April 1, 2002 surpassed it.

In the hope to avoid a federal default, President Bush asked Congress to raise the limit by $750 billion, which would cover borrowing into 2004 ('O'Neill Set to Prevent Federal Default', *Guardian*, March 19, 2002). Largely owing to the continued economic slowdown, coupled with the big tax cuts undertaken by the Bush administration in 2001 and 2002, the budget deficit was growing at an alarming pace. The current account deficit in the US was set to reach $600 billion in 2003. It should be highlighted that, in order to feed this deficit, the US needs to attract around a net $2.7 billion of overseas inflows every working day ('Dollar's Fall Giving Investors the Jitters', *Financial Times*, May 12, 2003). The inability of the US to live within its own means while imposing this same fiscal discipline on excluded states not only creates a crisis of confidence regarding prudent fiscal management; in addition, America's current account deficit poses one of the biggest risks to the world economy, according to the IMF ('The O'Neill Doctrine', *The Economist*, April 27, 2002). According to some observers, this deficit is being paid by foreign investors. In 2002, for example, 97 per cent of the American current account deficit was financed by net foreign purchases of bonds other than government bonds, such as US Treasury bonds. A consequence of this situation, in which the growing current account deficit is fed by increasingly short-term credit financing, is yet more insecurity (in the form of growing dependence on foreign sources of financing) for the US economy (*Monthly Review*, 2003: 26).

The lacklustre economy not only served to aggravate the security/insecurity paradox in the US, but also in the South. Despite the rhetoric of empowering development, private flows, which make up the bulk of capital streaming to developing countries, have also been affected by the global economic slowdown (The Conference Board, 2003). This decline in foreign investment to the South is demonstrated in the World Bank's *Global Development Finance* 2003 report (see Table 5.1). According to this document, the decline in foreign investment flows to the South since 1997 has occurred primarily in net capital flows from the private sector, particularly in the debt component (bank loans and bonds). From the peak years of 1995–96, when net debt inflows from the private sector were about $135 billion per year, they have dropped steadily, becoming net outflows in 2001 and 2002 (World Bank, 2003: 7). According to the Washington-based Center for Economic and Policy Research, most developing countries are now large exporters of capital, due to, for example, payments of interest and profits (Morissey and Baker, 2003). The US recessionary environment proved to be even bleaker for HIPCs – areas of the South that, at the best of times, have been experiencing decreasing public aid levels from the world's largest source of bilateral assistance.

Against this backdrop, the American economy in the immediate post-bubble era posed two important hurdles for the reproduction of neoliberal globalization. On the one hand, for the ruling class[15] in the US, the immediate problem was how to continue to legitimize neoliberal globalization in the face of deteriorating economic and social conditions both in the US and in the South. As David Kotz puts it: 'One hindrance to the US ruling class agenda of creating a neoliberal world system has been the glaring absence of convincing evidence that neoliberal restructuring produces the benefits claimed by its promoters' (Kotz, 2003: 16). In the week prior to 9/11, for example, President Bush's standing in opinion polls was at its lowest point ever, with only 50 per cent of respondents giving him a positive

Table 5.1   Net Capital Flows to Developing Countries, 1997–2003 ($ billions)

	1997	1998	1999	2000	2001	2002e	2003f
Current Account	–91.4	–113.6	–10.7	61.9	27.6	48.3	26.2
Balance as % of GDP	–1.5	–2.0	–2.0	1.0	0.5	0.8	0.4
Financed by:							
Net Equity Flows	196.4	181.9	194.3	186.7	177.6	152.3	158.0
Net FDI Inflows	169.3	174.5	179.3	160.6	171.7	143.0	145.0
Net Portfolio							
Equity Inflows	26.7	7.4	15.0	26.0	6.0	9.4	13.0
Net Debt Flows	102.1	57.4	13.9	–1.0	3.2	7.2	5.0
Official Creditors	13.0	34.1	13.5	–6.2	28.0	16.2	0.0
World Bank	9.2	8.7	8.8	7.8	7.5	1.5	–
IMF	3.4	14.1	–2.2	–10.6	19.5	14.5	–
Others	0.5	11.2	6.9	–3.4	1.0	0.2	–
Private Creditors	89.1	23.3	0.5	5.1	–24.8	–9.0	5.0
Net medium–long-term							
debt flows	84.0	87.4	21.9	14.5	–8.6	2.9	–
Bonds	38.4	39.7	29.6	17.4	10.1	18.6	–
Banks	43.1	51.4	–5.9	2.6	–11.8	–16.0	–
Others	2.5	–3.6	–1.8	–5.5	–7.0	–5.5	
Net short-term							
debt flows	5.3	–64.2	–21.4	–9.4	–16.2	–6.1	–
Bilateral aid grants	26.7	28.2	29.4	29.6	29.5	32.9	32.0

Note: e = estimate; f= forecast.
Source: World Bank, 2003: 8.

rating ('Trading on Fear', *Guardian*, July 12, 2003). On the other hand, given the economic slump at home, the US needs to expand production and financial activities beyond its domestic market. To do so it requires co-operative governments in the South, who are willing to devise and implement policies that support and protect the interests of transnational capitals, such as a well-disciplined labour market, slack environmental and taxation standards, and so on. Given the dismal state of the American economy, it has become more vital that official development agendas achieve economic freedom and rule of law in excluded states.

While the events of 9/11 are commonly seen as the main impetus for renewed US unilateralism, I suggest that it was the combination of mounting problems of legitimacy associated with the tumultuous American and global economy, the presence of a hawkish neoconservative administration, and the inability of the White House to refine clearly a strategy to tackle the economy, that led to the creation of a more intense form of imperialism. Neoconservative pundits like Robert Kagan, for instance, have argued that America's return to power-politics in important geopolitical areas such as economic and military concerns occurred well before the attacks on the World Trade Center and the Pentagon. We should bear in mind that, before 9/11, the Bush administration had moved towards a more overt and unabashed unilateralist stance. Some examples are the withdrawal from the Kyoto Protocol on global warming, the pushing of National Missile Defense in violation of the ABM treaty with Russia, and the scrapping of proposed enforcement measures in the Biological and Toxic Weapons Convention in favour of unilateral US enforcement (Mahajan, 2002: 22).

In a January 2000 issue of *Foreign Affairs*, the future National Security Advisor to George W. Bush, Condoleezza Rice, criticized the Clinton administration for replacing national interests with humanitarian interests and the interests of the international community. Instead, Rice suggested that the US should take the attitude that what is in its own interests is good for the world (Rice, 2000).[16] For the incoming Bush administration, the solution to the above problems was to tighten further the belts of the golden straitjacket. Interestingly, this was to be achieved through increased economic and military coercion, and with little consensus-formation or compromise.

The intensification and justification of a more repressive and unabashed unilateralism: US foreign policy after 9/11

> America's cause is the cause of all mankind.
> Benjamin Franklin, quoted in
> Robert Kagan, *Of Paradise and Power*, 2003.

The catastrophic events of 9/11 not only served to justify military expansion and American imperialism under the aegis of the 'war on terrorism', but also to legitimize more direct and repressive forms of intervention into 'strategic' areas of the South. On the surface, America's war on terrorism – both inside and outside national boundaries – was justified by the construction of a favourite American myth: the equation that the universal good coincided with American morals. Kagan captures this logic well: 'When Americans sought legitimacy for their actions abroad, they sought it not from supranational institutions but from their own principles. That is why it was always so easy for so many Americans to believe, as so many still believe today, that by advancing their own interests they advance the interests of humanity' (Kagan, 2003: 88). This sentiment is directly reflected in Bush's National Security Strategy, which was drafted one year after 9/11. The US possesses unprecedented – and unequalled – strength and influence in the world. Sustained by faith in the principles of liberty, and the value of a free society, this position comes with unparalleled responsibilities, obligations, and opportunity. The great strength of this nation must be used to promote a balance of power that favours freedom. In other words, 'The United States must defend liberty and justice because these principles are right and true for all people everywhere' ('Unprecedented Power, Colliding Ambitions', *The Economist*, September 28, 2002).

Aside from temporarily boosting both the president's approval ratings to an astounding 82 per cent, and consumer spending under the mantra of 'I am American' advertisements, at a deeper level the constructed myth surrounding American internationalism and 'the other' assisted in legitimizing increased coercion both at home and in what the government considered to be 'strategic' areas of the South – namely, failed states. With blatant and reckless disregard for the country's already high levels of indebtedness, President Bush's proposed 2004 budget is a case in point: the 'inescapable conclusion' the budget reaches is that 'the federal government must restrain the growth in any spending not directly associated with the physical security of the nation' (Office of Management and Budget, 2003). To this end, half of the $28 billion increase over 2003 discretionary spending was to go to defence. Specifically,

> The administration of President George W. Bush is requesting $399.1 billion for the military in fiscal year 2004 ($379.9 billion for the Defense Department and $19.3 billion for the nuclear weapons functions of the Department of Energy). This is $16.9 billion above current levels, an increase of 4.4 percent. In all, the administration plans to spend $2.7 trillion on the military over the next six years – and this as both the Office of Management and Budget and the Congressional Budget Office project a federal deficit as high as $200 billion to $300 billion next year [2004] (Center for Defense Information, 2004).

It is interesting to note that the focus of the federal budget was more on addressing the military dimensions of insecurity than on its social and economic dimensions. The federal government has shifted more of the financial burden of social service provisions to the states, leaving state and local governments with an aggregate budget deficit of almost $100 billion during fiscal year 2003 ('Doubts Arise Over

Scope for US Reforms', *Financial Times,* February 13, 2003). This move has served to embed further what many consider to be not only the most regressive welfare system for poor people among developed countries, but also the most punitive in terms of subjecting welfare recipients to personal intrusions and continuous surveillance (Platt, 2003; Fox Piven and Cloward, 1997).

The other dimension of the NSS involved the deepening and widening of internal state coercion in the US through the rollback of civil liberties. These are not only reflective of the government's attempt to straddle the security/insecurity paradox internally by, for example, curtailing civil liberties and political rights at home through the Patriot Act,[17] but also have important implications in the way in which the US government deals with this domestic paradox externally, especially with regard to the 'non-integrating' gap. Thus, before turning our attention to the MCA, it is instructive to look briefly at the Patriot Act, because it throws light on who exactly is to benefit from the MCA's attempt to construct and police civil liberties and political rights in the South. The justification for the Patriot Act, which was passed by Congress in October 2001, was to unite and strengthen America by providing the tools required to intercept and obstruct terrorism. The means of achieving this end was to authorize unprecedented leeway in the surveillance and incarceration of both citizens and non-citizens. More specifically, the Patriot Act

> expand[s] the ability of police to spy on telephone and Internet correspondence in anti-terrorism investigations and in routine criminal investigations. It authorized secret government searches, enabling the FBI and other government agencies to conduct searches without warrants and without notifying individuals that their property has been searched. It created a broad new definition of 'domestic terrorism' under which political protesters can be charged as terrorists if they engage in conduct that 'involves acts dangerous to human life'. It also put the CIA back in the business of spying on US citizens and allowed the government to detain non-citizens for indefinite periods of time without trial. The Patriot Act was followed in November 2001 by a new executive order from Bush, authorizing himself to order a trial in a military court for any non-citizen he designates, without a right of appeal or the protection of the Bill of Rights ('Trading on Fear', *Guardian,* July 12, 2003).

These unilateral tendencies, reproducing US dominance, as well as the ongoing economic crisis both at home and throughout the world, have led to a pre-emptive foreign policy not only in terms of security, but also in terms of the wider official development agenda. According to Saskia Sassen, the US is attempting to move away from its previous commitments to global governance and multilateralism, while seeking to shut down 'progressive', not-for-profit NGOs and their growing influence, especially with those social forces opposed to neoliberal globalization. The former is illustrated by the American Enterprise Institute, an influential think-tank closely associated with the Bush administration, which launched a neoconservative attack on the WTO with a conference in Washington in 2003,[18] attended by at least 42 senior representatives of the Bush administration. Civil society is slowly being shut out of development issues by moves to grant more contracts to private companies instead of non-profit organizations ('New Lords of Africa', *Guardian*, July 9, 2003).

Deepening economic and security threats both within and outside US borders have reshaped the regulatory landscape of a key issue of development: the management of poverty in failed states. It is from this context that a new official agenda emerges: pre-emptive development, and its ultimate aim of ensuring that the poorest countries are firmly fitted into the golden straitjacket. As we will see, despite its novelty, the basic premise of this new form of the official development agenda is strikingly similar to that of its predecessors – namely, that the path to increased growth and prosperity lies in countries' willingness and ability to adopt policies that promote economic freedom and the rule of law.

THE MILLENNIUM CHALLENGE ACCOUNT: MANAGING THE SECURITY/INSECURITY PARADOX

There is no longer any agreement on the main lines of economic policy between the current US administration and the international financial institutions.

> John Williamson, (inventor of the term 'Washington consensus')
> 'From Reform Agenda to Damaged Brand Name', 2003: 10–13.

Excluded states, poverty and the national security strategy

According to the 2002 NSS, failed states pose a direct threat to US national security. Before continuing, it is helpful to elaborate briefly on the term 'failed states'. While there is far from a consensus on the meaning of the term, failed states, such as Nigeria, Afghanistan, Sierra Leone, Iran, Bosnia, and Somalia, are defined by the US government as 'countries in which the central government does not exert effective control over, nor is it able to deliver vital services to, significant parts of its own territory due to conflict, ineffective governance [for which read: failure to adhere to the tenets of neoliberalism], or state collapse' (Rice, 2003). Following this logic, not only are failed states believed to provide convenient operational bases and safe havens for international terrorists; the lack of 'development' (economic freedom for capitals and the rule of law) inherent in failed states could also intensify political discontent and violence against foreign capitals, which could have wider repercussions, such as the terrorist attacks of 9/11 (White House, 2002). The justification for treating these countries with increased coercion and surveillance stems from the position that other countries have the right to act against the failed states in order to prevent the terrorism that could otherwise harm the other countries.[19] To understand the nature of the MCA, it is instructive to explore briefly what the US government sees as the main cause of excluded states.[20]

Although cautious not to draw a simple correlation between poverty and terrorism, the US government strongly suggests that the higher the poverty rates the higher the potential for that environment to breed terrorism. As the National Security Strategy makes clear, 'the events of September 11, 2001, taught us that weak states, like Afghanistan, can pose as great a danger to our national interests as strong states. Poverty does not make poor people into terrorists and murderers. Yet poverty, weak institutions, and corruption can make weak states vulnerable to terrorist networks and drug cartels within their borders' (Daalder et al., 2002). From this perspective, in order to deter future terrorist aggression against America, the government has to gain more control over what occurs within these countries so as to reproduce and protect US dominance in the global political economy, by ensuring that failed states adopt market-led policies and embrace globalization so that they may overcome poverty. To date, there have been two main ways in which the poorest regions of the world are being forced to slip on the golden straitjacket: one is by attempting to discipline failed states by shifting loans into measurable grants through the World Bank's International Development Association (IDA); the other is the MCA.

Intensifying capital's discipline through aid? Transforming IDA lending practices

According to the Bush administration, a more efficient way of ensuring that the poorest countries adopt neoliberal principles is through unilateral-inspired solutions administered by a multilateral lending institution, such as the IDA. The latter, which forms a key component of the World Bank Group (see Pincus and Winters, 2002), was created in 1960 to assist the world's poorest countries reduce poverty by providing 'credits', which are loans at zero-interest with a ten-year grace period, and maturities of 35–40 years.[21] To achieve maximum control over the development process, the US government has insisted that the IDA should convert its loans to grants. US Treasury Under-Secretary John Taylor sums up the logic behind this proposal in the following manner:

> [A] novel proposal we have suggested to the World Bank – to have shareholders' contributions tied to measurable results. *Grants can be tied more effectively to performance in a way that longer-term loans simply cannot. You have to keep delivering the service or you don't get the grant.* Every three years, the United States and other shareholders in the World Bank contribute a certain amount to this IDA program. The United States has reduced its contributions to IDA in the 1990s. We intend to reverse this trend. We want to increase our contributions to IDA, but we think it is essential to do so in a way that gears the contribution to results (Taylor, 2002; emphasis added).

While far from a novel idea, the concept of performance-based grants instead of traditional loans was enthusiastically supported by the neoconservative sectors of prestigious and highly influential American think-tanks such as the Heritage Foundation, as well as the International Financial Institution Advisory Commission, also known as the Meltzer Commission.[22] According to long-time advocates of grants, Adam Lerrick and Allan H. Meltzer, performance-based grants provide a more effective form of control and surveillance over states and markets of the South than traditional loans. On the one hand, grants can be project-linked and executed under competitive bids (which includes foreign market participants), with payments shared by both the World Bank and the beneficiary. On the other, the grant scheme would allow for an independent audit and payments based on clearly quantifiable basic needs aimed at improving the quality of life and, relatedly, economic growth: primary education, health, sanitation and water, as well as the numbers of babies vaccinated, improvement of literacy rates, and so on (Lerrick and Meltzer, 2002). It should be stressed that the imposition of performance-based grants through the Bank's IDA is not based on an inter-state consensus, as many G-7 countries stand in opposition to this proposal (Sanford,

2002). Thus, in keeping with its non-hegemonic status, the US seeks to implement policy in highly coercive and unilateral terms.

In 2002, the US government proposed additional funding as an incentive contribution if IDA satisfactorily initiated work on a results measurement system, and had delivered key country diagnostic assessments. According to US Treasury Secretary John Snow, '[f]or the first time IDA donors are able to link a portion of their contributions to the achievement of results. The US committed to increase its budgetary request by 18 per cent for IDA. Of the $2.85 billion US contribution to IDA, $300 million is contingent on improving results in a concrete and measurable way.' Convinced that the IDA has met conditions for additional funding, Snow announced his intention to request an additional $100 million in funding for the IDA in April 2003 (Office of Public Affairs of the US Treasury Department, 2003).

The MCA: the new compact for global development

In September 2000, heads of state committed themselves to reducing poverty in the world by 2015. To meet this objective of the Millennium Declaration, the UN Secretary-General, Kofi Annan, called for a Financing for Development (FfD) conference to take place in Monterrey, Mexico in March 2002.[23] It was during this meeting that President Bush proposed a dramatic increase in US foreign assistance for poor countries to meet the Millennium Development Goals. This momentous offer calls for an additional increase in official development assistance (ODA) by $5 billion a year, phased in over a three-year period: $1.7 billion in fiscal year (FY) 2004, $3.3 billion in FY 2005, and $5 billion in FY 2006 and each year thereafter (USAID, 2002). While Congress reduced Bush's proposed budget by 1.8 billion, it was still only 6 per cent higher than the amount approved for foreign operations for the current fiscal year (US Department of State, 2003).[24] What is more, the budgetary limitations of the MCA do not lessen its impact as a trend-setting method of managing aid. For one thing, the Millennium Challenge Corporation (MCC), as opposed to USAID, will govern the MCA's funds, although USAID is to be a 'key partner' of the MCA in the sense that it is to act as the implementing agency for many MCA programmes. The White House is trying to establish the MCC as an independent corporation, whose head will be chosen by the US president. Congress, on the other hand, would like to see the MCC fall under the jurisdiction of the State Department, thereby curbing its independence. Moreover, unlike traditional forms of development assistance, the programme, in the manner of IDA performance-based grants, seeks to reward performance and measure results so as to create an operational action plan aimed at ensuring that the goals set by the NSS are reached. In the words of President Bush:

> Countries that live by these three broad standards – ruling justly, investing in their people, and encouraging economic freedom – will receive more aid from America. And, more importantly, over time, they will really no longer need it, because nations with sound laws and policies will attract more foreign investment. They will earn more trade revenues. And they will find that all these sources of capital will be invested more effectively and productively to create more jobs for their people ... I challenge other nations, and the development banks, to adopt this approach as well (Citizens' Network on Essential Services, 2003).

The MCA is to provide aid to those countries who have successfully demonstrated, largely through quantifiable scores, that they meet *all* 16 indicators spanning three broad eligibility criteria: (1) ruling justly; (2) investing in people; and (3) economic freedom (see Table 5.2). While these conditions reflect the concerns of the official development discourse – reproducing the imperative of economic growth, open current and capital accounts, sound macroeconomic fundamentals, good governance, and democratic values – the 'empowering' features seem to be overshadowed by the pre-emptive nature of the MCA, not to mention the complementary scheme of pre-emptive conditionality imposed by the IDA. The execution of the MCA shares the discourse of good governance, including such ideas as ownership and social inclusion (partnership, participation) while further disciplining and controlling failed states to the dictates of the market. The concern for empowering individuals is limited to ensuring that the reform, along the lines of the 16 criteria listed in Table 5.2, is home-grown. Drawing their lessons from the ineffectiveness of IMF and World Bank conditionalities, the architects of the MCA stress the need for a strong domestic commitment to change. Yet, as the following quote reveals, the manner in which this reform is to be achieved is a classical 'top-down' manner with intensified US surveillance. According to the State Department, the partnership between the MCA and recipient countries is to be established in the following manner:

> the MCA will use time-limited, business-like contracts that represent a commitment between the United States and the developing country to

meet agreed performance benchmarks. Developing countries will set their own priorities and identify their own greatest hurdles to development. They will do so by engaging their citizens, businesses and government in an open debate, which will result in a proposal for MCA funding. This proposal will include objectives, a plan and timetable for achieving them, benchmarks for assessing progress and how results will be sustained at the end of the contract, delineation of the responsibilities of the MCA and the MCA country, the role of civil society, business and other donors, and a plan for ensuring financial accountability for funds used. The MCA will review the proposal, consulting with the MCA country. The Board will approve all contracts (Citizens' Network on Essential Services, 2003).

In stark contrast with the spirit of multilateralism demonstrated by Clinton's 'engagement and enlargement' strategy, as well as empowering development, all the institutions actually performing assessment on these 16 criteria are either largely neoconservative American organisations, such as the Heritage Foundation and the Freedom House, or US-dominated IFIs. As such, the power to pass judgment on the criteria would be based on a uniquely American perspective of what constitutes, for example, political rights and civil liberties. It should be emphasized that neither the NSS nor the MCA are clear on what is meant by these criteria, which in turn leads to much discretionary power being wielded by these institutions. Prejudicial, Western-based, Christian values thus predominate alongside a highly discretionary means of arriving at the definitions of each criterion. Moreover, given the increasingly repressive environment in the US itself, witnessed in the Patriot Act, it is questionable what is understood under the definition of 'civil liberties'. The effect of this rather subjective process is the construction of terms that appear to be an inert fact of nature (Said, 1979). The following quote provides greater insight into the linkages between the Heritage Foundation, an authoritative voice on financial matters, and the *Wall Street Journal*, not only reproduce common sense assumptions of the importance of economic freedom and rule of law in the South, but also act as a disciplinary strategy in the interests of capital:

The *Index of Economic Freedom* grades 10 factors for 161 countries with 1 being the best score and 5 being the worst score. These factors are: trade policy, fiscal burden of government, government intervention in the economy, monetary policy, capital flows and foreign investment, banking and finance, wages and prices, property rights, regulation, and black market activity. Those

Table 5.2   Eligibility Criteria for the MCA

Indicator	Source
I. Ruling Justly	
1. Control of Corruption	World Bank Institute[25]
2. Rule of Law	World Bank Institute
3. Voice and Accountability	World Bank Institute
4. Government Effectiveness	World Bank Institute
5. Civil Liberties	Freedom House[26]
6. Political Rights	Freedom House
II. Investing in People	
7. Immunization Rate: DPT and Measles	WHO/World Bank
8. Primary Education Completion Rate	World Bank
9. Public Primary Education Spending/GDP	World Bank
10. Public Expenditure on Health/GDP	World Bank
III. Economic Freedom	
11. Country Credit Rating	Institutional Investor
12. Inflation	IMF
13. Regulatory Quality	World Bank Institute
14. Budget Deficit/GDP	IMF/World Bank
15. Trade Policy	Heritage Foundation[27]
16. Days to Start a Business	World Bank

Source: 'Fact Sheet: Millennium Challenge Account', distributed by the administration on November 25, 2002, available at www.cgdev.org. Quoted in Radelet, 2003: 175.

10 scores for these factors are then averaged to give an overall score for economic freedom. Countries are designated 'free', 'mostly free,' and 'mostly unfree,' and 'repressed' based on these overall scores. As shown in the *Index*, free countries on average have a per capita income twice that of mostly free countries, mostly free countries have a per capita income more than three times that of mostly unfree and repressed countries. This relationship exists because countries maintaining policies that promote economic freedom provide an environment that facilitates trade and encourages entrepreneurial activity, which in turn generates economic growth (Schaefer, 2003: 3).

From the above perspective, it becomes clear not only how the MCA will operate, but also, and more importantly, that the golden straitjacket is far from a market-driven phenomenon, but is rather a political strategy designed to serve particular interests. A failing grade on the Heritage Foundation's *Index of Economic Freedom*, published annually by the *Wall Street Journal*, signals a higher risk for capitalists. They, in turn, punish countries by either capital flight or investment strikes. The assumptions inherent in these scores are also highly subjective. To be sure, the correlation between economic freedom, growth, and democracy has not been substantiated by history. Authoritarian Chile under the Pinochet regime produced the so-called neoliberal model in the South during the 1980s, while the 'developmental states' in East Asia helped produce the 'miracle economies'. Likewise, the assumption that economic freedom will quell historically and culturally rooted civil wars, oppression and human suffering in many of the failed states is not only based on flawed Eurocentric ideals, but also justifies the increasing physical and economic coercion undertaken in withholding private investment, and now public aid, from these states.

On another level, the MCA represents a change from a neoliberal to a neoconservative straitjacket. As Harvey notes, unlike the neoliberal agenda, the primary objective of neoconservativism

> is the establishment of and respect for order, both internally and upon the world stage. This implies strong leadership at the top and unwavering loyalty at the base, coupled with the construction of a hierarchy of power that is both secure and clear. To the neo-conservative movement, adherence to moral principle is also crucial (Harvey, 2003b: 190).

While there are various schools within conservative thought (authoritarian conservativism, paternalistic conservativism), I believe that the type to which Harvey is referring is libertarian conservativism. This strand advocates the greatest possible economic liberty and the least possible government regulation of social life, echoing laissez-faire neoliberalism. Unlike the latter, however, libertarian conservativism harnesses this to a belief in a more traditional, conservative social philosophy that stresses the importance of authority and duty, as embodied in the MCA and its reversal of the traditional aid formula: instead of giving aid to get the hoped-for reforms, it is based on reform before aid. Libertarian neoconservativism thus acts as a complementary stabilizer to the neoliberal straitjacket by justifying the need for greater and more explicit economic and physical coercion to stabilize laissez-faire forms of neoliberal global restructuring.

The MCA is infused with cultural and ideological dimensions. The recreation of the 'us' and 'them' divide, along the lines of the 'coalition of the willing' and the 'axis of evil', has acted to fill the vacuum left by Cold War rhetoric (the frequent characterization by Western governments and media of Communist regimes as unjust, backward, and diabolic) and distorts and blurs the growing contradictions of neoliberal globalization and American imperialism over the past several decades. As we will see, the MCA has appropriated the altruistic goals set out in the MDG and twisted the means to serve the ends of the American empire. While this new global development compact operates primarily through coercive means, it is legitimized to the American people and international system through the construction and reproduction of a discourse that views 'the other' as a passive and silent homogeneous unit that is unwilling to embrace neoliberal modernization, and thus remains a potential threat to the 'West'. Rather, such discourse as is found in the MCA renders the people of the colonized culture as powerless objects. Following Edward Said, the culture of powerlessness is enforced by a definition that anything written by those individuals located in the excluded states is deemed by the wider media, IFIs, bilateral donors, and private creditors and investors as illegitimate, non-knowledge, and nonsense (Said, 1979). The result of the culture of the 'powerless other' in official development discourse, particularly the MCA, has been the common-sense assumption that there is only one way to 'develop': by embracing the tenets of neoliberal globalization and Western democracy.

All told, the underlying logic of pre-emptive development evolves around the security/insecurity paradox: to safeguard neoliberal globalization and American imperial dominance it is vital to ensure that those states that have suffered most under market-led growth embrace the same neoliberal discipline that has led to high levels of insecurity in the first place.

CONCLUSION

The rise of pre-emptive development, as represented by the MCA, constituted the third and final window through which we could explore the capitalist nature of global governance. By drawing on an historical-materialist framework, I have argued that, while the MCA represents a new departure in terms of a more intrusive, coercive, and overtly US-led form of development, its content resembles that of the preceding official development agendas. Through the application of an historical-materialist perspective, the genesis and inner nature of the MCA were exposed as moments of the restructuring of US imperialism within neoliberal-led globalization. In attempting to deconstruct the MCA, I sought to go beyond the common-sense assumption that the MCA was a direct result of the tragic events of 9/11, in order to reveal the content of the MCA, as well as to shed more light on the increasingly coercive and intrusive expressions of US empire towards the Third World. To this end, I demonstrated that Bush's pre-emptive development agenda emerged from a combination of at least three factors – all of which were augmented, not caused, by the events of 9/11. First, there is a perceived crisis of confidence not only regarding neoliberal governance in the US, particularly in the post-speculative bubble era, but also regarding neoliberal governance in excluded states. Income levels have plunged in most parts of the developing world, poverty rates are on the rise, and the income gap between rich and poor countries has widened. Second, excluded states continue to receive very little in the form of private capital flows and bilateral aid. Third, the US economy, which has acted as the growth engine for the world, has been experiencing a deep economic slowdown since the bursting of its bubble after August 2000. Increased levels of unemployment not seen since 1994, spiralling budget and trade deficits, and unsustainable consumer and corporate debt levels, indicate a weak economy, which can no longer serve as the engine of growth for the rest of the world.

This discussion was useful not only in revealing the inner nature of the MCA, but also the basic thrust underlying the shifting nature of official development agendas, which in turn helps us grasp the capitalist dimension of global governance. As we saw, the MCA represents a heightened expression of coercion by the US of the poorest countries in the South. This growing coercion is tied to the conflict-led attempts by capitalists and states to restructure the social relations of capitalism in such a manner as to overcome the crisis of overaccumulation, while at the same time guaranteeing the conditions for the reproduction of these very social relations. This should give us pause regarding the conceptualizations of global governance advanced by enthusiasts such as the Commission on Global Governance.

As this chapter has demonstrated, while imperialism may take on different expressions under a Democratic or Republican administration, one thing remains constant: the compulsion for the

US to cling onto its power in global capitalism, so that capitalists may continue to influence the shape and direction of neoliberal restructuring strategies to ensure that they reap the highest material rewards, particularly in the face of general stagnation. Whether the MCA, combined with the World Bank's good governance principles of empowering development, will be able to stave off further aggression toward the US and its passive revolution remains to be seen, and, of course, will be contingent on struggle. What is clear is that, while the official development agenda continues to push all parts of the South to the exigencies of foreign capital by forcing these countries to adopt new forms of Anglo-American neoconservativism or risk the loss of any capital investment and aid, the present discontent with the existing governance structures, both at national (Brazil's Landless Peasants' Movement, the Zapatistas) and international (e.g., the World Social Forum, Seattle, and Cancun Protests) levels, will continue to grow in the South. This will in turn not only increase the already unsustainably low levels of legitimacy for the neoliberal programme, but also further constrict the golden straitjacket from which the US extracts much of its dominance (or 'imposed leadership'). In contrast to the rhetoric surrounding America's 'war on terrorism', the increasing security concern of the US government lies more in its need to intervene constantly, in an increasingly coercive manner, into the states and markets of the Third World in order to protect its interests, as opposed to its much-touted attempts at spreading democracy and freedom in the world. It appears that the trend towards intensified economic and military coercion appears to be the strategy to achieve the American Century propagated in the NSS, and not aspirations toward global economic governance.

On June 1, 2005, Paul Wolfowitz, former Deputy Secretary of Defense, and one of the key architects of the 2002 National Security Strategy, was appointed, with great support from President Bush, to head the World Bank. While, at the time of writing, it is too soon to make predictions of the nature of the 'third-generation' reforms, this appointment does send a very strong message to the development community and leaders of the Third World. We can be sure, however, that these reforms will rest on the same contradictions as their predecessors and will involve emphasis on a greater push towards political conformity through 'regime change', so as to serve better the interests of foreign capital while protecting capital interests at home. As I noted above, regime change does not translate into democracy, but rather political stability. The extent to which the inevitable forging of third-generation reforms under the Wolfowitz reign will take hold in the South depends, as always, on how well political groups organize to roll back and continue to delegitimize the neoliberal agenda.

6
Conclusion: Beyond Global Governance?

But our dominant feeling is of hope. We believe the most notable feature of the past 50 years has been the emancipation and empowerment of people. People today have more power to shape their future than ever before, and that could make all the difference.
    Commission on Global Governance, *Our Global Neighbourhood*, 1995: xiii.

Even by conservative estimates, 800 million people go to bed hungry. Would you allow this to happen if they were your own children? Yes, 30,000 children die every single day before they reach the age of five – just because they do not have enough food or medicine. Every 3.6 seconds another person dies of starvation. They are made to die. At the same time the world spends $1 trillion a year to make bombs and guns and to prepare for war.
    John Samuel, Keynote Address to the World Social Forum, April 2005.

THE ARGUMENT REVISITED

In contrast to the dominant mainstream debates about global economic governance, I have argued that this term must be grasped as a moment of global capitalism. This implies that its genesis and nature are shaped by the struggles and conflicts that are inherent in capital accumulation, particularly the tendency towards crisis and subsequent global restructuring strategies. This perspective allows us to deconstruct global governance, so as to understand its formation within these wider contradictions. The latter are closely linked to the changing nature of American empire and capitalist power in the world. An historical-materialist approach also helped us to grasp how the CGG's notion of global governance acts to normalize, neutralize, and legitimize increasingly austere forms of capitalist restructuring and expansion, which may be regarded as a deepening and broadening of neoliberalism that has taken place over the past several decades.

I suggested that there are at least three common-sense assumptions embedded in the mainstream understanding of global governance, primarily represented here by James Rosenau's work and the CGG. A critique of these assumptions was applied in each of the chapters, and it is worth listing them once again. The first assumption holds that globalization is an omnipotent external force that is inevitable. The second promotes the understanding that struggles take place on a level playing field, persuading a pluralist understanding of the world. And the third posits that global governance has positive consequences for the development of the global South. Through the implicit application of an historical-materialist approach, I sought to deconstruct these three common-sense assumptions that underpin global neoliberal restructuring.

In contrast to these mainstream assumptions, the three components of my version of historical materialism were (1) the social relations of capitalist production, (2) the inherent tendency to crisis of overaccumulation and restructuring, and (3) the role of state power exercised through neoliberal restructuring strategies, especially the part played by US imperialism. Taken together, these three interlocking axes formed the analytical frame I used as my primary tool to penetrate the apparently smooth and even surface of global governance by exposing the class-led struggles and contradictions that lie at the heart of this multi-level project. Drawing on this historical-materialist framework, I presented three windows through which to examine salient, although largely neglected, features of global governance, particularly as they pertained to North–South relations in the post-Bretton Woods era. The first window (Chapter 3) was represented by macro-strategies of corporate social responsibility, most notably the UNCTAD-sponsored Code for TNCs, and, more recently, the UN-led Global Compact. During this discussion, I focused on illuminating the similarities of these two seemingly divergent strategies. The second window corresponded to the transnational debt architecture. In Chapter 4, I attempted to describe and explain how the informal and *ad hoc* nature of transnational debt, especially in emerging markets, has emerged as a reaction to the ongoing crisis of overaccumulation, as it facilitates what David Harvey refers to as strategies of accumulation by dispossession. The third window related to official development strategies, such as President Bush's Millennium Challenge Account (MCA). In Chapter 5, I suggested that, while the form of the MCA represents an unabashed articulation of US-led imperialism with regard to the poorest regions in the South, the content of this allegedly novel strategy reflects the same attitudes that underlies the neoliberal agenda – namely, that the path to increased growth and prosperity lies in countries' willingness and ability to adopt policies that promote economic freedom and the rule of law.

Each window served the purpose of not only casting a different critical light on global governance, but also demystifying the common-sense assumptions tied to this term. There are several conclusions that may be drawn from our discussion. First, mainstream assumptions underpinning global governance assist not only in supporting, but also legitimizing the relations of power associated with the dominant US state. In doing so, global governance freezes the mounting contradictions tied to the crisis of hegemony. This has important implications for progressive social movements that are currently challenging neoliberal forms of global restructuring, as global governance builds false hope and false empowerment for these groups. Second, and more significantly, as our discussion of the Global Compact in Chapter 3 demonstrated, neoliberal strategies tied to global governance seek to co-opt and thus depoliticize radical grass-roots movements, as these strategies seek to mask American imperialism. However, this does not imply that all progressive struggles against capitalist exploitation and neoliberal dominance are doomed to failure. On the contrary, as our discussion of the aftermath of the Bretton Woods system demonstrated, the crisis of hegemony can open up new spaces for struggle towards a more equitable future. However, without critically understanding the competing strategies, such as neoliberal-led global governance, the objectives of these more progressive struggles towards a structural transformation of global capitalism may be either ignored, or, worse, relegated to confined spaces, such as the internet and 'open' summits (Johannesburg, 2002, on Sustainable Development, the UN Conference on Financing for Development in Monterrey, 2002) or 'closed' high-level summits (Quebec City Forum for the Free Trade Area of the Americas, 2001, the G-8 summits, the WTO Ministerial Conference in Doha, Qatar, in 2001, or the annual World Economic Forum in Davos, Switzerland) in which the ruling class only pays lip-service to the demands of those hurt the most by neoliberal-led globalization –the working poor, peasants, the homeless – so as to legitimize the status quo.

And third, as the crisis of US hegemony becomes aggravated by mounting contradictions and protests tied to neoliberal-led capitalist restructuring, such as the tensions between social and financial risks discussed in Chapter 4, or the MCA in Chapter 5, the ruling class in the US and its counterparts in other nation-states that reap material rewards from the continuation of neoliberal restructuring, become more coercive (economically and militarily). Indeed, after three decades of global neoliberal restructuring, all three topics discussed in this book point to a third, more malignant phase of neoliberalism, signalling not only deeper forms of economic, including environmental, exploitation, but also a rising level of legitimacy surrounding this form of political domination.

Despite the increasingly naked face of US imperialism, 'global governance' theorists, as well as international policy-makers, continue to employ, and thereby reproduce, the common-sense assumptions tied to this incredibly vague term. Yet it is precisely the popularity of the emptiness inherent in global governance that conceals, and thereby legitimizes, increased economic coercion by capitals and bourgeois states over vulnerable populations in the Third World. Why has such an empty buzzword gained so much appeal among academics, bureaucrats and diplomats? Why, even in the face of increased American unilateralism in the areas of global development and military intervention, both ruled by the overarching theme of the 'war on terrorism', have so many mainstream and radical academics chosen to ignore the power-laden and contradictory aspects of global governance? Why, in a world with increasing authoritarianism both in the South and in the developed world (e.g., the Patriot Act in the US), of protectionism witnessed not only in the backlash against the EU constitution by the Netherlands and France in 2005, but also mounting sentiments within the WTO, as well as rampant racial violence all over the globe, has the hegemonic position of the common values underpinning global governance not been challenged?

Although I focused on several issues that were neglected in the global economic governance literature in this book, there are many examples that highlight the anachronism of this term as an adequate descriptor of our times. The list of items showing the blatant lack of co-ordination, transparency, and accountability between the key actors of global governance such as the NGO sector, TNCs, international organizations, and national governments is long, but in the interests of space, we will look at two recent examples. The first pertains to the failure of the international community to intervene effectively in the genocidal activities in the Darfur region of Western Sudan. These activities, which have affected about 2 million people so far, and which have largely been carried out by government-supported militias, the 'Janjaweed', have conducted a frenzied attack on entire communities of African tribal farmers through slaughter, rape, starvation, and displacement. The international community remains paralysed in its indecision over the need to respect the sovereignty of the Sudanese state. Such consideration was not extended to Afghanistan in 2001 or Iraq in 2003. The second example relates to the inability or unwillingness of the international community to respond effectively to the Indian Ocean tsunami. Indeed, it has become blatantly clear that, six months after the tragedy little has been done, aside from immediate relief efforts, to help the victims and their families. The camps still lack adequate cooking and sanitation facilities; there remains a desperate need for counselling, as well as safety mechanisms to protect women and children in the camps; the housing conditions are still temporary and sub-standard (Nordic tents and perforated steel huts), and so on. One of the key issues in this case, as in the Darfur situation, is not the lack of funding, but the absence of co-operation and co-ordination among the national governments, international organizations, and powerful international NGOs, like the International Committee of the Red Cross, which controls approximately $400 million of relief aid in Sri Lanka alone. Indeed, it has an operating budget larger than the Sri Lankan government and some official donors in Sri Lanka.[1]

There is a plethora of examples that could be added to these two cases. The point here is not to create a shopping list of how private and public actors in the international community have continued to fail the poorest and most vulnerable. Sadly, this would be too easy a task. The point is that, without an adequate historical grasp of the power relations and contradictions from which neoliberal projects like the Commission on Global Governance and its many offshoots emerge, radical NGOs, development practitioners, grass-roots movements, students and academics will continue to struggle to reform the surface phenomena of capitalist society, as opposed to turning their attention to transforming the very foundation upon which ever-changing forms of political domination rest. Progressive struggles need not only to strive to understand and challenge the roots of power and oppression, but also to bridge the theory–practice divide. The 2005 campaign by G-8 countries to cancel the debt of 18 HIPCs is a case in point. This initiative by the leaders of the G-8 countries and their unlikely bedfellows – Hollywood, pop music icons, and progressive NGOs ('Make Poverty History') – is, to some, a successful and innovative attempt at dealing with poverty in the Third World. However, the simple removal of debt with the stroke of a pen by politicians of wealthy countries will not eradicate the historically embedded contradictions and power relations inherent in trade relations, the transnational debt architecture, or the increasing coercion in the international aid regime. Malnutrition, illness due to lack of clean water, HIV/AIDS, and other poverty-related problems will continue to plague the people of the HIPCs long after the debt has been eliminated. This, in turn, will lead to the need for more debt, with its accompanying Golden Noose.

NEW THEORETICAL DIRECTIONS IN THE STUDY OF WORLD POLITICS

There remains much room for new and critical scholarship aimed at challenging global governance, especially in the areas not covered by this book, such as race, gender, identity, culture, environment, food and agricultural regimes, new security issues, and labour studies. Given the complexity of these issues, it is of vital importance that those studying global governance issues, most of whom are students of international relations, begin to move beyond its narrow confines, including mainstream international political economy theories, which are rooted in the main concerns of political science – government power and policies – and seek to complement their state-centric analyses with historically informed empirical and theoretical work that seeks to draw on important analytical innovations in various disciplines and sub-disciplines, such as legal studies, economic geography, globalization studies, and social theory within the disciplines of sociology, cultural studies, and human anthropology. At the same time, students interested in radically exploring the various facets of global economic governance would do well to widen and deepen their analytical scope by relying on an historical-materialist framework that is informed by, although not limited to, the teachings of Marx, as this approach is the only perspective that allows the analyst to transcend the surface appearances of global capitalism so as to make sense of the underlying class-led conflicts, contradictions, and strategies that, in the final analysis, seek to reproduce the exploitative conditions inherent in capital accumulation. There are many scholars of what many now refer to as global political economy who not only differentiate themselves from traditional international political economy scholars, but also signal their sensitivity towards the importance of new actors, issues, and configurations of power. They have made great strides in their attempts to 'push the envelope' of traditional ways of thinking about and explaining the world. More work needs to be done, however, in our attempts at forging new and open interdisciplinary frameworks especially with regard to issues affecting social, cultural, religious, gender, racial, and political oppression, and exploitation within the national boundaries of global capitalism.

Innovatively eclectic, yet logically consistent, theoretical frameworks are necessary to make sense of an increasingly complex and unequal world. Likewise, new theoretical directions must be found if we are to deconstruct the common-sense assumptions behind ideologically driven concepts like global governance, and expose their inner nature and the specific interests for which they have been created. This is an important first step in understanding the world, so that we can work towards changing it.

Notes

1 GLOBAL GOVERNANCE IN QUESTION

1. The G-77 refers to a loose coalition of Third World countries, which came together in 1964 under the 'Joint Declaration of the Seventy- Seven Countries', which was issued at the United Nations Conference on Trade and Development. The G-77 was designed to promote greater strength in international negotiations with regard to trade and other development initiatives. Since 1964, the G-77 has expanded to 133 member countries. In March 2005, the G-20+ consisted of 21 nations: Argentina, Brazil, Bolivia, Chile, China, Cuba, Egypt, Guatemala, India, Indonesia, Mexico, Nigeria, Pakistan, Paraguay, Philippines, South Africa, Tanzania, Thailand, Uruguay, Venezuela and Zimbabwe. The G-20+ should not be confused with the G-20, which was formed at the G-7 Cologne Summit of 1999 to include 'systematically important' emerging markets (see Soederberg, 2004). For more information about the WTO and the various Ministerial Meetings, see http://www.wto.org/english/thewto_e/whatis_e/whatis_ e.htm. For more critical discussions about this multilateral institution, see the World Development Movement: www.wdm.org.uk and the Third World Network: http://www.twnside.org.sg/trade.htm.

2. Indeed, there are many issues that cast a critical light on notions of global governance, such as international civil society (Colás, 2002; Anheier et al., 2002), encompassing both global and local struggles, particularly urbanization studies (Davis, 1992; 2004; Keil, 1998; Brenner, 2004; Drainville, 2004); gender relations (Bakker, 1994); the environment (Lipschutz and Mayer, 1996; Hempel, 1996; Young, 1997); and new wars (Duffield, 2001; Kaldor, 1999).

3. The following excerpt is an excellent explanation of currency speculation:

> Short-selling, simply put, is the process by which you sell something that you do not own. Typically, this is stock, but it can also be currency, as we will see later. Short-selling goes against the 'buy low, sell high' logic that most associate with the stock market (known as 'selling long'). Instead, it involves borrowing stock, for a fee, from a broker. You then sell this stock, hoping that the price of the stock drops before you must return the stock to its owner. You then buy back the stock at its lower price (at a profit) and return it to its owner.
>
> The reason that selling short is seen as riskier than selling long is because when you buy a share of stock at $50, the maximum risk to you is $50, because the price can only drop to $0. However, when you short-sell that same stock, there is no limit to how high the price of the share can rise (instead of falling, as desired). Hence, the potential for your loss is without limit.

For this reason, short-selling alone is typically a luxury of the wealthy, however a combination of short-selling and long-selling is often used to 'hedge the bets' of both, in what are aptly named 'hedge funds'.

Downloaded on September 1, 2004. Available at: http://chris.quietlife. net/archives/000328.html. (For more discussion about speculation, see Harmes, 2001; 2002; Soros, 1987.)

4. 'Most favoured nation' refers to a clause in a trade agreement between two countries providing that each is to extend to the country the same trading privileges it extends to its other trading partners. Most favoured nation clauses are generally subject to exceptions for free trade areas (such as NAFTA) and customs unions (such as the European Union).

5. Quoted from the United Nations Educational, Scientific, and Cultural Organization (UNESCO) on September 1, 2004. Available at: http://www. unesco.org/culture/industries/trade/html_eng/question11.shtml.

6. OPEC members currently include: Algeria, Indonesia, Iran, Iraq, Kuwait, Libya, Nigeria, Qatar, Saudi Arabia, the United Arab Emirates, and Venezuela. For more information about OPEC, see its official website: http://www.opec.org/homepage/frame.htm.

7. According to the Organization for Economic Co-operation and Development (OECD), in a definition which is also largely shared by the WTO, foreign direct investment (FDI) may be described in the following manner:

the objective of obtaining a lasting interest by a resident entity in one country ('direct investor') in an entity resident in an economy other than that of the investor ('direct investment enterprise'), which can be either a public or private actor that is either incorporated or unincorporated. The lasting interest implies the existence of a long-term relationship between the direct investor and the enterprise and a significant degree of influence on the management of the enterprise.

Direct investment involves the initial transaction between the two entities, and all subsequent capital transactions not only between these entities but also among affiliated enterprises, both incorporated and unincorporated (OECD, 1999: 7–8). 'Ordinarily, the threshold for FDI is ownership of "10 percent or more of the ordinary shares or voting power" of a business entity' (IMF Balance of Payments Manual, 1993, cited at http://www.globalization101.org/issue/investment/1–1.asp).

8. Foreign portfolio investment (FPI) represents a

category of investment instruments that are more easily traded, may be less permanent, and do not represent a controlling stake in an enterprise. These include investments via equity instruments (stocks) or debt (bonds) of a foreign enterprise which does not necessarily represent a long-term interest. Although FDI, almost by definition, tends to be undertaken by multinational corporations, FPI comes from more diverse sources, and may originate, for example, from a small company's pension fund or through mutual funds held by individuals. The returns that an investor acquires on FPI usually take the form of interest payments or non-voting dividends. Investments in FPI that are made for less than one year are distinguished as short-term portfolio flows ... (Quoted from http://www.globalization101.org/issue/investment/1–1.asp).

9. The original name of this organisation was the Economic Commission of Latin America (ECLA). The ECLA became the ECLAC (United Nations Economic Commission for Latin America and the Caribbean) in 1984.
10. For more information see the UNIFEM website: http://www.unifem.org/.
11. The Report of the Brandt Commission is available at http://www.brandt21forum.info/BrandtCommission2.htm.
12. For more information, see http://www.trilateral.org/about.htm.
13. The G-8 Information Centre at the University of Toronto is an excellent source for publications and meetings: http://www.g7.utoronto.ca/what_is_g8.html.
14. It is worth noting that Dr Boutros-Ghali's second term was not renewed due to a veto by the US government. One of the main reasons for this veto was that the US government perceived Dr Boutros-Ghali as a controversial figure, especially with regard to his alignment with the Third World. The former Secretary-General has stated that it is his 'duty to defend the "orphans" (the poor countries) against the ethnocentrism of the dominant powers'. This stance, in turn, threatened to reveal the power structures within the UN. 'Why Washington wants rid of Mr Boutros-Ghali,' *Le Monde Diplomatique*, November 1996. Available at: http://mondediplo.com/1996/11/un.
15. Although some writers make a distinction between multinational corporations and transnational corporations, these terms will be used interchangeably in this book (Hirst and Thompson, 1996; Radice, 1975). I discuss these actors in more detail in the next chapter.

2   TRANSCENDING COMMON SENSE: TOWARDS AN HISTORICAL-MATERIALIST CRITIQUE OF GLOBAL GOVERNANCE

1. Hirst and Thompson list the following main points of their argument:

    i)   The present highly internationalized economy is not unprecedented: it is one of a number of distinct conjunctures or states of the international economy that have existed since an economy based on modern industrial technology began to be generalized from the 1860s. In some respects, the current international economy is *less* open and integrated than the regime that prevailed from 1870 to 1914.

    ii) Genuinely transnational companies (TNCs) appear to be relatively rare. Most companies are nationally based and trade multinationally on the strength of a major national location of production and sales and there seems to be no major tendency towards the growth of truly international companies.

iii) Capital mobility is not producing a massive shift of investment and employment from the advanced to the developing countries. Rather, foreign direct investment is highly concentrated among the advanced industrialised economies and the Third World remains marginal in investment and trade, a small minority of newly industrialised countries [such as China and India] apart.

iv) As some extreme advocates of globalization recognize, the world economy is far from being genuinely 'global'. Rather, trade, investment and financial flows are concentrated in the Triad of [the Europe Union], Japan and North America and this dominance seems set to continue.

v) These major economic powers, the G3, thus have the capacity, especially if they co-ordinate policy, to exert powerful governance pressures over financial markets and other economic tendencies (Hirst and Thompson, 1996: 2–3).

2. Italian Statistician Corrado Gini invented a measure of income inequality. The Gini coefficient is a number between zero and one. Zero means perfect equality in terms of income, whereas one means perfect inequality (where one person possesses all the income, and everyone else has nothing). For more information, see http://en.wikipedia.org/wiki/Gini_coefficient.

3. It should be kept in mind that the external and internal relations of power are not mutually exclusive. The configurations of relations of power between, for example, state officials, labour groups, and capitals in any given country are shaped by the country's economic and political interactions with other states – especially, although not limited to, more powerful countries such as the US. For the example of Mexico, see Soederberg (2001) 'State, Crisis and Capital Accumulation in Mexico', *Historical Materialism*, No. 9. For the example of Canada, see Soederberg (2001) 'Political Restructuring of Exploitation: An Historical Materialist Account of the Emergence of Neoliberalism in Canada', *Cultural Logic*, Vol. 3 (1). Available at: http://eserver.org/clogic/3–1&2/soederberg. html.

4. Macroeconomics is a branch of economics that examines the behaviour of an economy through a wide-angled lens (or aggregate level), as opposed to studying the behaviour of specific individuals and firms (microeconomics). Macroeconomics focuses on issues such as inflation, unemployment, and industrial production. It also concerns itself with the study of the effect of government policy (or, more specifically, macroeconomic policy) on these factors. Two key macroeconomic policies are: monetary policy (central bank policies determining the interest rate and controlling the country's money supply) and fiscal policy (taxation and spending levels of the government). To ensure that debtor countries are adhering to 'sound' macroeconomic fundamentals, the IMF has launched Public Information Notices (or PINs). PINs are posted regularly on the IMF website. PINs act as a means of achieving transparency by disseminating information about the condition of debtor countries' macroeconomic fundamentals PINs also serve as a means of surveillance. For more information, see the PINs website at http://www.imf.org/cgi-shl/create_x.pl?pn+1999. For a more theoretical analysis of the PINs and the changing nature of the IMF, see

Soederberg, 'Grafting Stability on to Globalization? Deconstructing the IMF's Recent Bid for Transparency', *Third World Quarterly*, Vol. 22 (5): 849–64.

5. 'Workers' remittances refer to transfers in cash or in kind from migrants [legal or illegal] to resident households in the countries of origin [normally located in the Third World]. Usually these are ongoing transfers between members of the same family, with persons abroad being absent for a year or longer.' Downloaded on June 2, 2004. Available at: Migration Information Source, http://www.migrationinformation.org/USfocus/display.cfm?ID=137.

6. Historical materialism may be regarded as the methodology of Marxism. Alternatively, historical materialism has been called a radical critique of political economy (cf. Bonefeld and Holloway, 1995; Bonefeld and Psychopedis, 2000; Saad-Filho, 2002), or, simply, radical political economy.

7. For a discussion of primitive accumulation in China and Russia, see N. Holstrom and R. Smith, 'The Necessity of Gangster Capitalism: Primitive Accumulation in Russia and China', *Monthly Review*, February 2000. Available at: http://www.findarticles.com/p/articles/mi_m1132/is_9_51/ai_59948726.

8. Unlike the classical theories of imperialism that sprang from the Second International (1889–1914), and which focused on territorial expansionism and inter-imperialist wars, the more recent wave of theories of imperialism, or what some refer to as the 'new imperialism', coincided with the end of direct colonial rule in many countries of the South in the 1950s and 1960s, and new capitalist strategies aimed at overcoming the crisis of overaccumulation in the 1970s (Poulantzas, 1974; 2000; Mandel, 1975; Radice, 1975; Brewer, 1980; Chilcote, 2000).

3   GLOBAL GOVERNANCE AND CORPORATE SOCIAL RESONSIBILITY

1. The World Business Council for Sustainable Development (WBCSD) was established in 1991 to represent business interests at the Rio Earth Summit. According to its website, 'the WBCSD is a coalition of 170 international companies united by a shared commitment to sustainable development through economic growth, ecological balance and social progress'. For more information, see http://www.wbcsd.ch.

2. For more information about Oxfam, see http://www.oxfam.org.uk/about_us/index.htm.

3. Australia's Consumer Association, 'In good company: social responsibility'. Downloaded on June 2, 2004. Available at: http://www.choice.com.au/viewArticle.aspx?id=104234&catId=100268&tid=100008&p=8.

4. 'TNCs' refers to incorporated (a firm that has been formed into a legal corporation) or unincorporated enterprises comprising parent enterprises and their foreign affiliates. A parent company (headquarters) controls assets of other entities in countries other than its home country, usually by owning an equity capital stake (cash or goods raised from owners) of 10 per cent or more of the ordinary shares or voting power is considered

the threshold for the control of assets. A foreign affiliate is defined as an incorporated or unincorporated enterprise in which an investor, who is a resident of another country, owns a stake that permits a lasting interest in the management of that enterprise, usually an equity stake of 10 per cent (UNCTAD, 2002). While we normally associate huge conglomerates employing 500 or more people with the term TNC, John Stopford, writing in the late 1990s, points out that the surge in TNC growth is driven by a spate of newcomers, many of whom are rather small. 'Most of the estimated 45,000 firms that operate internationally employ fewer than 250 people. It is commonplace to find service companies that maintain fewer than 100 employees operating across more than 15 countries' (Stopford, 1998: 14). Nonetheless, the market is still dominated by 500 large TNCs.

5. 'Beggar-thy-neighbour policies' refers to those policies undertaken by governments to increase their country's prosperity (usually by reducing its unemployment) at the expense of prosperity in other countries (especially by increasing their unemployment). For example, the government of country A subsidizes its domestic industries. This in turn allows its industries to lower their costs of manufacturing, and thus enables the company of country A to sell its products at a cheaper price on the international market, consequently undercutting the prices of other companies in other countries, who did not receive government subsidy. Thus, a company from country B can no longer compete with country A's exports, and thus must lay off workers. This strategy also includes competitive currency devaluations, which were rampant in the post-1973 era of floating exchange rates.

6. TNCs did not emerge during this period – indeed, according to some observers, they date back to 1867 (Sklair, 2002). What's more, while most TNCs are based in advanced industrialized countries and are owned and controlled by capitalists and shareholders of those countries, Leslie Sklair and Peter Robbins demonstrate that major corporations from the global South operate abroad as well, albeit in low-technology sectors (Sklair and Robbins, 2002; cf. Tolentino, 2000).

7. In their seminal work, Paul Baran and Paul Sweezy sought to understand the generation and absorption of the surplus under conditions of monopoly capitalism in the form of large corporations. For Baran and Sweezy, surplus is

the difference between what a society produces and the costs of producing it. The size of the surplus is an index of productivity and wealth, of how much freedom a society has to accomplish whatever goals it may set for itself. The composition of the surplus shows how it uses that freedom: how much it invests in expanding its productive capacity; how much it consumes in various forms, how much it wastes and in what ways (Baran and Sweezy, 1966: 9–10).

8. 'FDI' describes any equity holding across national borders that affords the owner substantial control over the entity. According to the OECD and UNCTAD, this is defined as a 10 per cent holding or greater, although,

through capitalist centralization strategies, most FDI ends up as 100 per cent ownership by a TNC (UNCTAD, 2003).

9. As Rhys Jenkins notes, TNCs are not necessarily a major source of new technology. 'In fact only about a fifth of a sample of post-war innovations were originally introduced by TNCs [see Vernon, 1977: 40], but they have played a major role in commercializing new technology' (Jenkins, 1987: 10).

10. A caveat is in order here. Although I draw on Prebisch's version of dependency, it should be stressed that there is not one homogeneous school of dependency theory, but various competing approaches and paradigms ranging in degrees of radicalness (see Frank, 1981; Cardoso and Faletto, 1979; Amin, 1974).

11. While apartheid laws were enacted in 1948, it wasn't until the UN arms embargo on South Africa became mandatory in 1977 that the world began to take notice of this practice of institutionalized racism and violence.

12. For more information about the ICCR see, http://www.iccr.org.

13. The US public pension funds, such as the California Public Employees' Retirement System or CalPERS, are a case in point. The sheer number of ethical mutual funds that have emerged over the past few decades is also indicative of the rise of a 'socially responsible investment movement'.

14. Although they never explicitly cite her work in their article, the term 'structural power' was coined by the late Susan Strange. This term captures the increasingly complex and competitive games being played out in the world between states and between economic enterprises. 'Structural power confers the power to decide how things shall be done, the power to shape frameworks within which states relate to each other, relate to people, or relate to corporate enterprises' (Strange, 1994: 25).

15. For more information see UNCTAD's Investment, Technology and Enterprise Development website at http://www.unctad.org/Templates/StartPage.asp?intItemID=2983&lang=1.

16. For more information see http://www.fairlabor.org.

17. For a listing of the ILO's Conventions see http://www.ilo.org/public/english/standards/norm/whatare/fundam/.

18. For more information see http://www2.coca-cola.com/citizenship/index.html.

19. For more information see http://www.shell.com/home/Framework?siteId=home

20. For more information see http://www.mcdonalds.com/corp/values/socialrespons.html.

21. For more information see http://www.globalreporting.org.

22. For more information see http://www.ceres.org/.

23. For more information see http://www.cepaa.org/SA8000/SA8000.htm.

24. For more information see http://www.princeofwales.gov.uk/trusts/bus_forum.html.

25. These guidelines are available online at http://www.wto.org/english/forums_e/ngo_e/guide_e.htm.

26. Founded in 1970, the pro-business World Economic Forum usually holds its annual meeting in Davos, Switzerland. The World Economic Forum's

members are mostly the world's 1,000 leading companies, along with 200 smaller businesses, many from the developing world, that play a potent role in their industry or region. For more information see http://www. weforum.org. It should be noted that the World Social Forum, which holds its annual meetings in the South (Porto Alegre, Brazil, Mumbai in India) , bringing together individuals, groups, and organizations who oppose the manifestations of global neoliberal-led capital restructuring. For more information about the World Social Forum, see: http://www. nadir.org/nadir/initiativ/agp/free/wsf.

27. John Gerard Ruggie, a Harvard professor of government, assumed the position of Assistant Secretary-General and Chief Advisor for strategic planning to the UN Secretary-General Kofi Annan. During his tenure at the UN, Ruggie was a key architect of the GC.

28. For more information, see http://www.unglobalcompact.org/ Portal/?NavigationTarget=/roles/portal_user/aboutTheGC/nf/nf/ theNinePrinciples.

29. For more information see http://www.unglobalcompact.org/ Portal/?NavigationTarget=/roles/portal_user/aboutTheGC/nf/nf/ theNinePrinciples.

30. For more information see http://www.unglobalcompact.org/ Portal/?NavigationTarget=/roles/portal_user/aboutTheGC/nf/nf/ theNinePrinciples.

31. For more information see http://www.iccwbo.org/home/menu_global_ compact.asp.

32. For more information see http://www.corpwatch.org/article. php?list=type&type=16.

4 MANAGING SOVEREIGN DEFAULT WITHIN THE TRANSNATIONAL DEBT ARCHITECTURE

1. A provisional or contingency clause within a contract between the bondholders and the purchasers of the bonds (governments, corporations, etc.) that makes performance under the contract conditional upon the occurrence of a bankruptcy or default. More importantly, collective action clauses, as defined by the IMF, imply that there are majority restructuring and majority enforcement provisions at the time of the sale. For instance, in the case of Argentina, it would be a majority of bondholders that should manage and determine repayment schedules and methods, as opposed to public bodies such as the IMF.

2. Middle-income countries, or, what is the same thing, emerging markets, will be the focus of this chapter for one important reason: unlike low-income countries, many of which are subsumed under the World Bank's 1996 Highly Indebted Poor Countries (HIPCs) Initiative, middle-income countries receive the highest amount of private loans in the form of foreign portfolio investment (see the IMF's *Global Development Finance*, various years). Based on gross national income (GNI), the World Bank uses three main categories of developing countries: low income ($735 or less); lower-middle income ($736–$2,935); upper-middle income

($2,936–$9,075); and high income ($9,076 or more). See, for example, http://www.worldbank.org/data/countryclass/countryclass.html.

3. External debt refers to 'debt owed to creditors outside the country. This includes debt owed to private commercial banks, debt owed to other governments or debt owed to the international financial institutions such as the IMF and World Bank.' Quoted in *Citizens' Network on Essential Services*, downloaded on June 3, 2004. from http://www.servicesforall.org/html/el_menu1.shtml#E.

4. 'Keynesianism' refers to ideas and policies derived from the theories of John Maynard Keynes (1883–1946). Unlike neoclassical economists, whose theories underpin the neoliberal agenda, Keynesians believe that government intervention in the economy – especially to promote demand – is an important strategy to stimulate business activity and increase employment. Keynes was one of the main architects of the BWS.

5. The second main feature of the BWS was the US dollar–gold fixed exchange rate system. This currency system had the effect of making currencies more predictable and thus stable for both trade and credit relations, by avoiding competitive currency devaluations at all costs. This imperative has been abandoned in the post-Bretton Woods era, where the values of freely floating exchange rates are, theoretically speaking, to be determined by supply and demand, but, in reality, are largely influenced by geo-political power relations, particularly in relation to the US dollar and currencies of the global South (see Cohen, 1998; 2003; Helleiner, 2003).

6. For more information about fetishism, see Marx's discussion of 'commodity fetishism' in the first chapter of Volume 1 of *Capital* (Marx, 1990).

7. For an excellent analysis of the drastic and negative transformation of the experience of work for the majority of Argentines since the convertibility regime in 1991, see Patroni, 2004. Marcus Taylor provides a similar historical account of labour in Chile under neoliberal rule (M. Taylor, 2002).

8. 'Current account' refers to part of a country's balance-of-payments accounts that records payments and receipts arising from trade in goods and services, and from interest and dividends earned by capital owned in one country and invested in another (Lipsey et al., 1991).

9. For example, Rosa Luxemburg, writing in the early 1900s, argued that public loans from what she termed older to younger countries assisted in capital accumulation, as these loans had various functions: '(a) it serves to convert money of non-capitalist groups into capital, i.e., money both as a commodity equivalent (lower middle-class savings) and as fund of consumption for the hangers-on of the capitalist class; (b) it serves to transform money capital into productive capital by means of state enterprises – railroad building and military supplies; (c) it serves to divert accumulated capital from the old capitalist countries to young ones' (Luxemburg, 2003: 401).

10. A Ponzi scheme is a fraudulent investment operation, illegal in many countries. Named after Charles Ponzi, it broadly entails paying returns to investors out of the money raised from subsequent investors. Through

his scheme, which ran from 1919 to 1920 in the US, Ponzi paid his investors 50 per cent interest on short-term investments. These payments were, however, being made with the money from new investors. As long as there is an adequate number of new investors, a Ponzi scheme can continue.

11. For more information on this responsibility, see http://www.imf.org/external/np/exr/facts/surv.htm.

12. The so-called 'Heimann decision' effectively assisted American banks to overcome the legal limits placed on lending practices to the South. For example, prior to this decision US banks were not permitted to lend more than 10 per cent of their capital to any single person, co-partnership (a partnership in which employees get a share of profits in addition to their wages), association, or corporation. In the context of American accounting practice, the Heimann decision allowed the interpretation of a legal person to apply to separate financial units. Thus, foreign governments (which were viewed as 'legal persons') could divide their bureaucracy into separate financial entities. Each bureaucratic unit (or department) was treated as a 'legal person'. As such, banks were able to lend to bureaucratic units without fear of hitting the overall 10 per cent limit. That is, as long as they remained within the 10 per cent limit per bureaucratic unit.

13. Unlike the primary market in which the original issuance of securities (i.e. stocks and bonds) occurs, a secondary market is a market in which an investor purchases securities indirectly from other investors, as opposed to the issuer.

14. A capital account is the part of the international balance-of-payments that covers investment and loans from one country to another.

15. According to the US Securities Exchange Act of 1934, a security is defined as

> [a]ny, note, stock, treasury stock, bond, debenture, certificate of interest or participation in any profit-sharing agreement or in any oil, gas, or other mineral royalty or lease, any collateral trust certificate, pre-organisation certificate or subscription, transferable share, investment contract, voting-trust certificate, certificate of deposit, for a security, any put, call, straddle, option, or privilege on any security, certificate of deposit, or group or index of securities (including any interest therein or based on the value thereof), or any put, call, straddle, option, or privilege entered into on a national securities exchange relating to foreign currency, or in general, any instrument commonly known as a security; or any certificate of interest or participation in, temporary or interim certificate for, receipt for, or warrant or right to subscribe to or purchase, any of the foregoing; but shall not include currency or any note, draft, bill of exchange, or banker's acceptance which has a maturity at the time of issuance of not exceeding nine months, exclusive of days of grace, or any renewal thereof the maturity of which is likewise limited.

Downloaded on March 2, 2004 from http://www.investorwords.com/4446/security.html.

16. Gross domestic product (GDP) refers to the market value of all goods and services produced in a year within a country's borders. The GDP is the standard measure of the overall size of a national economy. As the Canadian government website suggests, 'GDP is a limited measure insofar as it does not take certain activities into account that are "outside the market" – for example, the value of work done within the home, or by volunteer workers, or the harmful effects on human health from air and water pollution.' Downloaded on June 1, 2004 from http://canadianeconomy.gc.ca/english/economy/gdp2.html.

17. According to Jack Boorman there were essentially four proposals under debate: (1) the SDRM, (2) the CACs, (3) to leave things 'as is' and to continue to muddle through, and (4) a two-step process tabled by J. P. Morgan, which involved the following: 'creditors would effectively exchange outstanding debt for claims which include CACs which could then be used, in step two, to facilitate a restructuring agreement between a sovereign debtor and those creditors' (Boorman, 2002). It is interesting to note that Boorman fails to acknowledge the alternative put forward by many representatives of global civil society organizations such as Jubilee 2002, and multilateral organizations such as UNCTAD – namely, Chapter 9 bankruptcy procedures.

18. Interestingly, the SDRM was not based upon Chapter 9 of the US legal code. Unlike Chapter 11, which applies to corporations, Chapter 9 applies to municipal and other public institutions. Chapter 9 recognizes that when a public government institution enters into insolvency, the subsequent debt restructuring must acknowledge the human and social rights of the population in the form of, for example, education, health, and other forms of welfare provision. For more information, see Susanne Soederberg and Marcus Taylor (2004) 'The Latin American Debt Crisis and its Implications for Managing Financial and Social Risk' – policy document prepared for the Canadian Foundation of the Americas (FOCAL) in March 2004, and available at: www.focal.ca.

19. The IMFC also welcomed the announcement that, by June 2003, those European Union countries issuing bonds under foreign jurisdictions would include CACs. The Mexican government was the first to include CACs in its sovereign bond issues in 2003. Time will tell whether CACs will be able to provide a buttress against the next crisis.

20. For a critique of the role played by the IMF in the Argentine default, see the Independent Evaluation Office (IEO) of the IMF's *Report on the Evaluation of the Role of the IMF in Argentina, 1991–2001*, available at http://www.imf.org/External/NP/ieo/2004/arg/eng/index.htm.

5   GLOBAL GOVERNANCE AND DEVELOPMENT ASSISTANCE: THE CASE OF AMERICA'S MILLENNIUM CHALLENGE ACCOUNT

1. For more information about the Millennium Development Goals, see http://www.developmentgoals.org.

2. Bush announced the creation of the MCA in March 2003. As of June 18, 2003, the Senate Foreign Relations Committee and the House

International Relations Committee have authorized the creation of the MCA.

3. It should be stressed that the amount of spending put forward by the Bush Administration is contingent on budgetary approval by Congress. Both House and Senate Budget Committees have cut ambitious amounts. This will be discussed in more detail in the second half of the chapter. For now, suffice it to say that, viewed through a wider lens, US levels of developmental aid, broadly defined, have been decreasing since the 1960s. The spending levels of the MCA are not as dramatic as the Bush administration makes them out to be. What concerns us here, however, is not the amount of aid, but the pre-emptive form in which this aid is distributed, and, in turn, its disciplinary characteristics (see Daalder et al., 2002: 5).

4. Interview with a Country Director at the Millennium Challenge Corporation, Arlington, Virginia, May 9, 2005.

5. The Project for the New American Century is a non-profit organization that is dedicated to promoting a 'few fundamental propositions: that American leadership is good both for America and for the world; that such leadership requires military strength, diplomatic energy and commitment to moral principle; and that too few political leaders today are making the case for global leadership'. For more information, see http://www. newamericancentury.org.

6. 'Terrorism' is a highly contested term. Its meaning is largely determined by who is doing the defining. 'Terrorist', for example, is a term of abuse generally used against groups who engage in violent behaviour, by people who oppose the goals of the group. It carries the connotation that suffering has been caused to helpless victims. As Peter Willetts rightly notes, the term 'terrorist' 'might be more appropriately applied to those, including governments, who use indiscriminate violence for the purpose of political intimidation' (Willetts, 1999: 297). Heather Turcotte and Ronnie Lipschutz provide an interesting examination of terrorism by exploring ways in which the concept 'terrorist' is constructed through textual analysis (Lipschutz and Turcotte, 2005).

7. In proportion to its size, the US spends the least of all the wealthy countries. In 2002, for example, it spent only 0.12 per cent of its GDP. To put this in perspective, Denmark donated almost 1 per cent of GDP in bilateral aid – quoted in 'The Solidarité Summit', *The Economist*, May 30, 2003.

8. See Mark Rupert's 'Anti-Friedman Page', at http://www.maxwell.syr.edu/maxpages/faculty/merupert/Anti-Friedman.htm.

9. In the early 1980s, for example, low-income countries experienced a decline in per capita income of 1.4 per cent, the number of people living on less than $1 a day increased from 1,197 million in 1987 to 1,214 million in 1998, and the 1999 UNDP Human Development Report notes that, whereas the income gap between the 20 per cent of the richest people in the wealthiest countries in the world and the 20 per cent of the poorest was 30:1 in 1960, the gap was 74:1 in 1997. UNDP, *Human Development Report 1999: Globalization with a Human Face*, at http://hdr.undp.org/reports/global/1999/en.

10. Aside from the 'celebrity critics', such as Joseph Stiglitz, Ravi Kanbur, and Jeffrey Sachs, the voices of conservative dissenters in Washington, who have long argued for the abolition of the IMF and World Bank, were not only becoming louder, but also had a growing and sympathetic audience. The Heritage Foundation (now a key player in the MCA) and the Cato Institute, for example, have charged the IMF with eliminating the discipline of risk in private markets (moral hazard) by interfering in the 'natural rationality' of markets through bailouts and aid packages. See, for example, Alan Reynolds of the Cato Institute, 'The IMF's Suffocating Embrace', at http://www.worldtrademag.com/CDA/ArticleInformation/features/BNP__Features__Item/0,3483,91669,00.html; Edwin J. Feulner, Jr., 'The IMF Needs Real Reforms, Not More Money', Heritage Foundation, *Backgrounder* No. 1175, May 9, 1998; Johnson and Schaefer, 'No New Funding for the IMF,' Heritage Foundation, *Backgrounder Update* No. 287, September 23, 1997.

11. It should be noted that the

> share of U.S. resources devoted to development, humanitarian or economic aid for other countries has generally fallen since the mid-1960s. The overall decline has been substantial, reducing such spending to exceptionally low levels for the United States. The share of national resources the United States contributes in aid to the world's poorest nations is now far lower than the share that any other industrialized country contributes, and is at one of the lowest levels in the post-World War II era.

The figures stated here are expressed in 2000 dollars and adjusted for inflation. Quoted in Shapiro, 2000.

12. IMF, *IMF Survey*, Vol. 30, No. 7, 2001: 104.

13. According to the US Labour Department, the unemployment rate rose in May to 6.1 per cent – its highest level since July 1994. 'Unemployment up to 6.1 per cent in May', *Financial Times*, June 6, 2003.

14. Since June 2004, however, the Federal Reserve has begun to raise interest rates, although it is still considered relatively low compared to previous historic periods.

15. It is worth highlighting that the ruling class is not understood here as a homogeneous social force that wields instrumental rule over the capitalist state. See Chapter 2 for more on the state and the capitalist class.

16. See, for example, PBS Frontline, http://www.pbs.org/wgbh/pages/frontline/shows/iraq/etc/wolf.html.

17. These two indictors are defined and quantitatively measured by Freedom House. For more information, see Freedom House's 2003 *Freedom in the World: Country and Territory Report*, at http://www.freedomhouse.org/research/freeworld/2003/countries.htm.

18. More information about the American Enterprise Institute is available at http://www.aei.org.

19. Of course, the highly subjective and self-serving aspects of this notion are not called into question by the US government. For a critical assessment, see Martin Khor, '"Failed States" Theory Can Cause Global Anarchy', *Third*

World Network, March 4, 2002 at http://www.twnside.org.sg/title/et0125.htm.

20. Of course, the exploitative and repressive nature of centuries of imperial and colonial rule are not brought into the official explanation as to why these states have 'failed' to serve dominant capitalist interests properly.

21. It should be mentioned that, from the early 1980s the United States began to exercise its muscle in a much more unilateral and pre-emptive manner towards the International Development Association – see Kapur, 2002.

22. See, for example, Schaefer, 2001.

23. For more details on the Millennium Declaration, see the United Nations website at http://www.un.org/millennium/declaration/ares552e.htm.

24. According the White House's summary and analysis of the President's 2005 budget,

> The budget includes $2.5 billion for this [MCA] initiative, $1.5 billion more than the funding provided for 2004. Funds from the MCA are made available on a competitive basis to countries with low and moderate per capita incomes. Countries receive MCA funds based on their performance on 16 economic and political indicators, grouped into three clusters: good governance, investment in people, and economic policy. The Administration has indicated its intention to request MCA levels adequate to provide $5 billion in annual assistance by 2006. Meeting this level in next year's budget would require an additional $2.5 billion beyond the levels in the 2005 budget.

Downloaded on September 5, 2004. Available at http://www.house.gov/budget_democrats/pres_budgets/fy2004/fy04update/fy2005/150.htm.

25. The World Bank Institute (WBI) is a part of the World Bank Group. The goal of the WBI is to create 'learning opportunities for countries, World Bank staff and clients, and people committed to poverty reduction and sustainable development. WBI's work program includes training, policy consultations, and the creation and support of knowledge networks related to international economic and social development.' See http://www.worldbank.org/wbi/.

26. According to its website, Freedom House, 'a non-profit, non-partisan organisation, is a clear voice for democracy and freedom around the world. Through a vast array of international programs and publications, Freedom House is working to advance the remarkable worldwide expansion of political and economic freedom.' Freedom House was established around the same time as the Bretton Woods Institutions, and is sponsored by, *inter alia*, the Soros Foundation, USAID, and the Ford Foundation. For more information, see http://www.freedomhouse.org.

27. The Heritage Foundation is a research and educational institution, founded in 1973. It is a think-tank 'whose mission is to formulate and promote conservative public policies based on the principles of free enterprise, limited government, individual freedom, traditional American

values, and a strong national defense'. For more information, see the Heritage Foundation website at http://www.heritage.org.

6   CONCLUSION: BEYOND GLOBAL GOVERNANCE?

1. Interview with the United Nations Organization for the Co-ordination of Humanitarian Assistance in Colombo, Sri Lanka, in March 2005. The official referred to the international NGOs in Sri Lanka as 'walking bags of money', which, in turn, makes these actors difficult development partners. What is implied, of course, is the element of new forms of competition between various local and international NGOs on what appears to be an increasingly uneven playing-field of the global aid industry.

Bibliography

Agnew, J. and S. Corbridge (1995) *Mastering Space: Hegemony, Territory, and International Political Economy* (London: Routledge).

Akyuz, Y. (2003) 'Some Reflections on the SDRM'. Remarks made at the International Policy Dialogue: New Sovereign Debt Restructuring Mechanism – Challenges and Opportunities, on February 21, 2003 in Berlin. International Development Economics Association (IDEAS). Available at: http://www.networkideas.org/misc/reg.htm.

Albo, G. (1994) 'Competitive Austerity and the Impasse of Capitalist Employment Policy', in R. Miliband and L. Panitch (eds) *The Socialist Register 1994* (London: Merlin Press): 23–38.

——(2003) 'The Old and New Economics of Imperialism', in L. Panitch and C. Leys (eds) *Socialist Register 2004* (London: Merlin Press): 88–113.

Altvater, E. (2002) 'The Growth Obsession', in L. Panitch and C. Leys (eds): *Socialist Register 2002* (London: Merlin Press): 73–92.

——(2003) 'The Privatization of Public Goods: The Impact on Governance and on the Co-ordination of Economic Policy. A case study: cross-border leasing' *Impressum rls (Rosa Luxemburg Stiftung.)* Policy Paper, 3/2003. Berlin: Rosa Luxemburg Stiftung.

Altvater, E. and B. Mahnkopf (1996) *Grenzen der Globalisierung: Ökonomie, Ökologie und Politik in der Weltgesellschaft* (Münster, Germany: Westfälisches Dampfboot).

——(2002) *Globalisierung der Unsicherheit: Arbeit im Schatten, schmutziges Geld und informelle Politik* (Münster, Germany: Westfälisches Dampfboot).

Ambrose, S. (2003) 'The IMF's Latest Ruse: Sovereign Debt Restructuring Mechanism', *50 Years is Enough – Economic Justice News Online*, vol. 6, no. 1, April 2003.

Amin, S. (1974) *Accumulation on a World Scale, Vol. 1* (New York: Monthly Review Press).

——(1999) 'For Progressive and Democratic New World Order', in Francis Adams et al. (eds) *Globalization and the Dilemmas of the State in the South* (London: Macmillan): 17–32.

——(2003) 'World Poverty, Pauperization & Capital Accumulation', *Monthly Review*, accessed on September 12, 2005, at http://www.monthlyreview. org/1003amin.htm.

Andreff, W. (1984) 'The International Centralization of Capital and the Re-ordering of World Capitalism,' *Capital & Class*, no. 22 (Spring): 58–80.

Anheier, H., M. Glasius and M. Kaldor (eds) (2002) *Global Civil Society 2002* (Oxford: Oxford University Press).

Annan, K. (1999) 'A Compact for a New Century', UN Secretary-General's Address to World Economic Forum in Davos, Switzerland, January 31, 1999. Press Release SG/SM/6881. Downloaded on 2 March 2000 from http://www. un.org/News/Press/docs/1999/19990201.sgsm6881.html.

Archibugi, D. and D. Held (1995) *Cosmopolitan Democracy: An Agenda for a New World Order* (Cambridge: Polity Press).

Archibugi, D., D. Held and M. Köhler, (eds) (1998) *Re-imagining Political Community: Studies in Cosmopolitan Democracy* (Cambridge: Polity Press).

Archibugi, D. and J. Michie (eds) (1997) *Technology, globalization and economic performance* (Cambridge: Cambridge University Press).

Arrighi, G. (1983) *The Geometry of Imperialism: The Limits of Hobson's Paradigm*, translated by P. Camiller (London: Verso).

——(1994) *The Long Twentieth Century: Money, Power, and the Origins of our Time* (London: Verso).

——(2004) 'Spatial and Other "Fixes" of Historical Capitalism'. Paper presented to the Conference on Globalization in the World System: Mapping Change over Time, University of California, Riverside, February 7/8, 2003, downloaded on May 2, 2004 from http://www.irows.ucr.edu/conferences/globgis/papers/Arrighi.htm#_ftn1.

Arrighi, G. and B. Silver (1999) *Chaos and Governance in the Modern World System* (Minneapolis: University of Minnesota Press).

Bakan, J. (2004) *The Corporation: The Pathological Pursuit of Profit and Power* (Toronto: Penguin).

Baker, A. (2005) *The Group of Seven: Finance Ministries, Central Banks and The Politics of Global Financial Governance* (London: Routledge).

Bakker, I. (ed.) (1994) *The Strategic Silence: Gender and Economic Policy* (London: Zed Books).

Bair, J. (2004) 'From the New International Economic Order to the Global Compact: Development Discourse at the United Nations'. Paper presented to the Annual Meeting of the International Studies Association, Montréal, March 17–20, 2004, mimeograph.

Baran, P. and P. Sweezy (1966) *Monopoly Capitalism: An Essay on the American Economic and Social Order* (New York: Monthly Review Press).

Barnett, R. and R. Müller (1974) *Global Reach: The Power of the Multinational Corporations* (New York: Simon & Schuster).

Beck, U. (1992) *Risk Society: Towards a New Modernity* (London: Sage).

——(2001) *World Risk Society* (Cambridge: Polity Press).

Bello, W. (2002) *Deglobalization: Ideas for a New World Economy* (London: Zed Books).

Berger, M. (2004) *The Battle for Asia: From Decolonisation to Globalization* (London: Routledge).

Berle, A. and G. Means (1932) *The Modern Corporation and Private Property* (New York: Macmillan).

Bhagwati, J. (ed.) (1977) *The New International Economic Order: The North–South Debate* (Cambridge, MA: MIT Press).

——(2004) *In Defense of Globalization* (New York: Oxford University Press).

Bichler, S. and J. Nitzan (2003) 'Dominant Capital and the New Wars', mimeograph, downloaded on November 4, 2003 from http://www.arts.yorku.ca/politics/nitzan/bnarchives/mimeographs/pdf/Dominant_Capital_the_New_Wars_03_5_28.pdf.

Boggs, C. (1976) *Gramsci's Marxism* (London: Pluto Press).

Bond, P. (2003) *Against Global Apartheid: South Africa Meets the World Bank, IMF and International Finance* (second edition) (London: Zed Books).

——(2004a) 'Bankrupt Africa: Debt Peonage Continues, Courtesy of Washington, Monterrey and NEPAD', *Historical Materialism*, in press.

——(2004b) 'Should the World Bank and the IMF be "Fixed" or "Nixed"? Reformist Posturing and Popular Resistance', *Nature, Capitalism, Socialism*, forthcoming.

Bonefeld, W. (1995) 'Money, Equality and Exploitation: An Interpretation of Marx's Treatment of Money', in Bonefeld and Holloway (eds) *Global Capital, National State, and the Politics of Money* (New York: St. Martin's Press): 178–209.

Bonefeld, W. and J. Holloway (eds) (1995) *Global Capital, the National State, and the Politics of Money* (New York: St. Martin's Press).

Bonefeld, W. and K. Psychopedis (eds) (2000) *The Politics of Change: Globalization, Ideology and Critique* (London: Palgrave).

Boorman, J. (2002) 'Sovereign Debt Restructuring: Where Stands the Debate?', speech by J. Boorman, Special Advisor to the Managing Director, International Monetary Fund, delivered at a conference cosponsored by the CATO Institute and *The Economist*, New York, October 17, 2002 (Washington, DC: IMF).

Brancato, C. (1997) *Institutional Investors and Corporate Governance: Best Practices for Increasing Corporate Value* (Chicago: Irwin).

Brennan, D. (2005) '"Fiduciary Capitalism", the "Political Model of Corporate Governance", and the Prospect of Stakeholder Capitalism in the United States'. *Review of Radical Political Economy*, vol. 37 (1): 39–62.

Brenner, N. (2004) *New State Spaces: Urban Governance and the Rescaling of Statehood* (Oxford: Oxford University Press).

Brewer, A. (1980) *Marxist Theories of Imperialism* (London: Routledge & Kegan Paul).

Brodie, J. (2003) 'Globalization, In/Security, and the Paradoxes of the Social', in I. Bakker and S. Gill (eds) *Power, Production and Social Reproduction* (London: Palgrave): 47–65.

Bull, H. (1977) *The Anarchical Society: A Study of Order in World Politics* (London: Macmillan).

Burnham, P. (1991) 'Neo-Gramscian Hegemony and the International Order', *Capital and Class*, 45: 73–94.

Cardoso, F. and E. Faletto (1979) *Dependency and Development in Latin America* (Berkley, CA: University of California Press).

Carnoy, M. (1984) *The State and Political Theory* (Princeton, NJ: Princeton University Press).

Carroll, W. (2004) *Corporate Power in a Globalizing World* (Toronto: Oxford University Press).

Carruthers, B. and S. Babb (2000) *Economy/Society: Markets, Meanings, and Social Structure* (Thousand Oaks, CA: Pine Forge Press).

Center for Defense Information (2004) 'FY04 Budget Request', *Center for Defense Information*, downloaded on October 1, 2004 from http://www.cdi.org/budget/2004/.

Cerny, P. (ed.) (1993) *Finance and World Politics: Markets, Regimes and States in the Post-hegemonic era* (Aldershot, UK: Edward Elgar).

——(1999) *The Changing Architecture of Politics: Structure, Agency, and the Future of the State* (London and Thousand Oaks, CA: Sage).

Chamberlin, M. (2003) 'Remarks of Michael M. Chamberlin', EMTA Executive Director, Third Annual Insolvency Conference, June 9, 2003, New York, International Insolvency Institute, School of Law, Fordham University.

Chamberlin, M., C. Dallara, R. Gray, M. Green, M. Lackritz, J. Langton and A. McKenna (2002) 'Letter to the Honorable Paul Henry O'Neill, Secretary of the Treasury'.

Chilcote, R. (ed.) (2000) *Imperialism: Theoretical Directions* (New York: Humanity Books).

Citizens' Network on Essential Services (2003) 'The U.S.'s Millennium Challenge Account: New Paradigm For Development Assistance?', by President G. W. Bush, March 14, 2002, *News & Notices for IMF and World Bank Watchers*, vol. 2, no. 8, Spring 2003, downloaded August 29, 2003 from http://www. challengeglobalization.org/html/news_notices/spring2003/INTRO.

Clarke, S. (1988) *Keynesianism, Monetarism, and the Crisis of the State* (Aldershot, UK: Edward Elgar).

——(ed.) (1991) *The State Debate* (New York: St. Martin's Press).

——(1994) *Marx's Theory of Crisis* (New York: St. Martin's Press).

Clinton, W. (1998) 'Remarks by the President to Opening Ceremony of the 1998 International Monetary Fund/World Bank Annual Meeting', October 6, downloaded on October 12, 2002 from http://www.usconsulate.org. hk/gf/1998/1006a.htm.

Cohen, R. (1986) *In Whose Interest? International Banking and American Foreign Policy* (New Haven, CT and London: Yale University Press for the Council on Foreign Relations).

——(1998) *The Geography of Money* (Ithaca, NY: Cornell University Press).

——(2002) 'Capital Controls: Why Do Governments Hesitate?', in L. Elliot Armijo (ed.) *Debating the International Financial Architecture* (Albany, NY: SUNY Press): 56–73.

——(2003) *The Future of Money* (Princeton, NJ: Princeton University Press).

Cohen, R., N. Felton, M. Nkosi and J. van Liere (eds) (1979) *The Multinational Corporation: A Radical Approach* (Cambridge: Cambridge University Press).

Colás, A. (2002) *International Civil Society: Social Movements in World Politics* (Cambridge: Polity Press).

Commission on Global Governance (1995) *Our Global Neighbourhood: The Report of the Commission on Global Governance* (New York: Oxford University Press).

Conference Board, The (2003) 'U.S. Economic Growth Will Slow in 2003; Globalization May be Stagnating', *The Conference Board*, April 3, downloaded on May 5, 2003 from http://www.conference-board.org/economics/press. cfm?press_ID=2115.

Cooper, R. (2002) 'Chapter 11 for Countries?' *Foreign Affairs*, July/August, vol. 81, issue 4: 90–104.

Cox, R. (1987) *Production, Power and World Order: Social Forces in the Making of History* (New York: Columbia University Press).

——(1993a) 'Gramsci, Hegemony and International Relations: An Essay in Method', in S. Gill (ed.) *Gramsci, Historical Materialism, and International Relations* (Cambridge: Cambridge University Press): 49–66.

——(1993b) 'Structural Issues of Global Governance: Implications for Europe', in S. Gill (ed.) *Gramsci, Historical Materialism and International Relations* (Cambridge: Cambridge University Press): 259–89.

——(ed.) (1997) *The New Realism: Perspectives on Multilateralism and World Order* (London: Macmillan).

Cypher, J. (2001) 'Developing Disarticulation within the Mexican Economy', *Latin American Perspectives*, vol. 28 (3): 11–37.

Daalder, I. et al. (2002) 'The Bush National Security Strategy: An Evaluation', *Policy Brief*, no. 109 (Washington, DC: The Brookings Institution).

Dahl, R. (1956) *A Preface to Democratic Theory* (Chicago: University of Chicago Press).

D'Arista, J. (1999) 'Benefits of Capital Flows: New Role for Public Institutions', *Foreign Policy In Focus*, November 1999, vol. 4 (32): 1–4.

Davis, M. (2002) *City of Quartz: Excavating the Future in Los Angeles* (New York: Vintage Books).

——(2004) 'Planet of Slums: Urban Involution and the Informal Proletariat', *New Left Review* 26 (March–April 2004): 5–34.

De Angelis, M. (1999) 'Marx's Theory of Primitive Accumulation: A Suggested Reinterpretation', March 1999, University of East London, downloaded on October 12, 2003, from http://homepages.uel.ac.uk/M.DeAngelis/PRIMACCA.htm.

De Soto, H. (2000) *The Mystery of Capital: Why Capitalism Triumphs in the West and Fails Everywhere Else* (New York: Basic Books).

Dinerstein, A. (2003) 'The Battle of Buenos Aires: Crisis, Insurrection and the Reinvention of Politics in Argentina', *Historical Materialism* vol. 10 (4): 5–38.

Donahue, J. and J. Nye Jr (eds) (2002) *Market-Based Governance: Supply Side, Demand Side, Upside, and Downside* (Washington, DC: Brookings Institution Press).

Donaldson, T. (1982) *Corporations and Morality* (Englewood Cliffs, N.J.: Prentice-Hall).

Drainville, A. (2004) *Contesting Globalization: Space and Place in the World Economy* (London: Routledge/Review of International Political Economy Series).

Duffield, M. (2001) *Global Governance and the New Wars: The Merging of Development and Security* (London: Zed Books).

Economic Policy Institute (2002) 'Economic Snapshots', downloaded on August 1, 2002 from http://www.epinet.org/index.html.

Eichengreen, B. (2002) *Financial Crises: And What to Do About Them* (New York: Oxford University Press).

Eichengreen, B. and A. Fishlow (1998) 'Contending with Capital Flows: What is Different about the 1990s?' in M. Kahler (ed.) *Capital Flows and Financial Crises* (Ithaca: Cornell University Press): 23–68.

Eland, I. (2002) 'The Empire Strikes Out: The "New Imperialism" and its Fatal Flaws', *Policy Analysis* no. 459, November 26 (Washington: Cato Institute), downloaded on June 5, 2004 from http://www.cato.org/pubs/pas/pa459.pdf.

Emmanuel, A. (1972) *Unequal Exchange: A Study of the Imperialism of Trade* (London: New Left Books).

Escobar, A. (1995) *Encountering Development: The Making and Unmaking of the Third World* (Princeton, N.J.: Princeton University Press).

——(2004) 'Beyond the Third World: Imperial Globality, Global Coloniality and Anti-globalisation Social Movements', *Third World Quarterly*, vol. 25 (1): 207–30.

Felix, D. (2002) 'The Economic Case Against Free Capital Mobility', in L. Armijo (ed.) *Debating the Global Financial Architecture* (New York: SUNY Press): 126–58.

Fine, B. (2001) 'Making the Post-Washington Consensus', in B. Fine et al. (eds) *Development Policy in the Twenty-first Century: Beyond the Post-Washington Consensus* (London: Routledge): 131–54.

Fine, B., C. Lapavitsas, J. Pincus (eds) (2001) *Development Policy in the Twenty-first Century: Beyond the Post-Washington Consensus* (New York: Routledge).

Fischer, S. (1999) 'On the Need for an International Lender of Last Resort'. Paper prepared for delivery at the joint luncheon of the American Economic Association and the American Finance Association, New York, January 3, 1999 (Washington, DC: IMF).

Fisher, W. and T. Ponniah (eds) (2003) *Another World is Possible: Popular Alternatives to Globalization at the World Social Forum* (London: Zed Books).

Fox Piven, F. and R.. Cloward (1997) *The Breaking of the American Social Compact* (New York: New Press).

Frank, A. (1981) *Crisis in the Third World* (London: Heinemann Books).

Friedman, Thomas (1999) *The Lexus and the Olive Tree* (New York: Farrar, Straus & Giroux).

Fröbel, F., J. Heinrichs and O. Kreye (1980) *The New International Division of Labour* (Cambridge: Cambridge University Press).

Fung, A., T. Hebb and J. Rogers (eds) (2001) *Working Capital: The Power of Labor's Pensions* (Ithaca, NY: Cornell University Press).

Germain, R. (2001) 'Reforming the International Financial Architecture: The New Political Agenda', Toronto: University of Toronto, downloaded on April 2, 2004 from http://www.library.utoronto.ca/g7/scholar/ germain2001/ Germain_G20.pdf.

Gill, S. (1991) *American Hegemony and the Trilateral Commission* (New York: Cambridge University Press).

——(ed.) (1997) *Globalization, Democratization and Multilateralism* (London: Macmillan).

——(2003) *Power and Resistance in the New World Order* (London: Palgrave).

——(2005) 'The Contradictions of US Supremacy', in L. Panitch and C. Leys (eds) *Socialist Register 2005* (London: Merlin Press): 24–39.

Gill, S. and D. Law (1993) 'Global Hegemony and the Structural Power of Capital', in S. Gill (ed.) *Gramsci, Historical Materialism, and International Relations* (Cambridge: Cambridge University Press): 93–124.

Gilpin, R. (2000) *The Challenge of Global Capitalism: The World Economy in the Twenty-first Century* (Princeton, NJ: Princeton University Press).

Global Policy Forum (2000) 'The Global Compact', UN Press Briefing by Assistant Secretary-General and Special Adviser to Secretary-General John Ruggie (July 20, 2000), downloaded on July 1, 2004 from http://www. globalpolicy.org/reform/ruggie.htm.

Global Urban Observatory (2003) *Slums of the World: The Face of Urban Poverty in the New Millennium?* (New York: Global Urban Observatory).

Gowan, P. (1999) *The Global Gamble: Washington's Faustian Bid for World Dominance* (London: Verso).

——(2003) 'US:UN' *New Left Review* 24 (November–December): 5–28.

Grabel, I. (1996) 'Marketing the Third World: The Contradictions of Portfolio Investment in the Global Economy', *World Development*, vol. 24 (11): 1761–76.

Graham, C. and P. Masson (2002) 'The IMF's Dilemma in Argentina: Time for a New Approach to Lending?' Policy Brief No. 111, *The Brookings Institution Policy Brief* (Washington, DC: The Brookings Institution).

Gramsci, A. (1971) *Selections from the Prison Notebooks* (New York: International Publishers).

Greider, W. (1997) *One World, Ready or Not: The Manic Logic of Global Capitalism* (New York: Simon & Schuster).

Gruber, L. (2000) *Ruling the World: Power Politics and the Rise of Supranational Institutions* (Princeton, NJ: Princeton University Press).

Hacher, S. (2004) 'Argentina Water Privatization Scheme Runs Dry', *Corpwatch*, downloaded on July 1, 2004 from http://www.corpwatch.org/article.php?id=10088.

Haley, M. (1999) 'Emerging Market Makers: The Power of Institutional Investors', in L. Armijo (ed.) *Financial Globalization and Democracy in Emerging Markets* (London: Macmillan): 74–90.

Hardt, M. and A. Negri (2000) *Empire* (Cambridge, MA: Harvard University Press).

Harmes, A. (2001) *Unseen Power: How Mutual Funds Threaten the Political and Economic Wealth of Nations* (Toronto: Stoddart).

——(2002) 'The Role of Portfolio Investors in the Asian Financial Crisis', in E. Aksu and J. Camilleri (eds) *Democratizing Global Governance* (London: Palgrave): 117–26.

Hartman, L., D. Arnold, and R. Wokutch (eds) (2003) *Rising above Sweatshops: Innovative Approaches to Global Labour Challenges* (Westport, CT: Praeger).

Harvey, D. (1989) *The Condition of Postmodernity: An Enquiry into the Origins of Cultural Change* (Oxford: Blackwell).

——(1999) *The Limits to Capital* (London: Verso).

——(2001) *Spaces of Capital: Towards a Critical Geography* (London: Routledge).

——(2003a) 'The "New" Imperialism: Accumulation by Dispossession' in L. Panitch and C. Leys (eds) *Socialist Register 2004* (London: Merlin Press): 63–87.

——(2003b) *The New Imperialism* (Oxford: Oxford University Press).

Held, D. (2003) 'Cosmopolitanism: Ideas, Realities and Deficits', in D. Held and A. McGrew (eds) *Governing Globalization* (second edition) (Cambridge: Polity Press): 305–24.

——(2004) *Global Covenant: The Social Democratic Alternative to the Washington Consensus* (Cambridge: Polity Press).

Held, D. and M. Koenig-Archibugi (eds) (2005) *Global Governance and Public Accountability* (Oxford: Blackwell Publishing).

Held, D. and A. McGrew (eds) (2002) *Governing Globalization* (Cambridge: Polity Press).

——(2003) 'Introduction' in D. Held and A. McGrew (eds) *Governing Globalization* (second edition) (Cambridge: Polity Press): 1–21.

Helleiner, E. (1994) *States and the Reemergence of Global Finance: From Bretton Woods to the 1990s* (Ithaca, NY: Cornell University Press).

——(2003) 'Dollarization Diplomacy: US Policy towards Latin America Coming Full Circle?' *Review of International Political Economy*, vol. 29 (3): 406–29.

Hempel, L. (1996) *Environmental Governance: The Global Challenge* (Washington, DC: Island Press).

Hettne, B., A. Inotai and O. Sunkel (eds) (1999) *Globalism and the New Regionalism*, (Basingstoke: Macmillan).

——(eds) (2000) *National Perspectives on New Regionalism in the South* (Basingstoke: Macmillan).

Hewson, M. and T. Sinclair (eds) *Approaches to Global Governance Theory* (Albany, NY: SUNY Press).

Hirsch, J. (1974) *Staatsapparat und Reproduktion des Kapitals* (Frankfurt/Main: Suhrkamp).

——(1990) *Kapitalismus ohne Alternative?* (Hamburg: VSA-Verlag).

——(1992) 'Politische Form, politische Institutionen und Staat', Fachberreich 3, Universität Frankfurt, mimeograph.

Hirst, P. and G. Thompson (1999) *Globalization in Question* (second edition) (Cambridge: Polity Press).

Hocking, B. and D. Kelly (2002) 'Doing the Business? The International Chamber of Commerce, the United Nations, and the Global Compact', in A. Cooper, J. English and R. Thakur (eds) *Enhancing Global Governance: Towards a New Diplomacy?* (Tokyo: United Nations University Press): 203–28.

Hoffman, S. (2002) 'Clash of Globalizations', *Foreign Affairs*, vol. 81, issue 4, (July/August): 25–41.

Holloway, J. (1995) 'Global Capital and the National State', in W. Bonefeld and J. Holloway (eds) *Global Capital, National State, and the Politics of Money* (New York: St. Martin's Press): 116–40.

Holman, O. (1996) *Integrating Southern Europe: EC Expansion and the Transnationalisation of Spain* (London: Routledge).

Holme, R. and P. Watts (2000) *Corporate Social Responsibility: Making Good Business Sense* (Geneva: WBCSD).

Hopkins, M. (1998) *A Planetary Bargain: Corporate Social Responsibility Comes of Age* (London: Macmillan).

Hymer, S. (1976) *The International Operations of National Firms: A Study of Direct Foreign Investment* (Cambridge, MA: MIT Press).

ILO (2004) 'Facts on Child Labour' (Geneva: ILO), downloaded on July 1, 2004 from http://www.ilo.org/public/english/bureau/inf/download/child/childday04.pdf.

IMF (2002a) 'Reports on the Observances of Standards and Codes', Washington, DC: IMF, available at http://www.imf.org/external/np/rosc/rosc.asp.

——(2002b) 'The IMF's Poverty Reduction and Growth Facility (PRGF)', downloaded on April 20, 2002 from http://www.imf.org/external/np/exr/facts/prgf.htm.

——(2003a) *Global Financial Stability Report: Market Developments and Issues* (Washington, DC: IMF).

——(2003b) *Global Development Finance: Striving for Stability in Development Finance* (Washington, DC: IMF).

——(2003c) 'Financial Markets Update', November 2003, International Capital Markets Department, Global Markets Analysis Division (Washington, DC: IMF).

——(2003d) 'Poverty Reduction Strategy Papers', downloaded on June 26, 2003 from http://www.imf.org/external/np/prsp/prsp.asp.

——(2003e) 'Reports on the Observances of Standards and Codes', downloaded on April 15, 2003 from http://www.imf.org/external/np/rosc/rosc.asp?sort=date.

——(2003f) *World Economic Outlook: Growth and Institutions*, Chapter 2: 'When Bubbles Burst', downloaded on September 24, 2003 from http://www.imf.org/external/pubs/ft/weo/2003/01/pdf/chapter2.pdf.

IMF and World Bank (2001) 'Reports on the Observance of Standards and Codes (ROSCs), Washington, DC: IMF, available at http://www.imf.org/external/np/rosc/2000/stand.htm.

Jenkins, R. (1984) 'Divisions over the International Division of Labour', *Capital & Class* 22: 28–57.

——(1987) *Transnational Corporations and Uneven Development: The Internationalization of Capital and the Third World* (London: Methuen).

Jenkins, R., R. Pearson and G. Seyfang (eds) (2002) *Corporate Responsibility and Labour Rights: Codes of Conduct in the Global Economy* (London: Earthscan Publications).

John, S. and S. Thomson (eds) (2003) *New Activism and the Corporate Response* (London: Palgrave).

Johnson, C. (2004) *The Sorrows of Empire: Militarism, Secrecy and the End of the Republic* (New York: Metropolitan Books).

Jones, K. (2004) *Who's Afraid of the WTO?* (Oxford: Oxford University Press).

Kagan, R. (2003) *Of Paradise and Power: America and Europe in the New World Order* (New York: Alfred Knopf).

Kahler, M. (1998) 'Introduction: Capital Flows and Financial Crises in the 1990s', in M. Kahler (ed.) *Capital Flows and Financial Crises* (Ithaca, NY: Cornell University Press): 1–22.

Kaldor, M. (1999) *New and Old Wars: Organised Violence in a Global Era* (Cambridge: Polity Press).

Kapstein, E. (1994) *Governing the Global Economy: International Finance and the State* (Cambridge, MA: Harvard University Press).

Kapur, D. (2002) 'The Changing Anatomy of Governance of the World Bank', in J. Pincus and J. Winters (eds) *Reinventing the World Bank* (Ithaca, NY: Cornell University Press): 54–75.

Keck, M. and K. Sikkink (1998) *Activists across Borders: Advocacy Networks in International Politics* (Ithaca, NY: Cornell University Press).

Keil, Roger (1998) *Los Angeles: Globalization, Urbanization, and Social Struggles*, (Chichester: John Wiley & Sons).

Kell, G. and J. Ruggie (1999) 'Global Markets and Social Legitimacy: The Case for the "Global Compact"', *Transnational Corporations*, vol. 8 (3) (December): 108–22.

Keohane, R. (1984) *After Hegemony: Cooperation and Discord in the World Economy* (Princeton, NJ: Princeton University Press).

Kindleberger, C. (1969) *American Business Abroad* (New Haven: Yale University Press).

——(1986) *The World Depression, 1929–1939* (Berkeley, CA: University of California Press).

Kirton, J. and G. von Furstenberg (eds) (2001) *New Directions in Global Economic Governance: Managing Globalization in the Twenty-First Century* (Aldershot: Ashgate).

Klein, N. (2000) *No Logo: Taking Aim at the Brand Bullies* (Toronto: Vintage Canada).

Körner, P., G. Maass, T. Siebold and R. Tetzlaff (1984) *The IMF and the Debt Crisis: A Guide to the Third World's Dilemma* (London: Zed Books).

Korten, D. (1995) *When Corporations Rule the World* (West Hartford: Kumarian Press and Berrett-Koehler Publishers).

Kotz, D. (2003) 'Neoliberalism and the US Economic Expansion of the 1990s', *Monthly Review*, vol. 54 (11): 10–28.

Krueger, A. (2002) 'A New Approach to Sovereign Debt Restructuring', Washington, DC: IMF, available at http://www.imf.org/external/pubs/ft/exrp/sdrm/eng/sdrm.pdf.

Lane, T. and S. Phillips (2001) 'IMF Financing and Moral Hazard', *Finance & Development*, June 2001, vol. 28 (2), available at http://www.imf.org/external/pubs/ft/fandd/2001/06/lane.htm.

——(2002) 'Moral Hazard: Does IMF Financing Encourage Imprudence by Borrowers and Lenders?', *Economic Issues*, no. 28, Washington, DC: IMF.

Langley, P. (2002) *World Financial Orders: An Historical International Political Economy* (London: Routledge, RIPE Series).

——(2004) '(Re)politicising Global Financial Governance: What's "New" about the "New International Financial Architecture"?' *Global Networks*, vol. 4 (1): 69–87.

Larkin, J. (2003) *Strategic Reputation Risk Management* (London: Palgrave).

Latham, R. (1999) 'Politics in a Floating World: Towards a Critique of Global Governance', in M. Hewson and T. Sinclair (eds) *Approaches to Global Governance Theory* (New York: SUNY Press): 23–53.

Lerrick, A. and A. Meltzer (2002) 'Grants: A Better Way to Deliver Aid', *Quarterly International Economics Report*, Gailliot Center for Public Policy, Pittsburgh, PA: Carnegie Mellon, downloaded on September 21, 2003 from http://www.house.gov/jec/imf/grant.pdf.

Leys, C. (1996) *The Rise and Fall of Development Theory* (Bloomington: Indiana University Press).

Lipietz, A. (1987) *Miracle and Mirages: The Crisis of Global Fordism*, translated by D. Macey (London: Verso).

Lipschutz, R. (2001) 'Regulation for the Rest of Us? Global Civil Society, Social Regulation, and National Impacts', paper presented at the Annual Meeting of the International Studies Association, February 20–24, 2001, Chicago, mimeograph.

——(2005) 'States of Terror: Framing Threats and Selling Texts', paper presented at the Annual Meeting of the International Studies Association, March 1–5, Honolulu, Hawaii, mimeograph.

Lipschutz, R. and J. Mayer (1996) *Global Civil Society and Global Environmental Governance: The Politics of Nature from Pace to Planet* (Albany, NY: SUNY Press).

Lipschutz, R. and Te treault, M. (2005) *Global Politics as if People Mattered* (Lanham, MD: Rowman & Littlefield).

Lipsey, R., D. Purvis and P. Steiner (1991) *Economics*, seventh edition (New York: HarperCollins).

Lipson, C. (1981) 'The International Organization of Third World Debt', *International Organization*, vol. 34, no. 4: 603–31.

——(1986) 'International debt and international institutions', in M. Kahler (ed.) *The Politics of International Debt* (Ithaca, NY: Cornell University Press).

Litwak, R. (2000) *Rogue States and US Foreign Policy: Containment after the Cold War* (Washington, DC: The Woodrow Wilson International Center).

Lodge, G. (2002) 'The Corporate Key: Using Big Business to Fight Global Poverty', *Foreign Affairs*, vol. 81 (4): 13–18.

Luxemburg, R. (2003) *The Accumulation of Capital* (London: Routledge Classics).

Mackenzie, D. (2004) 'The Big, Bad Wolf and the Rational Market: Portfolio Insurance, the 1987 Crash and the Performativity of Economics', *Economy and Society*, vol. 33 (3): 303–34.

Mahajan, R. (2002) *The New Crusade: America's War on Terrorism* (New York: Monthly Review Press).

Makki, F. (2004) 'The Empire of Capital and the Remaking of Centre–Periphery Relations' *Third World Quarterly*, vol. 25 (1): 149–68.

Mandel, E. (1975) *Late Capitalism* (London: New Left Books).

Marx, K. (1976/1990) *Capital – Volume 1* (London: Penguin).

——(1981) *Capital – Volume 3* (London: Penguin).

——(1986) 'The Eighteenth Brumaire of Louis Bonaparte', in K. Marx and F. Engels, *Selected Works* (New York: International Publishers): 97–180.

Marx, K. and F. Engels (1964) *The Communist Manifesto* (New York: Washington Square Press).

McDonald, D. and J. Pape (eds) *Cost Recovery and the Crisis of Service Delivery in South Africa* (London: Zed Books).

McMichael, P. (2004) *Development and Social Change: A Global Perspective* (Thousand Oaks, CA: Pine Forge Press).

Meltzer, A. (1984) 'The International Debt Problem', *Cato Journal*, vol. 4 (1): 63–9.

Miller, M. (2002) 'Sovereign Debt Restructuring: New Articles, New Contracts – or No Change?', International Economic Policy Brief, No. PB02–3 (April 2002).

Monbiot, G. (2003) *The Age of Consent: A Manifesto for a New World Order* (London: Flamingo).

Monks, R. and N. Minow (2003) *Corporate Governance* (second edition) (Oxford: Blackwell Publishing).

Moody, K. (1997) *Workers in a Lean World* (London: Verso).

Moran, M. (1991) *The Politics of the Financial Services Revolution: The USA, UK and Japan* (London: Macmillan).

Morgenthau, H. (1978) *Politics among Nations: The Struggle for Power and Peace* (New York: Knopf).

Morrissey, M. and D. Baker (2003) 'When Rivers Flow Upstream: International Capital Movements in the Era of Globalization', March 22 (Washington, DC: Center for Economic and Policy Research).

Murphy, C. (1984) *The Emergence of the NIEO Ideology* (Boulder, CO: Westview Press).

——(1994) *International Organization and Industrial Change: Global Governance since 1850* (Cambridge: Polity Press).

——(2000) 'Global Governance: Poorly Done and Poorly Understood', *International Affairs*, no. 76 (4): 789–803.

Mussa, M. (2002) *Argentina and the Fund: From Triumph to Tragedy* (Washington, DC: Institute for International Economics).

Mutume, G. (2001) 'US Congressional Commission Pushes for Deeper IMF, World Bank Reforms', downloaded October 15, 2001 from http://www.1worldcommunication.org/deeperreforms.htm.

Naim, M. (1999) 'Fads and Fashion in Economic Reforms: Washington Consensus or Washington Confusion?', working draft of a paper prepared for the IMF Conference on Second Generation Reforms, Washington, DC, downloaded on June 23, 2000 from http://www.imf.org/external/pubs/ft/seminar/1999/reforms/Naim.HTM.

Newhouse, J. (2003) *Imperial America: The Bush Assault on the World Order* (New York: Alfred A. Knopf).

O'Brien, R., A. Goetz, J. Scholte and M. Williams (2000) *Contesting Global Governance: Multilateral Economic Institutions and Global Social Movements* (Cambridge: Cambridge University Press).

Ocampo, J. (2000) 'A Broad Agenda for International Financial Reform', in J. Ocampo et al. (eds) *Financial Globalization and the Emerging Economies* (Santiago, Chile: United Nations Economic Commission for Latin American and the Caribbean): 41–62.

OECD (1999) *OECD Benchmark Definition of Foreign Direct Investment* (third edition) (Paris: OECD).

Office of Management and Budget (2003) 'Charting a Course for the Federal Budget', Washington, DC: the White House, June 15, 2003, downloaded on September 3, 2003 from http://www.whitehouse.gov/omb/budget/fy2004/charting.html.

Office of Public Affairs of the US Treasury Department (2003) 'Treasury Secretary John Snow Announces Request of an Additional $100 million for the International Development Association, Affirms Progress on Goals and Measurable Results', April 13, 2003, Washington, DC: US Treasury Department, downloaded on May 11, 2003 from http://www.ustreas.gov/press/releases/js186.htm.

Ohmae, K. (1990) *The Borderless World* (London and New York: Collins).

——(1995) *The End of the Nation State: The Rise of Regional Economies* (New York: New Press).

Osborne, D. and T. Gaebler (1992) *Reinventing Government: How the Entrepreneurial Spirit is Transforming the Public Sector, from Schoolhouse to Statehouse, City Hall to the Pentagon* (Reading, MA: Addison-Wesley).

Overbeek, H. (2004) 'Global Governance, Class, Hegemony: A Historical Materialist Perspective', Working Papers Political Science No. 2004/01, Vrije University, Amsterdam, February.

Paine, L. (2003) *Value Shift: Why Companies Must Merge Social and Financial Imperatives to Achieve Superior Performance* (New York: McGraw-Hill).

Palan, R. (2003) *The Offshore World: Sovereign States, Virtual Places, and Nomad Millionaires* (Ithaca, NY: Cornell University Press).

Palloix, C/ (1977) 'The Self-Expansion of Capital on a World Scale', *Review of Radical Political Economics*, vol. 9 (2): 1–28.

Panitch, L. (1994) 'Globalisation and the State', in R. Miliband and L. Panitch (eds) *Socialist Register 1994* (London: Merlin Press): 11–29.

——(2000) 'The New Imperial State', *New Left Review* (March–April): 45–56.

Panitch, L. and S. Gindin (2003) 'American Empire and Global Capitalism' in L. Panitch and C. Leys (eds) *Socialist Register 2003* (London: Merlin Press): 1–42.

Patomäki, H. (2001) *Democratising Globalisation: The Leverage of the Tobin Tax* (London: Zed Books).

Patroni, V. (2004) 'Disciplining Labour, Producing Poverty: Neoliberal Structural Reform and Political Conflict in Argentina', *Research in Political Economy*, vol. 21: 34–50.

Pauly, L. (1996) *The League of Nations and the Foreshadowing of the International Monetary Fund* (Princeton, NJ: Princeton University Press).

——(1997) *Who elected the bankers? Surveillance and Control in the World Economy* (Ithaca, NY: Cornell University Press).

Pearson, R. and G. Seyfang (2001) 'New Hope or False Dawn? Voluntary Codes of Conduct, Labour Regulation and Social Policy in a Globalizing World', *Global Social Policy*, vol. 1 (1): 49–78.

Pender, J. (2001) 'From "Structural Adjustment" to "Comprehensive Development Framework": Conditionality Transformed?' *Third World Quarterly*, vol. 22 (3): 397–411.

Perelman, M. (1984) *Primitive Accumulation and the Social Division of Labour* (Totowa, NJ: Rowman & Allanheld).

——(2000) *The Invention of Capitalism: Classical Political Economy and the Secret History of Primitive Accumulation* (Durham, NC: Duke University Press).

Pettifor, A., L. Cisneros and A. Olmos Gaona (2001) 'It Takes Two to Tango: Creditor Co-responsibility for Argentina's crisis – and the need for independent resolution' (London: Jubilee Plus).

Phillips, N. (2004) *The Southern Cone Model: The Political economy of Regional Capitalist Development in Latin America* (London: Routledge/RIPE Series in Global Political Economy).

Pincus, J. and J. Winters (2002) 'Reinventing the World Bank', in J. Pincus and J. Winters (eds) *Reinventing the World Bank* (Ithaca, NY: Cornell University Press): 1–25.

Platt, T. (2003) 'The State of Welfare: United States 2003', *Monthly Review*, vol. 55 (5): 13–27.

Poulantzas, N. (1974) *Classes in Contemporary Capitalism* (London: New Left Books).

——(2000) *State, Power, Socialism* (London: Verso).

Prebisch, R. (1967) *Hacia una dinámica del desarrollo latinamericano* (Montevideo: Ediciones de la Banda Oriental).

Radelet, S. (2003) 'Will the Millennium Challenge Account be Different?' *Washington Quarterly*, vol. 26 (2) (Spring): 175.

Radice, H. (ed.) (1975) *International Firms and Modern Imperialism* (Harmondsworth: Penguin).

Raghavan, C. (2001) 'Review Global Compact partnership with ICC, says study', *South–North Development Monitor (SUNS)* and Third World Network, downloaded on January 8, 2003 from http://www.twnside.org.sg/title/icc.htm.

Reich, R. (1992) *The Work of Nations* (New York: Vintage).

Reiffel, L. (2002) 'A Note on the International Debt Commission' (Washington, DC: The Brookings Institution).

Rice, C. (2000) 'Promoting the National Interest', *Foreign Affairs*, January/February, vol. 79 (1) 45–63.

Rice, S. (2003) 'The New National Security Strategy: Focus on Failed States', Policy Brief No. 116 (Washington, DC: The Brookings Institution).

Rittberger, V. (ed.) (2001) *Global Governance and the United Nations System* (Tokyo: United Nations University Press).

Robinson, W. (2002) 'Remapping Development in Light of Globalisation: From a Territorial to a Social Cartography,' *Third Word Quarterly*, vol. 23, no 6: 1047–71.

——(2004) *A Theory of Global Capitalism: Production, Class, and State in a Transnational World* (Baltimore and London: Johns Hopkins University Press).

Rock, D. (2002) 'Racking Argentina', *New Left Review* 17: 55–86.

Rodrik, D. (1997) 'Has Globalization Gone Too Far?' (Washington, DC: Institute for International Economics).

——(1999) 'Making Openness Work: The New Global Economy and the Developing Countries' (Washington, DC: Overseas Development Council).

——(2003) 'Why Financial Markets Misbehave', in A. Pettifor (ed.) *Real World Economic Outlook: The Legacy of Globalization – Debt and Deflation* (London: Palgrave): 188–91.

Roemer, J. (1988) *Free to Lose: An Introduction to Marxist Economic* (Cambridge, MA: Harvard University Press).

Rogoff, K. and J. Zettelmeyer (2002) 'Bankruptcy Procedures for Sovereigns: A History of Ideas, 1976–2001, *IMF Staff Papers*, no. 3 (Washington, DC: IMF).

Rosenau, J. (1992) 'Governance, Order, and Change in World Politics', in J. Rosenau and E. Cziempel (eds) *Governance without Government: Order and Change in World Politics* (Cambridge: Cambridge University Press): 1–29.

——(1995) 'Governance in the Twenty-first Century', *Global Governance*, vol. 1 (1): 13–43.

——(1997) *Along the Domestic–Foreign Frontier: Exploring Governance in a Turbulent World* (Cambridge: Cambridge University Press).

Rosenberg, J. (2000) *The Follies of Globalisation Theory: Polemical Essays* (London: Verso Press).

Rothstein, R. (1979) *Global Bargaining: UNCTAD and the Quest for a New International Economic Order* (Princeton, NJ: Princeton University Press).

Ruggie, J. (1982) 'International Regimes, Transactions and Change: Embedded Liberalism in the Post-war Economic Order', *International Organization*, vol. 36 (2): 89–114.

Ruggie, J. (ed.) (1993) *Multilateralism Matters: The Theory and Praxis of an Institutional Form* (New York: Columbia University Press).

——(2000) 'Globalization, the Global Compact and Corporate Social Responsibility', *Transnational Associations*, vol. 52 (6) (November–December): 54–69.

——(2001) 'global_governance.net: The Global Compact as Learning Network', *Global Governance*, vol. 7 (4): 371–8.

——(2002) 'The Theory and Practice of Learning Networks: Corporate Social Responsibility and the Global Compact', *Journal of Corporate Citizenship*, 5 (Spring): 27–36.

——(2004) 'Reconstituting the Global Public Domain – Issues, Actors, and Practices', *European Journal of International Relations*, vol. 10 (4): 499–531.

Ruigrok, W. and R. van Tulder (1995) *The Logic of International Restructuring* (London: Routledge).

Saad-Filho, A. (2002) *The Value of Marx: Political Economy for Contemporary Capitalism* (London: Routledge).

Saad-Filho, A. and D. Johnston (2005) 'Introduction', in A. Saad-Filho and D. Johnston (eds) *Neoliberalism: A Critical Reader* (London: Pluto Press): 1–6.

Said, E. (1979) *Orientalism* (New York: Vintage Books).

Sakamoto, Y. (1994) *Global Transformation: Challenges to the State System* (New York: United Nations University Press).

Sanford, J. (2002) 'World Bank: IDA Grants or IDA Loans', February 8, 2002 Washington, DC: Bank Information Center, downloaded on March 15, 2002 from http://www.bicusa.org/usgovtoversight/Sanford%20_IDA_loans_or_grants.pdf.

Santoro, D. (2004) 'The "Aguas" Tango: Cashing in on Buenos Aires' Privatization', Centre for Public Integrity, downloaded on July 3, 2004 from http://www.publicintegrity.org/water/report.aspx?aid=50&sid=100.

Sassen, S. (1996) *Losing Control? Sovereignty in the Age of Globalization* (New York: Columbia University Press).

——(1998) *Globalization and its Discontents* (New York: New Press).

Saull, R. (2001) *Rethinking Theory and History in the Cold War: The State, Military Power and Social Revolution* (London: Frank Cass).

Schaefer, B. (2001) 'Real Help for Poor Nations: President Bush's World Bank Grant Proposal', Backgrounder #1466, Washington, DC: The Heritage Foundation, downloaded on September 27, 2003 from http://www.heritage.org/Research/TradeandForeignAid/BG1466.cfm.

Schaefer, B. (2003) 'Promoting Growth and Prosperity in the Developing World through Economic Freedom', *Economic Perspectives*, downloaded on September 5, 2003 from http://usinfo.state.gov/journals/ites/0303/ijee/schaefer.htm.

Schechter, M. (ed.) (1999) *Future Multilateralism: The Political and Social Framework* (New York: St. Martin's Press).

Schmitter, P. (1975) *Corporatism and Public Policy in Authoritarian Portugal* (Beverly Hills, CA: Sage Publications).

Scholte, J. (2002) *Global Civil Society Voices and the International Monetary Fund* (Ottawa: North–South Institute).

Secretariat of the League of Nations (1935) *The Aims, Methods, and Activity of the League of Nations* (Geneva: Secretariat of the League of Nations).

Shapiro, I. (2000) 'Trends in US Development Aid and the Current Budget Debate', Washington, DC: Center on Budget and Policy Priorities, September 2000, downloaded on August 2, 2003 from http://www.cbpp.org/4-25-00bud.htm.

Shamir, R. (2004) 'The De-Radicalization of Corporate Social Responsibility', *Critical Sociology*, vol. 30 (3): 669–89.

Showstack Sassoon, A. (1980) *Gramsci's Politics* (New York: St. Martin's Press).

Shiller, R. (2000) *Irrational Exuberance* (Princeton, NJ: Princeton University Press).

Siebert, H. (ed.) (2003) *Global Governance: An Architecture for the World Economy* (Berlin: Springer Verlag).

Simbulan, R. (2002) 'US Military Intervention in the Philippines: A New Phase', lecture delivered to the Department of Social Sciences, College of Arts & Sciences, University of the Philippines, Manila (http://www.yonip.com/main/articles/war_01.html).

Sinclair, T. and M. King (2001) 'Grasping at Straws: A Ratings Downgrade For The Emerging International Financial Architecture', Centre for the Study of Globalisation and Regionalisation, University of Warwick, Coventry. Working Paper No. 82/01.

Sinclair, T. (2003) *'Global Monitor: Bond Rating Agencies' New Political Economy*, vol. 8 (1): 147–61.

Sklair, L. (2002) *Globalization: Capitalism and its Alternatives* (Oxford: Oxford University Press).

Sklair, L, and P. Robbins (2002) 'Global Capitalism and Major Corporations from the Third World', *Third World Quarterly* 23, no. 1: 81–100.

Slaughter, A. (2004) *A New World Order* (Princeton, NJ: Princeton University Press).

Soederberg, S. (2000) 'Political Restructuring of Exploitation: An Historical Materialist Account of the Emergence of Neoliberalism in Canada', *Cultural Logic*, vol. 4 (1), downloaded on January 15, 2003 from http://eserver.org/clogic/3-1%262/soederberg.html.

——(2001) 'Deconstructing the Neoliberal Promise of Prosperity and Stability: Who Gains from the Maquiladorization of the Mexican Society?', vol. 4 (2), downloaded on January 15, 2003 from http://eserver.org/clogic/4-2/soederberg.html.

——(2002a) 'From Neo-liberalism to Social Liberalism: Situating the National Solidarity Program within Mexico's Passive Revolutions', *Latin American Perspectives*, vol. 28 (3): 104–23.

——(2002b) 'A Historical Materialist Account of the Chilean Capital Control: Prototype Policy for Whom?' *Review of International Political Economy*, vol. 9 (3): 490–512.

——(2002c) 'The New International Financial Architecture: Imposed Leadership and Emerging Markets', in L. Panitch and C. Leys (eds) *Socialist Register* (London: Merlin Press): 175–92.

——(2004) *The Politics of the New International Financial Architecture: Reimposing Neoliberal Dominance in the Global South* (London: Zed Books).

Soederberg, S., G. Menz and P. Cerny (eds) (2005) *Internalizing Globalization: The Rise of Neoliberalism and the Erosion of National Models of Capitalism* (London: Palgrave).

Soros, G. (1987) *The Alchemy of Finance: Reading the Mind of the Market* (New York: John Wiley & Sons).

Sparkes, R. (2002) *Socially Responsible Investment: A Global Revolution* (Chichester: John Wiley & Sons).

Stiglitz, J. (2002) *Globalization and its Discontents* (New York: W.W. Norton).

Stopford, J., S. Strange, with J. Henley (1992) *Rival States, Rival Firms: Competition for World Market Shares* (Cambridge: Cambridge University Press).

Stopford, J. (1998) 'Multinational Corporations: Think Again', *Foreign Policy* (December): 12–24.

Strange, S. (1986) *Casino Capitalism*, (Manchester: Manchester University Press).

——(1994) *States and Markets* (second edition) (London: Pinter).

——(1996) *The Retreat of the State: The Diffusion of Power in the World Economy* (New York: Cambridge University Press).

——(1998) 'New world of debt', *New Left Review* 1(230): 91–114.

Surendranath, C. (2004) 'Coca-Cola: Continuing the Battle in Kerala', India Resource Center/CorpWatch, downloaded on July 1, 2004 from http://corpwatch.radicaldesigns.org/article.php?id=7528.

Taylor, M. (2002) 'An Historical Materialist Critique of Neoliberalism in Chile', *Historical Materialism* 10 (2): 45–76.

——(2004) 'Responding to Neoliberalism in Crisis: Discipline and Empowerment in the World Bank's New Development Agenda', *Research in Political Economy* vol. 21: 3–30.

——(2005) 'Opening the World Bank: International Financial Institutions and the Contradictions of Global Capital', *Historical Materialism* 13 (1): 153–70.

Taylor, J. (2002) 'Improving the Bretton Woods Financial Institutions', by John B. Taylor, Under Secretary of Treasury for International Affairs, Annual Mid-Winter Strategic Issues Conference Bankers Association for Finance and Trade, February 7, 2002, *Citizens' Network on Essential Services*, downloaded on June 2, 2003 from http://www.challengeglobalization.org/html/econ_lit/treasury_feb02.shtml.

The Conference Board (2003) 'U.S. Economic Growth will Slow in 2003; Globalization may be Stagnating', April 3, 2003, downloaded on May 5, 2003 from http://www.conference-board.org/economics/press.cfm?press_ID=2115.

The Editors (2003) 'What Recovery?' *Monthly Review*, vol. 54 (11): 3–14.

Thérien, J.-P. and V. Pouliot (2004) 'The Global Compact: UN's Bid for a World Social Contract', paper presented at the 45th Annual Convention of the International Studies Association, Montréal, March 17–20, 2004, mimeograph.

Thomas, C. (2002) 'Global governance and human security', in R. Wilkinson and S. Hughes (eds) *Global Governance: Critical Perspectives* (London: Routledge): 113–31.

Tolentino, P. (ed.) (2000) *Multinational Corporations: Emergence and Evolution* (London: Routledge).

Transnational Resource and Action Centre (2000) *Tangled Up in Blue: Corporate Partnerships at the United Nations* (San Francisco: Transnational Resource and Action Centre).

UNCTAD (1996) *World Investment Report 1996: Investment, Trade and International Policy Arrangement Overview* (New York: United Nations).

——(1998) *World Investment Report 1998: Trends and Determinants* (New York: United Nations).

——(2000) *World Investment Report 2000: Cross-border Mergers and Acquisitions and Development* (New York: United Nations).

——(2001) *Social Responsibility* (New York: United Nations).

——(2002) *World Investment Report 2002 – Transnational Corporations and Export Competitiveness* (New York: United Nations).

——(2003) *World Investment Report: FDI Policies for Development – National and International Perspectives* (New York: United Nations).

UNCTC (1985) *Transnational Corporations in World Development*, Third Survey United Nations Centre on Transnational Corporations (London: Graham & Trotman).

Underhill, G. (1997) 'Private Markets and Public Responsibility in a Global System: Conflict and Co-operation in Transnational Banking and Securities Regulation', in G. Underhill (ed.) *The New World Order in International Finance* (London: Macmillan Press, 1997): 17–49.

UNDP (1994) *Human Development Report* (Oxford: Oxford University Press).

——(2002) *Human Development Report: Deepening democracy in a fragmented world* (New York: Oxford University Press).

UN-HABITAT (2003) *UN-HABITAT's new Global Report on Human Settlements 2003 – The Global Challenge of Slums* (Oxford: Oxford University Press).

United States Agency for International Development (USAID) (2002) 'Millennium Challenge Account Update', June 3, 2002, downloaded on July 5, 2002 from http://usinfo.state.gov/journals/ites/0303/ijee/usaidfs/htm.

US Department of the Treasury (2000) 'Response to the Report of the International Financial Institution Advisory Commission', Washington, DC: Department of Treasury, downloaded on August 15, 2002 from http://www.ustreas.gov/press/releases/reports/response.pdf.

US Department of State (2003) 'House Panel Approves $17.1 Billion Foreign Spending Bill', July 11, 2003, Washington, DC: US Department of State, downloaded on August 20, 2003 from http://usinfo.state.gov/xarchives/display.html?p=washfile-english&y=2003&m=July&x=20030711103326e mmoccmk7.867068e-02&t=usinfo/wf-latest.html.

van der Pijl, K. (1984) *The Making of an Atlantic Ruling Class* (London: Verso).

——(1998) *Transnational Classes and International Relations* (London: Routledge).

Vernon, R. (1971) *Sovereignty at Bay* (London: Penguin Books).

——(1977) *Storm Over the Multinationals: The Real Issues* (London: Macmillan).

Von Braunmühl, C. (1978) 'On the Analysis of the Bourgeois Nation State within the World Market Context', in J. Holloway and S. Picciotto (translators and editors) *State and Capital: A Marxist Debate* (London: Edward Arnold): 160–77.

Waltz, K. (1979) *Theory of International Politics* (Reading, MA: Addison-Wesley).

Wayne, A. (2003) 'The MCA Promotes Sound Economic Policies', *Economic Perspectives* (Washington, DC: US State Department).

Webber, M. and D. Rigby (1996) *The Golden Age Illusion: Rethinking Postwar Capitalism* (New York: The Guilford Press).

Weber, M. (1946) 'Politics as a Vocation', in *From Max Weber: Essays in Sociology*, H. Gerth and C. Wright Mills (translators and editors) (New York: Oxford University Press).

Weisbrot, M. and D. Baker (2002) 'What Happened to Argentina?', January 31, 2002, Center for Economic and Policy Research, accessed on November 1, 2003 from http://www.cepr.net/IMF/what_happened_to_argentina.htm.

White House (2002) 'National Security Strategy of the United States of America', Washington, DC: the White House, September 2002, downloaded on November 4, 2002 from http://www.whitehouse.gov/nsc/nss1.html.

Wilkinson, R. (2000) *Multilateralism and the World Trade Organisation: The Architecture and Extension of International Trade Regulation* (London: Routledge).

——(2002) 'Global Governance: A Preliminary Interrogation', in R. Wilkinson and S. Hughes (eds) *Global Governance: Critical Perspectives* (London: Routledge): 1–14.

Wilkinson, R. and S. Hughes (eds) (2002) *Global Governance: Critical Perspectives* (London: Routledge).

Willetts, P. (1997) 'Transnational Actors and International Organizations in Global Politics', in J. Baylis and S. Smith (eds) *The Globalization of World Politics: An Introduction to International Relations* (Oxford: Oxford University Press): 287–310.

——(1999) 'Actors in Global Politics', in J. Baylis and S. Smith (eds) *The Globalization of World Politics: An Introduction to International Relations* (Oxford: Oxford University Press): 287–310.

Williamson, J. (ed.) (1990) *Latin American Adjustment: How Much has Happened?* (Washington, DC: Institute for International Economics).

——(2000) 'What Should the World Bank Think About the Washington Consensus?', *World Bank Research Observer* (Washington, DC: The International Bank for Reconstruction and Development), vol. 15, no. 2 (August): 251–64.

——(2003) 'From Reform Agenda to Damaged Brand Name', *Finance & Development*, September: 10–13.

Wood, E. (1990) 'The Uses and Abuses of "Civil Society"' in R. Miliband and L. Panitch (eds) *Socialist Register 1990* (London: Merlin Press): 60–84.

——(1995) *Democracy against Capitalism: Renewing Historical Materialism* (Cambridge: Cambridge University Press).

Woods, N. (2003) 'The United States and International Financial Institutions: Power and Influence in the World Bank and the IMF', in R. Foot, N. MacFarlane and M. Mastanduno (eds) *US Hegemony and International Organisations* (Oxford: Oxford University Press): 59–73.

World Bank (2001) *Global Development Finance 2001: Building Coalitions for Effective Development Finance* (http://www.worldbank.org/prospects/gdf2001/vol1.htm).

——(2002a) *World Development Report 2002: Building Institutions for Markets* (New York: Oxford University Press).

——(2002b) *Global Development Finance: Financing the Poorest Countries* (Washington, DC: World Bank).

——(2003) *Global Development Finance: Striving for Stability in Development Finance* (Washington, DC: World Bank).

World Business Council for Sustainable Development (2000) *Corporate Social Responsibility: Making Good Business Sense* (Geneva: WBCSD).

Young, B. (2003) 'Financial Crises and Social Reproduction: Asia, Argentina and Brazil', in I. Bakker and S. Gill (eds) *Power, Production and Social Reproduction* (London: Palgrave Macmillan): 103–23.

Young, O. (ed.) (1997) *Global Governance: Drawing Insights from the Environmental Experience* (Cambridge, MA: MIT Press).

Zarembka, P. (2002) 'Primitive Accumulation in Marxism: Historical or Trans-Historical Separation from Means of Production?', *The Commoner*, March 2002 (www.thecommoner.org).

Index

Compiled by Sue Carlton

Printed and bound by CPI Group (UK) Ltd, Croydon, CR0 4YY

16/04/2025

14658481-0001